Confronting Public Health Risks

A Decision Maker's Guide

Laura C. Leviton
Carolyn E. Needleman
Maurice A. Shapiro

SAGE Publications
International Educational and Professional Publisher
Thousand Oaks   London   New Delhi

For information:

SAGE Publications, Inc.
2455 Teller Road
Thousand Oaks, California 91320
E-mail: order@sagepub.com

SAGE Publications Ltd.
6 Bonhill Street
London EC2A 4PU
United Kingdom

SAGE Publications India Pvt. Ltd.
M-32 Market
Greater Kailash I
New Delhi 110 048 India

Printed in the United States of America

Library of Congress Cataloging-in-Publication Data

Leviton, Laura C.
   Confronting public health risks: A decision maker's guide / by
Laura C. Leviton, Carolyn E. Needleman, and Maurice A. Shapiro.
     p. cm.
   Includes bibliographical references and index.
   ISBN 0-8039-5356-9 (cloth : acid-free paper). — ISBN
0-8039-5357-7 (pbk.: acid-free paper)
   1. Health risk communication—United States—Case studies.
2. Public health—United States—Citizen participation—Case
studies. 3. Public relations—Health planning—United States—Case
studies. I. Needleman, Carolyn Emerson, 1941- . II. Shapiro,
Maurice A. III. Title.
   RA423.2.L48 1998
   614.4'273—dc21   97-33795

98 99 00 01 02 03 10 9 8 7 6 5 4 3 2 1

Acquiring Editor:	C. Deborah Laughton
Editorial Assistant:	Eileen Carr
Production Editor:	Sanford Robinson
Production Assistant:	Lynn Miata
Typesetter:	Danielle Dillahunt
Indexer:	Teri Greenberg
Cover Designer:	Ravi Balasuriya
Print Buyer:	Anna Chin

CONTENTS

ACKNOWLEDGMENTS

This book would not have been written without the advice and vision of Dana Phillips. Then a program officer of the Howard Heinz Endowment, she was intrigued by our experiences in coping with serious public health risks. She also wanted to explore further some major success stories in which professionals and community members had taken leadership on public health problems. The Heinz Endowments/ Pittsburgh Foundation eventually funded 14 case studies, 6 of which appear here.

This book was transformed by deepening experiences in work with communities. Thanks are owing to Robert A. Bruce of the W. K. Kellogg Foundation for the opportunity to participate in the planning year of the Kellogg Foundation's Community-Based Public Health Initiative. Thanks are also due to Karen Feinstein and to N. Mark Richards of the Jewish Health Care Foundation of Pittsburgh for their financial support to our community planning process and for several opportunities to study the process of confronting risk. Most important, thanks are owing to the community partners in these episodes, who were willing to share their understanding.

Maggie MacDonald provided essential help in numerous phases of the case study process, and Russell G. Schuh was largely responsible for assuring that they would be conducted in time and within budget. Excellent guidance on how to construct case studies was provided by Beaufort Longest Jr. Paul Schulte of the National Institute for Occupational Safety and Health (NIOSH) provided a thoughtful analysis on ways to improve public health practice. Theodore Marmor, Charles Perrow, and Sandra Panem also provided early advice in the planning process. To Martin Needleman, Stephanie Larison, and MaryAnn Petersen, thanks for your ideas, encouragement, patience, and enthusiasm for this project. Thanks are also due to the doctoral students in the Occupational and Environmental Health Concentration at Bryn Mawr College's Graduate School of Social Work and Social Research, for many spirited discussions of the issues raised in this book.

CHAPTER 1

CONFRONTING RISK

A Value-Laden Activity

CAROLYN E. NEEDLEMAN

LAURA C. LEVITON

Bad news is never welcome. When people learn of public health risks in their communities, their reactions can be unexpected and sometimes very unpleasant. Henrik Ibsen's 1882 play, *An Enemy of the People* (Heritage Edition, 1965), was prophetic of the problems many public health and environmental professionals face today in community-based interventions. Ibsen vividly portrayed the pressures battering a well-meaning doctor who discovered that a new spa, likely to attract many tourists, was contaminated by waste from nearby tanneries.

Dr. Stockman: It is I that have the real good of the town at heart! I want to lay bare the evils that, sooner or later, must come to light. Ah! You shall see whether I love my native town.

Burgomaster: You, who, in your blind obstinacy, want to cut off the town's chief source of prosperity!

Dr. Stockman: That source is poisoned, man! Are you mad? We live by trafficking in filth and corruption! The whole of our flourishing social life is rooted in a lie!

Burgomaster: Idle fancies—or worse. The man who scatters broadcast of such offensive insinuations against his native place must be an enemy of society. (Ibsen, 1965, p. 41)

Public health risks in a community often remain unrecognized, concealed, accepted, or denied until some event precipitates change. Like the Norwegian town in Ibsen's play, most community settings include diverse interest groups with different levels of receptivity to information about public health risks. Some residents may stand to lose significantly by disclosures about risks, either financially or in terms of social considerations such as public image. For example, local leaders in an inner-city neighborhood may deny an escalating rate of AIDS, not wanting to reinforce negative stereotypes about the community. Homeowners may resist risk information about health threats related to residential radon, asbestos, or lead contamination because of anticipated adverse effects on the price and marketability of their property. Communities can be sharply divided between those who want to know as much as possible about whatever public health risks they face and those who desperately want such information suppressed or at least minimized.

The aim of this book is to assist professionals and students in public health and environmental protection to anticipate and cope with the social complexity of working with communities threatened by serious health hazards. Professionals often feel unprepared for such roles. Like the community residents at risk from the hazard, they sometimes find themselves enmeshed in social and political situations that they do not understand, or they feel powerless to change the situations they do understand. This book provides case examples and specific tools for analyzing and dealing with such predicaments.

The hard fact is, risk communication and public health problem solving are not necessarily viewed by all as benign, desirable interventions. Therefore, the role of the health or environmental professional is not value neutral. Like it or not, professionals are taking sides in a political contest in which the much desired win/win solution is not always possible. In and of itself, the decision to raise community awareness about a public health risk and to begin addressing the problem is a moral choice, with the health professional unavoidably cast to some degree as an advocate and champion for public health in opposition to other contrary local interests.

If pressed, most of us would probably say we approve of the choice to deal with community health hazards openly, and we consider the role of public health advocate to be an honorable one. But professionals charged with risk communication and disease prevention often fail to recognize the implications of these value choices. Instead of anticipating and planning for complex, varied reactions from different audiences in the community, they expect a uniform and basically positive community response to their intervention. When target communities become divided, hostile, and difficult to deal with, their residents are said to be acting irrationally (National Research Council, 1989; Wandersman & Hallman, 1993). In truth, the charge of irrationality might apply with greater accuracy to the health professionals who expected the bad news to be received calmly.

There is at least some good news about the bad news: Confronting environmental risk is often very healthy for communities, in a social as well as a medical sense. As the case studies in this book show, such problems present opportunities as well as costs. Sometimes, by confronting risks, communities can initiate or enhance the usefulness of public debate about a variety of community problems. Sometimes confronting risk serves as a catalyst to transform the definition of these problems, or to improve the way that community institutions operate to solve them. Confronting risk can also encourage the emergence of new leadership on important public health problems.

In practice, public health professionals often recognize and sometimes act on these opportunities. Yet, with some important exceptions, this area of public health practice takes place outside the conceptual frameworks currently guiding professional training. It relies instead on.

an oral tradition of what might be called "craft knowledge" or "practice wisdom" concerning how to work interactively with communities around environmental risk issues. These experience-based strategies get shared informally in professional circles and passed along verbally from teachers to their students. They seldom become explicit (although Chess, Hance, & Sandman, 1988, provide a notable exception to the rule). Public health and environmental protection are not unusual in this respect, of course. All sciences and professions have their own body of informal craft knowledge, whether they recognize it or not.

In recent years, as communities have grown more aware and concerned about environmental hazards, public health problems, and environmental justice issues, this particular kind of craft knowledge has become critically important. Under these circumstances, skills for working with communities should logically begin to find a place in formal professional training. But this has not yet happened. As a result, many public and environmental health professionals still find themselves unprepared for and genuinely puzzled by negative community reactions to their proposals for handling risks. Without understanding quite how it happened, they fall into the "enemy of the people" role (Harris, 1984; Kohler, 1990; Sigmund, 1989; Ward, 1972), feeling the kind of anger and frustration expressed by Ibsen's hero, Dr. Stockman: "What? Isn't it the truth that I tell them? Don't they turn all ideas upside down? Don't they stir up right and wrong into one hotch-potch? Don't they call lies everything that I know to be the truth?" (1965, p. 91).

Fortunately, although existing resources for improving this situation are underused, they are already numerous and rich in potential. For example, conceptual frameworks developed by social scientists for analyzing risk perception are clearly relevant (e.g., Fischhoff, 1989; Fischhoff, Bostrom, & Quadrel, 1993; Slovic, Fischhoff, & Lichtenstein, 1987). Analyses of community dynamics and social processes related to public health risks and environmental hazards have a direct bearing on the issue (Becker, 1996; Edelstein & Wandersman, 1987; Erikson, 1976; Kasperson et al., 1988; Silver, 1992; Wandersman & Hallman, 1993, 1994). Materials developed to assist risk communicators—for example, the list of "dos and don'ts" produced by Rutgers University faculty in conjunction with the state of New Jersey—are bound to be useful (e.g., Chess, Hance, & Sandman, 1988; Covello, Sandman, & Slovic, 1988).

From the case studies in this book, it seems clear that many aspects of craft knowledge could be systematized and placed into existing frameworks of sociology, organizational behavior, interpersonal relations, community organization, political science, and ethics.

RISK CONFRONTATION: A FOURTH LEVEL OF EFFORT

This book is entitled *Confronting Public Health Risks* in order to emphasize that it deals with a level of professional effort different from the more familiar activities of *assessing, managing,* or *communicating* risk. *Confronting* seems more descriptive of the complex interactions involved when professionals in public health, environmental protection, and health education actually begin to engage with communities to address local problems that represent serious health risks.

The risks discussed here are public health problems. The specific illustrations involve environmental hazards, occupational health exposures, and treatment of people living with HIV. However, specifics matter less than the basic issues. The focus is not on these substantive topics, but on the process whereby public health problems become (or potentially might become) focal points of community concern. We could have chosen other public health problems, such as cancer clusters, infant mortality, or even the polio epidemic. The book does not address other kinds of risks with high priority at the local level, such as crime or economic insecurity. Even though some of the processes described may have broader applicability, we have concentrated exclusively on examples from the United States in order to keep some consistency in the political context.

Risk confrontation is defined as a problem-solving process. This does not imply that the problem will actually be resolved, but rather, that professionals and community members will come together to address the problem and options for a solution. To achieve a problem-solving process that might be deemed successful—from anyone's perspective—a broad range of skills is required.

Skills for risk confrontation are not entirely formalized or even recognized. Policy makers and program managers may need to handle crises that call for skills in public relations and crowd control. They may need to negotiate agreements among competing parties and work constructively with mass media concerning publicity and news coverage. When restoring public confidence seems to call for opening up a more participatory risk-management process, they may need to deal with skeptical supervisors and constraining norms within their own organizations. Professionals may need to help exposed or health-impaired individuals and their families cope with anger, anxiety, hesitation about participating in health screening, and legal concerns about compensation.

Such challenges hover in the background of the three-phase risk response framework outlined by the National Research Council (1989): risk assessment, risk management, and risk communication. The Council defines *risk assessment* as "the characterization of potential adverse effects of exposures to hazards" (p. 321). Although it is generally viewed as a technical activity to be carried out by professionals, even this phase is not totally insulated from nonscientific concerns. Scientific values, public pressure, and politics play at least some role in determining what constitutes a risk worth assessing.

Risk management, taking a step closer to overt politics, is "the evaluation of alternative risk control actions, selection among them . . . , and their implementation" (p. 322). This also is sometimes viewed as a purely technical activity; however, to the degree that making these choices involves negotiation among professionals and various interest groups, it cannot remain strictly technical.

The third phase, *risk communication,* is defined by the Council (1989) as

> an interactive process of exchange of information and opinion among individuals, groups, and institutions; often involves multiple messages about the nature of risk or expressing concerns, opinions, or reactions to risk messages or to legal and institutional arrangements for risk management. (p. 322)

Conceived of in this way—as an interactive process rather than as a one-way information disclosure—risk communication can be quite complex socially. As a dialogue between professionals and laypersons addressing community concerns, it includes many nontechnical considerations.

The National Research Council (1989) acknowledges that the assessment, management, and communication of risk takes place in a larger context. This larger context, which we are calling confronting risk, should be treated as a *fourth level of effort* in dealing with community health hazards. Professionals responsible for assessing, managing, and communicating public health risks are usually well equipped with scientific and technical expertise. But *confronting risk* involves community-based problem solving, inherently social in nature; training for this part of the process is often lacking. To prepare professionals appropriately, the organizational and political dimensions of risk confrontation need to be recognized, understood, accepted as normal, and actively incorporated into planning public health interventions.

Viewing confronting risk as a distinct focal point of effort has a number of advantages. First, the term draws attention to the interactive aspects of dealing with community health risks, where various interest groups with different agendas work at problem solving along with professional experts, and proposed solutions get hammered out through political processes. The technical aspects of risk assessment, risk management, and risk communication as traditionally conceived certainly play a role. However, as shown in the case studies that follow, nonrational social and community forces are at least as important as the technical judgments of professionals. In the real world, reason and science do not necessarily prevail. Bargains must be struck; community support must be finessed; and resources must be mobilized to carry out the proposed solutions. In risk confrontation, inclusion of the community is not merely good public relations or window dressing. Instead, it is a genuine alliance with interested parties in the community as significant, necessary, and sometimes exasperating partners.

A second reason to emphasize confronting risk is that, in these case studies at least, the very nature of the health risk itself is defined not by science alone, but rather through negotiation in a muddled and shifting social environment. Traditional conceptions of risk assessment and risk management imply that science and technology can tell us from the very start what the risk is and what priority it should have for attention. Yet, the community may see things very differently. Substantial research suggests that some perceived risks are not real, whereas some real risks are not perceived as such (e.g., Fischhoff, 1989). The case studies presented here bear this out, offering examples of perceived risks that have little basis in reality and true risks for which the public feels little concern. In risk confrontation (as opposed to assessment, management, and communication), the objective truth is not the main point. What matters—and what has real consequences, valid or not—is the social consensus reached on how to define and deal with the risk.

A third reason to focus on confronting risk is that various factions of professionals, as well as various factions of community residents, may hold divergent views about what "solving" a public health problem actually means. For some, the problem is solved when a sizable proportion of the affected individuals are informed of the health hazard so that intelligent choices can be made, or official actions related to hazard control can be justified. For others, solving the problem requires setting up accessible service programs to assure education, prevention, disease detection, and medical treatment. Still others will not consider the problem solved until ongoing exposures to the hazard are successfully abated. Some may consider the problem solved when negative publicity dies down, even if the hazard still exists. The kind of end-point being sought is central to the social process of risk confrontation, causing enormous confusion if unrecognized disagreement exists.

A final advantage of the term confronting risk is that it implies an ongoing process. Many public health problems contain intractable dilemmas. They may not ever be totally resolved; but they will not go away. Communities will continue to live with the health hazards and struggle to cope with them, but the problems may persist because of the diversity of community interests involved and the magnitude of the resources required to meet the community's needs fully. Certainly in the case studies presented here, not everyone is totally pleased with the outcomes, and the work of risk confrontation continues.

To summarize, health risks not only need to be assessed, managed, and communicated; they also need to be confronted in a social and political sense. Confronting risk means handling public health problems in ways that fit the community's social realities, reconciling inconsistent interests sufficiently to move toward actual disease prevention. In risk confrontation, the situations into which professionals and policy makers are thrown may involve complicated relationships and unaccustomed roles; solutions may require cooperation from community interest groups with strong agendas unrelated to health. To deal with problems of this sort, public health professionals need the kinds of skills that have been identified as key features of leadership in public health: developing good definitions of the problems, convening stakeholders, and developing a range of options for solving public health problems (Institute of Medicine, 1988).

THE SOCIAL CONSTRUCTION OF PUBLIC HEALTH PROBLEMS

To address a *public health problem,* one must first understand the complexity of the concept itself. On one level it seems simple enough. In contrast to medicine's emphasis on individual care, public health focuses on improving conditions that affect the health of whole populations—ensuring safe food and drinking water, controlling infectious diseases, reducing toxic exposures, preventing accidents, changing unhealthy lifestyles, and improving living conditions and service access for the disadvantaged. Assessing the status of public health effort in the United States in 1988, the Institute of Medicine (a branch of the National Academy of Sciences) described the goals of public health in these broad terms: to identify problems that affect entire communities or populations, marshal support to address those problems, and assure that solutions get implemented. The U.S. Public Health Service has incorporated these concerns into a plan for improving the health of the nation, known as the Year 2000 Objectives (Public Health Service, 1990).

In general formulations of this kind, the task itself sounds daunting, but the concept, public health problems, is presented as fairly unambiguous. It is assumed that public health problems have an objective reality that is measurable in scientific terms by experts in medicine or epidemiology. For example, health professionals in the community have detected a disease cluster—say, a specific kind of cancer occurring at a rate higher than that expected for the general population. Or a careful test of the drinking water shows a specific kind of contamination, measurable in parts per million, that exceeds a scientifically determined standard of safety for human health. Presumably, these are the facts, self-evidently true. The professionals' task is to help the community understand and address them.

But in community settings, things are seldom so clear-cut. Like all social problems, public health problems are socially constructed (Johnson & Covello, 1987). To a large extent, they exist in the eye of the beholder, and not all beholders see the same reality.

The importance of recognizing that public health problems are socially constructed was brought home to two of the authors in a way we will never forget, by a visit to Leadville, Colorado. Leadville, a small town perched amid spectacular peaks in the Rocky Mountains, was once one of the nation's richest mining centers. During the 19th century, legendary fortunes were made from the area's phenomenal deposits of silver and other metals, including the lead that gives the town its name. The larger mines around Leadville are played out now, and a number of residents have turned to small, owner-operated mining activities. The town's present economy also depends heavily on the tourists drawn to this high-altitude remnant of America's Wild West. With a well-practiced blend of pride and cynicism, some local residents earn income by steering visitors through the town's museum houses and gift shops, pointing out the old Opera House and the sites of celebrated gunfights. They regale the tourists with stories of Leadville's colorful and scandalous boom years, when leading citizens flaunted their wealth and their mistresses in grand style. For the benefit of tourists on special occasions, the town puts on dance-hall entertainments, reenacts stagecoach robberies, and parades mule trains through its main streets.

Unfortunately, at the time of our visit, the community of Leadville was also dealing with what we understood to be fairly serious lead contamination related to its mining history. While attending a government-sponsored conference on risk communication in the summer of 1990, we found ourselves in the general vicinity of Leadville and could not resist a visit. We knew that the U.S. Environmental Protection Agency (EPA) had recently taken action to clean up toxic mine tailings and alert Leadville's residents to their public health problem, and we were curious about how the community was responding. We expected the reaction to be somewhat mixed, because the EPA was reportedly requiring the small mine owners to clean up not only their own waste, but also a century's worth of mine tailings and waste left by former operators. The small mine operations were not profitable enough to carry this expense, and their owners could be forced out of business. With this further erosion of the town's economic basis, other community people also stood to lose jobs.

We rented a car and drove up through the Continental Divide to see Leadville for ourselves. What we found was a complete disconnect between different interpretations of reality. Many of the residents we talked to—shopkeepers, people in the street, mothers walking their children home from school—regarded the EPA as the devil incarnate. Grimly, they recounted how government bureaucrats had invaded their town uninvited, threatening residents with the prospect of condemned property, involuntary relocation, and unwelcome new legal requirements for small mine owners. And all, they claimed, over a hazard that "doesn't exist."

Asked about the plans for testing blood lead levels among the town's children, some residents seemed receptive. But others assured us that no one in the community would cooperate with this "stupid idea." "Don't they think we'd know it if something was making our own children sick?" one shop owner demanded, brandishing the postcards she was in the process of selling us.

> Don't they think we care? Nobody here has noticed any health problems. Who are these bureaucrats to come in and tell us that we're ignorant, that we don't know as much as they do? How dare they tell us we shouldn't live here! This town is our home. A lot of us have grown old here, and our health is just fine!

Her hands trembled as she spoke, in what might have been anger, or maybe the wrist weakness that sometimes signals lead poisoning.

Leadville's residents may have denied they had lead problems because of self-interest of the sort that Ibsen wrote about—a calculated effort to cover up a public health hazard, which if acknowledged would mean economic loss in tourist dollars, property values, and mining profits. But we felt something deeper was involved. Some of these townspeople truly believed, sincerely and passionately, that no hazard and no risk existed. Their own health and the health of their children were important to them. But they had constructed reality in a way that simply had no room for the idea of danger from their familiar community environment. They were totally closed to arguments of fact and the evidence that might have come from community blood testing, because they felt the outside experts did not understand the community's history, respect its culture, or care about its best interests. In truth, EPA had not done much, at that date, to change their impression. If the solution to the problem was going to be annihilation of their social world, they wanted no part of it and refused even to entertain the thought that a hazard might actually exist.

How can we explain Leadville's and EPA's vastly different versions of the facts? Writing in the 1920s, the sociologist W. I. Thomas (1966) noted that any given set of circumstances can be interpreted in radically different ways, each of which will seem self-evidently true to those holding that particular interpretation; these definitions of the situation are what influence social action, whether they are objectively true or not. In working with communities, it is important to understand exactly how the local public health problems are being defined by all of those involved, both professionals and residents. One's own interpretation may seem obviously correct, and the interpretation of others may seem patently absurd—but both have a certain validity within their respective frameworks as ways of looking at reality. Being socially constructed and therefore to some extent reflecting values and ideology, none of the differing definitions (including that of the technical expert) represents the final word on objective truth (Berger & Luckmann, 1967).

When a number of individuals in the community develop a particular definition of the situation over time, that definition acquires a social reality and no longer represents merely the personal opinions of individuals. Even if directly contradicted by the available scientific evidence, it influences how people in a community actually react and behave. Such definitions are a large part of what must be understood by professionals in order to work constructively with a community.

These realities help explain why public health professionals and community residents sometimes feel they are talking past each other.

Practitioners and policy makers may be trying hard to heighten community awareness about a hazard they deem very serious, whereas the community residents are defining the same hazard as relatively minor in the face of their total life situations. Alternatively, the public may view a risk as extraordinarily important and become frustrated that public health officials do not see it in the same light.

Even where agreement exists on the perception of risk, bureaucracies and communities may be responding to different constraints and priorities. A good illustration is violence prevention. Interpersonal violence appears at the very top of many communities' list of health concerns—yet public health agencies are forced by their mandates and funding to concentrate instead on health concerns that have a lower community priority. Clearly, solving public health problems is not always straightforward, and both the definition of problems and the proposed solutions involve more than technical or medical considerations.

SIX CASE STUDIES OF RISK CONFRONTATION

In the chapters that follow, six case studies are presented: two from environmental health, two from occupational health, and two from the AIDS epidemic. They reflect original research by the authors conducted between 1990 and 1992. Many of the people we talked to were promised anonymity; this enabled them to speak with unusual candor, making the case studies particularly detailed and revealing. However, to assure the confidentiality of their remarks, we needed to change the names of some people and places. As a result, we are barred from providing the typical cites and references that might accompany such material. If we were to include references to reports or newspaper articles, for example, we would be revealing the identities we have otherwise worked to disguise. Documentation exists for all quotations and references and was reviewed by the advisory committee for this project.

The situations described in these case studies are fluid and complex; they represent problems that, in organizational behavior literature, have been called "messes" (Gray, 1989). The characteristics of such problems are shown in Figure 1.1. *Mess* seems a good term to describe what many

1. The problems are ill defined, or there is disagreement about how they should be defined.

2. Several stakeholders have a vested interest in the problems and are interdependent.

3. These stakeholders are not necessarily identified a priori or organized in any systematic way.

4. There may be a disparity of power and/or resources for dealing with the problems among the stakeholders.

5. Stakeholders may have different levels of expertise and different access to information about the problems.

6. The problems are often characterized by technical complexity and scientific uncertainty.

7. Differing perspectives on the problems often lead to adversarial relationships among the stakeholders.

8. Incremental or unilateral efforts to deal with the problems typically produce less than satisfactory solutions.

9. Existing processes for addressing the problems prove insufficient and may even exacerbate them.

Figure 1.1. Characteristics of "Messy" Problems
Source: Barbara Gray, *Collaborating,* San Francisco: Jossey-Bass, 1989, p. 10. Reprinted by permission.

practitioners and decision makers face when they try to confront risks. Not only are the problems ill defined initially, but new issues of community power, perceptions, actions, and feelings continually arise to keep things unpredictable and to create a climate antithetical to rationally planned technical solutions.

When community residents, local leaders, and outside professionals confront an environmental or public health risk, they are usually trying to solve several associated problems at the same time. The ostensible focus is the direct impact of the risk on human health—that is, the effects traditionally considered central in risk assessment, risk management, and risk communication. However, as these cases show, other important problems may arise from the way the risk is perceived by various interested parties, as well as from proposed solutions. These problems may touch on health effects, but they also reflect other social, political, and economic issues.

Community definitions of the situation often include concerns that professionals tend to leave out—in particular, the possibility that addressing the public health problem could have some unintended adverse social consequences (Needleman, 1993). For example, those at risk commonly worry that publicity about the problem will cost them losses in property value or stigmatize them for future employment and insurability. There may be objective truth in these fears, but that is not the point. These concerns need to be taken seriously, even if health professionals think they are unwarranted. If such concerns are dismissed as irrelevant, the community being "helped" will feel under attack instead and will react accordingly—as did the community in Leadville.

Risk problems evolve over time; so do professional relationships with the community. For ease of discussion, each of the case studies is introduced with a *timeline* to give a sense of how events unfolded—when and how the problem was defined and the time periods in which particular strategies were used and new issues arose. Many case studies of risk intervention deal only with a very brief moment in the history of the problem, leaving the impression that the issue arose quickly and was resolved after the period studied. By contrast, the case studies presented here all cover a long time span. Over a period of years, events create the risk; the risk becomes defined as a problem (or several problems); effort is aimed at bringing attention to the risk; conflict and negotiation may or may not take place; resources, often meager, are allocated to address the problem; and communities deal with the benefits and inadequacies of the outcome. Professionals need to become familiar with the way that risk problems unfold over time, because they may develop relationships with communities and confront risk problems at many different points in the evolution of the problem. As the Institute of Medicine (1988) has pointed out, maintaining a good working relationship between professionals and the community is at least as important as solving any particular public health problem.

A list of the active *stakeholders* is also supplied at the start of each case. Stakeholder is a term that originated in political science, but one that has been adopted in the organization literature and in evaluation of public programs (Gray, 1989; Shadish, Cook, & Leviton, 1991).

Stakeholders are defined as all parties (including professional experts) likely to be affected either positively or negatively by the perceived risk and by the proposed solutions. Understanding various stakeholders' perspectives is important because their perceptions, history, interests, capacities, and relationships enter into shaping the possibilities for risk confrontation. Some stakeholders gain recognition because of their official positions and expertise, others because they control financial and other resources, others because they are directly affected by the hazard. Not all affected parties actually become active in risk confrontation; therefore, for each case example, we have listed only those stakeholders who played a visible social and political role.

Finally, each case is followed by a discussion section highlighting a *key issue* that the case illustrates particularly well. The issues are built around concepts drawn eclectically from the fields of sociology, organizational behavior, community organization, and ethics. Although key issues are presented in connection with a specific case, they can all be applied more broadly, and should be. To facilitate this broader application, some *general questions* have also been supplied for each case to draw attention to its lessons for similar situations. The aim is to leave the reader in a better position to make informed choices about the process of confronting health risks more generally.

OUTLINE OF THE CASES

In Chapter 2, "Health Risk Notification in a Small Town," Laura C. Leviton shows how workers and community coped with exposure to a notorious, well-understood chemical carcinogen. The case study shows how occupational health problems can spill over to become community problems as well. It also illustrates how health risks can generate a variety of muddled social problems, even when scientific understanding of the hazard seems complete. In this case, the community split sharply over how the issue should be handled. Tensions increased, along with a feeling that federal and state authorities had betrayed the town. Lawsuits divided the community, and many concerns ancillary to health kept surfacing. Only later, after the crisis period had exhausted everyone, did a different kind of problem-solving process become possible. The key issue discussed in relation to this case is *the social construction of risk*.

In Chapter 3, "Science Versus Service in a Community-Based Lead Screening," Carolyn E. Needleman and Martin L. Needleman show how well-meaning scientists ran into unexpected community indifference concerning an environmental health risk. Because the hazard was lead, widely known to pose special health risks to children, the apparent lack of interest was all the more surprising. To clarify why the health department's lead screening failed to gain the target population's cooperation, the authors examine the methods that were used to work with the community. Their analysis shows how important it is to identify appropriate community leaders and approach them correctly. It also shows how scientific research goals can conflict with public health service, in ways that undermine the community's motivation to cooperate. The key issue discussed in relation to this case is *the central importance of community support.*

Chapter 4, by Laura C. Leviton, is titled "Worker Health in Black and White" because of its strong racial overtones and also its seemingly clear-cut opposition of good and evil. The case involves occupational exposure to the same well-understood carcinogen discussed in Chapter 2. However, the way this community confronted the risk could not have been more different. The exposed workers were primarily African American, in a Southern town governed almost exclusively by whites; charges of racism arose in relation to both the exposure and subsequent events. The workers' plight became a national symbol, but local community leaders seemed not to care. At least, that is what the federal experts thought. They may well have been wrong. So many differences in perception abound in this case that we may never get to the bottom of them. In the meantime, who decides where the public interest lies, or what kind of professional intervention best promotes social justice? The key issue discussed in relation to this case is the *ethics of public health actions.*

Chapter 5, by Laura C. Leviton and Regina R. Reitmeyer, is entitled "HIV and the Schools in a High Prevalence Community." Although public hysteria has generally subsided over HIV-positive children in the schools, a festering distrust of school leadership can take its place when HIV-related policies are not implemented well. The problems of confidentiality, support services for children, HIV prevention, and staff training loom especially large in inner-city school districts such as the one discussed here, where AIDS is a prevalent problem and resources are scarce. Yet, even in this needy community, some surprising resources were brought to bear with positive results. The key issue discussed in relation to this case is *building community capacity*.

In Chapter 6, "Superfund Showdown," Stephen E. Kauffman chronicles the conflict between the U.S. Environmental Protection Agency and a well-organized suburban community over the cleanup of a Superfund site. This case shows how the process of problem solving, and also the relationships between communities and bureaucrats, evolves over time. In this case, risk communication began as a one-way message from "experts" to "the public." Because the cleanup method was controversial, however, activists forced a two-way communication process. The eventual resolution illustrates the importance of building in good mechanisms for public participation and also the importance of informal relationships among stakeholders. The key issue discussed in relation to this case is *fostering community participation*.

In Chapter 7's case study, "Community Teamwork on AIDS Care," Laura C. Leviton analyzes a community-wide problem-solving effort to improve service access for people living with AIDS. This community undertook the "risk" of placing people with AIDS in local nursing homes, at a time when most communities were still struggling over discrimination against AIDS patients within hospitals. The novel solutions developed in this case show what can be accomplished through genuine collaboration between professionals and community leaders. The key issue discussed in relation to this case is *the process of negotiation*.

In Chapter 8, "Risk Confrontation: Tasks, Criteria, and Evaluation," Laura C. Leviton and Maurice A. Shapiro offer a conceptual framework that can be used to evaluate the six case studies, as well as other instances in which health professionals, community leaders, and others confront risks. This final chapter, meant as a summary, assumes that the reader has already considered the key issues addressed at the end of individual chapters.

A NOTE ON SKILL BUILDING

Understanding an issue does not impart skill in dealing with the issue. There is no automatic translation to know what to do and how to go about it. Public health and environmental professionals who want to assist communities in confronting risk will need to develop the practical skills described or implied by the cases in this book—identifying community leaders, mediation, conflict resolution, program development, resource mobilization, communication, counseling, strategic planning, and ethical analysis.

This kind of skill development is beyond the scope of the present book. However, relevant resources may be close at hand. The Internet provides many resources; for example, a search of the term *conflict resolution* through a web browser revealed no less than 743,876 websites on the subject. Workshops on conflict resolution and negotiation are plentiful. Another resource is people and their experience. Veterans of past campaigns in public health include the nurses who were active in tuberculosis care and maternal and child health care, as well as veteran sexually transmitted disease officers. Many of these professionals are close to retirement or in retirement, but they can describe how their organizations and communities developed capacity and infrastructure to deal with these problems. To explore value-based choices more deeply, the reader may want to invite input from medical ethicists, who are present on the staff or faculty of many medical schools and universities. These individuals have been trained to articulate how abstract ethical principles apply in practice and could speak to ethical dilemmas in public health. One of the authors (Leviton) has consulted an ethicist in more than one public health project.

Instructors using this casebook are encouraged to develop exercises to assist students in developing skills, or at least in understanding the importance of developing them. The authors have made use of some of the cases in teaching graduate students in social work and health behavior programs and have found that several studies make a particularly good basis for role play experiences. For example, the case studies presented in Chapters 2, 4, and 6 are useful for role playing related to conflict resolution and negotiation. Chapters 2 and 7 serve well to support role-playing exercises that illustrate principles of collaboration and joint problem solving. Targeting a local area affected by health risk problems, students can use Chapter 3 and the Key Issue discussion at its conclusion to inform an exercise in carrying out preliminary social reconnaissance, identifying community leadership, and relating community concerns to a planned intervention. Chapter 5 can be used as background for an exercise aimed at mapping community capacity for problem solving. Finally, we have found it extremely useful for students to talk directly with environmental activists and public health advocates in the local area, experts who are invited as class speakers to discuss their views on how professionals can best work constructively with communities around environmental and public health risks.

CHAPTER **2**

HEALTH RISK NOTIFICATION IN A SMALL TOWN

LAURA C. LEVITON

INTRODUCTION[1]

This case study describes the events leading up to a chemical worker health risk notification and health protection
program in a small town, as well as the implementation and
evolution of the program. The chemical company that hired
these workers went bankrupt in 1981, and the site was
placed on the federal Superfund cleanup list. Today, the
plant has been razed to the ground. A barbed-wire fence
blocks access to the site. No vegetation grows inside the
perimeter; the playground next door is deserted. One sees
cars whizzing by on the superhighway leading into downtown. It's a very small Superfund site. Who would have
thought it would have started all that trouble?

AUTHOR'S NOTE: Portions of this case study appeared in brief form in the *American
Journal of Public Health* (Leviton, Marsh, et al., 1971).

KEY ISSUE AND GENERAL QUESTIONS

This case study illustrates how the social definition given to a health risk can become just as important as the medical or physical definition, in terms of its consequences for communities. Health professionals need to plan how they will deal with the social definition as they confront the "real" risk. The discussion following the case describes how risk perceptions differ among the interested parties and why the social definition of risk can produce so much stress. Specifically, the discussion addresses these questions:

▲ What does it mean for a risk to have a social reality as well as a physical reality?

▲ Why does the layperson not perceive risk in the same way as the scientist?

▲ Why does the social reality of risk so often induce conflict and stress?

STAKEHOLDERS

Former workers—whether activist or not

City and county civic leadership

CLEAN—Citizens League for Environmental Action Now

Participants in lawsuit against company assets

Plant owners: Hilltown Chemical Company previously owned by Dutch Country Chemical Company

National chemical companies

Business community of Hilltown

State Department of Environmental Resources (DER)

State Department of Health (DOH)

Federal Environmental Protection Agency (EPA)

Federal Agency for Toxic Substances and Disease Registry (ATSDR)

National Institute for Occupational Safety and Health (NIOSH)

University research group

TIMELINE

1940	Health effects of betanaphthylamine (BNA) are established
1947-1962	Dutch Country plant manufactures BNA
1961	Hilltown newspaper reports BNA effects
1965	Site leased by Hilltown Chemical Company
1973-1981	Hilltown plant is cited for violation of health and safety regulations
Late 1970s	Central State Chemical Company provides medical surveillance to its workers
1981	Closure and bankruptcy of Hilltown Chemical
1982	Hilltown site is nominated to Superfund list
	Emergency cleanup ordered by EPA
1983	Formation of CLEAN organization
	Closure of Central State Company and another major employer
	Governor vetoes state appropriation for health screening
1983-1985	DOH health screening of workers and residents
1985	ATSDR funds DOH for new screening effort
1986	University contract for screening is awarded

SECTION I

BACKGROUND: CHALLENGES AND OPPORTUNITIES

DESCRIPTION OF THE COMMUNITY

Located on the Susquehanna River in the mid-Atlantic states is Hilltown, a community of approximately 12,000 people. The surrounding county has 37,000 people. The town, nestled in a scenic valley between mountains, is surrounded by rural woodlands and farms. Bears have been known to wander into the downtown area, and deer are commonplace. The town, perhaps a bit rundown, is charming and old-fashioned, with many historic homes lining the riverfront. A superhighway brought improved access to the town in the late 1970s.

The population of Hilltown describes itself as a mixture of European immigrants and "hillbillies." As one resident quipped, "With this mountain range here, I'd say we're mountain billies." The town is fairly conservative in outlook. Relatively few younger people leave town, in spite of limited job opportunities. A small teachers college, light manufacturing, and nearby coal and paper manufacturing industries predominate. A major state university is located nearby, but it exerts no influence on the culture of the town.

In the 19th century, the town was a major hub of the lumbering industry—a boomtown with extremely wealthy residents. It boasted visits by celebrities such as Mark Twain, and the Queen of Spain bought a hotel there for investment purposes. However, the town was stratified socially between the wealthy lumbering families who ran the operation and the lumberjacks who performed the work.

As in many small towns, social division persists to the present day. Family roots define who people are and what they will become, according to one longtime resident. One public health professional described Hilltown as "a sad little town," noting that the town appeared to have all the problems and none of the advantages of a small town. Community residents seldom have a good thing to say about each other; on the other hand, loyalties run deep, and people willingly help neighbors and friends.

Hilltown is plagued with chronic unemployment due to its location and the decline in both the manufacturing and the coal industries. A 30% unemployment figure was cited in the mid-1980s, and few businesses have expanded since then. Many people hold down two jobs to make ends meet because of the low pay scales. Employees of one paper company went on strike in 1987. Within 2 months, the company replaced all of the strikers with other local residents and broke the strike. This situation caused tremendous ill feeling between strikers and new employees, and between employers and workers.

The townspeople have a distinctive view of employment and employers. It is not unusual for employees to expect mistreatment, or for employers and supervisors to give it. Employees can be extremely fearful of being replaced, and unions are on the decline locally. The expectation and confirmation of an authoritarian relationship occurs both on an individual basis and within organizations. When one chemical company closed, workers received $500 severance pay, if they were fortunate. Workers formed a picket line to protest, but it did no good. The town expected little else.

Politics also demonstrates social divisions between "haves" and "have nots." For example, periodic flooding from the bordering riverfront affects about three quarters of the town. This flooding could be prevented by construction of levees, but the construction would cost a great deal of money. Currently, individual home owners have to spend a good deal to prevent flood damage. Flooding does not affect historic riverfront homes of the well-to-do, who feel that a levee would impair the scenic view of the river. Several residents have said that the riverfront residents kept levees off the town agenda for decades. Finally, the issue came up for a vote last year. One longtime resident baldly called this debate "a class struggle."

HISTORY OF THE
HILLTOWN CHEMICAL COMPANY

Chemical companies have located their operations in Hilltown since the 1850s. An excellent water supply and cheap water power made it a desirable area for chemical manufacturing. An 8-acre site located just outside the downtown area has been the site of a chemical company throughout most of this century. In 1940, the Dutch Country Chemical Company was established on the site. In 1962, the Dutch Country company was purchased by a national corporation, and, in 1965, the Hilltown Chemical Company leased the site. The Dutch Country and Hilltown companies manufactured intermediate specialty chemicals for producers of dyes, pharmaceuticals, cosmetics, herbicides, and pesticides.

The original investors in the Dutch Country plant included a Hilltown University chemistry professor and a local surgeon who sits on the hospital board. There may have been other local stockholders in these companies from time to time. A prominent citizen and city council member leased nearby land for ground disposal of chemical wastes. For reasons that will be seen later, these intertwining interests posed some problems for the community.

From 1947 to 1962, when its use was banned in the state, the Dutch Country company manufactured betanaphthylamine (BNA), an aromatic amine, for use as an intermediate in manufacturing dyes and antioxidants. It is suspected, however, that, after 1962, small amounts of BNA may have been synthesized by Hilltown Chemical as a residual product in the manufacture of Broenner's acid, which was produced in large quantities until the plant closed in 1981. Furthermore, some workers have alleged that BNA continued to be used illegally by Hilltown Chemical after the 1962 ban. In addition to BNA, company invoices show that benzidine was used throughout the 1960s and into early 1970. Several other carcinogens and suspected carcinogens were used on-site.

BNA causes bladder cancer. It is one of the most potent chemical carcinogens known to occupational medicine, increasing the risk of bladder cancer by as much as 90 times. It is also one of the best-known occupational carcinogens. By the late 1800s, it was known that dye workers were much more likely than the general population to suffer from bladder cancer. Since 1940, the role of BNA in this has been established. Yet, manufacture of BNA at Hilltown Chemical began in 1947. The plant was one of only two (possibly three) locations in the United States in which BNA was manufactured after 1960. Although there is a less dangerous alternative to BNA in chemical manufacturing, BNA is cheaper to make. There were allegations that the owners of the Dutch Country company knew about the effects of BNA when they began manufacturing it. As with so many allegations in the history of this plant, it has not been possible to confirm the owners' prior knowledge.

At the request of the International Union Against Cancer, the State Department of Health (DOH) investigated the Dutch Country plant and a neighboring plant that used the chemicals. A report in a scientific journal identified 11 bladder cancer cases among these workers, a far greater incidence than the expected rate among the general population. The local newspaper quoted these findings in 1961. According to the scientific article, "As a result of the findings of these eleven cases and because it was believed impossible to obtain a voluntary discontinuation of the manufacture of beta-naphthylamine, the manufacture, use and storage of beta-naphthylamine was outlawed in (the state)." There was apparently no criminal penalty attached to violation of the ban. The company was purchased by a major chemical corporation shortly after, and, in 1965, the site was leased from this corporation by the owners of the Hilltown Chemical Company.

Dust containing BNA was dispersed into the atmosphere of the plant, and workers were exposed through breathing, skin contact, and ingestion. The company did not require workers to wear respirators and provided only short rubber gloves as protective equipment. Several of those interviewed said that the workers did not know or understand the dangers of breathing the dust. Yet, no one worked at Hilltown Chemical for long if he had any other options. The pay was low, and conditions were dangerous and uncomfortable. Men who worked at the plant often would have urine the same color as the dyes with which they worked.

Additionally, a social stigma was attached to working at the plant. Hilltown Chemical employed unskilled laborers, many of whom reportedly had alcohol problems. Some were illiterate, and some were mildly retarded. In the late 1970s, the Teamsters finally organized this workforce.

The Hilltown Chemical Company was always viewed by community leaders as "a shoestring operation." Even at its height, the plant never employed more than 100 people—only a total of 406 during the entire history of its operation. Hilltown management's knowledge of chemistry was variously described as pre-1946 and high school level by people familiar with their manufacturing processes. The owner exhibited signs of heavy-metal poisoning. Management knew little about toxicology and occupational health. From 1973 through 1981, the company was cited several times for violation of safety and health regulations.

One worker described the owner as a very religious man who would not deliberately put the workers in dangerous situations. The owner believed there were risks, but the risks were worth it, given the economic benefits of the jobs. Many respected citizens agreed with him. In the Hilltown area, the bottom line was jobs. Most Hilltown Chemical products were harmless as end products, but the process of manufacturing them created dangers. For example, banned chemicals were sometimes created in the process of manufacturing others. No one quite realized the impact of this process.

Many of the major U.S. chemical companies contracted with Hilltown Chemical for the production of items that were new, those for which only small quantities were needed, or those that allegedly posed possible health and safety liability they did not want themselves. According to an engineer, other chemical companies were "scared of Hilltown" due to the risks they ran in health and safety. Larger manufacturers had much higher standards for their own workers.

Hilltown Chemical had constant problems, particularly explosions. A public health nurse stated that people knew there were dangerous chemicals in the plant, some of which were probably toxic, but they accepted the situation. No one really considered it abnormal when, almost every week, a cloud of unknown material floated over the plant. Most people believed then, as now, that, if they were doing something wrong at Hilltown Chemical, the government would stop it.

Many rumors circulated in town about the chemicals that were actually manufactured at Hilltown Chemical. Several workers had allergic reactions to an orange herbicide with properties similar to Agent Orange, so many people believed that it was manufactured there. Others suspected that nerve gas was manufactured, but our informants say it is unlikely. They add, however, that such a chemical combination could occur accidentally.

The Hilltown Chemical site is 3 minutes from downtown Hilltown and adjacent to the river, with a park and playground nearby. Several community residents recall swimming as children in the on-site lagoons used by Hilltown to dispose of chemicals. In later years, a superhighway leading into town was constructed next to the site, and a senior citizen apartment building and a discount store were built nearby.

The Central State Company, another, larger, chemical manufacturer located next to the Hilltown Chemical site, used the BNA produced by Dutch Country/Hilltown for many years. Waste from this plant was dumped in various locations around Hilltown. To this day, the dumping locations remain uncertain.

PLANT CLOSURE, BANKRUPTCY, AND EMERGENCY CLEANUP

In the late 1970s and early 1980s, there was declining demand for dyestuff in the United States. Furthermore, Hilltown Chemical was increasingly scrutinized for violations of state and federal laws pertaining to the environment and to worker safety and health. In April 1979, the State Department of Environmental Resources (DER) required a change in the handling and disposal of solid waste and in the disposal of sludge and wastewater. In August 1980, an initial inspection of Hilltown Chemical by the federal Environmental Protection Agency (EPA) identified leaking drums, liquid waste in lagoons, and lack of security fencing, noting that "leachate leaving property has left a path 5 yards wide devoid of vegetation." Between January 1981 and January 1982, DER conducted eight inspections and attempted to get the owner to clean up the site. In March 1981, a contractor estimated the cost of cleanup to be more than the company could afford.

In May 1981, the National Institute for Occupational Safety and Health (NIOSH) investigated complaints about unsafe conditions and a variety of ailments workers were experiencing. The NIOSH report mentioned that although no known bladder carcinogens were in evidence during the inspection visit, the manufacture of Broenner's acid, which was common on-site, could theoretically produce small amounts of BNA. NIOSH concluded that remediation of health and safety hazards would require extensive modernization of the plant and that enforcement of the use of respirators would be needed as an interim step.

Hilltown Chemical stopped production the day after the NIOSH visit. Production ceased permanently in July, and Hilltown Chemical filed for bankruptcy in August. In December 1981, the local gas company shut the gas line to the Hilltown company because the gas bill had not been paid. Chemicals "cooking" in the reactor vessels were left standing, and everyone vacated the plant.

Around that time, the Superfund program was established by the federal government, and states were being solicited to nominate sites to the priority list. The DER viewed Superfund as a possible source of funding for cleanups and nominated the Hilltown Chemical site to the Superfund list.

An EPA assessment team went into the site, came out immediately, and declared an emergency in February 1982. The waste lagoons were leaching into a bordering creek, which fed the river. Furthermore, there were drums and tanks full of unknown materials on-site. The decision to declare an emergency was based on a 10-point document that was completed in 1 hour. Hilltown Chemical became the first Superfund site in the state and one of the first in the country. The Hilltown site was at that time at the top of EPA's priority list.

A state official who had been involved with the emergency phase put some perspective on EPA's subsequent actions. He was the on-site coordinator for the DER, Bureau of Waste Management, when the EPA declared the Hilltown emergency. He pointed out that, in 1982, when the EPA was first called into the Hilltown Chemical case, the agency had just faced three major national incidents, two of which were in the same state. The DER geared up dramatically during this time to face these problems. Also, federal regulations and new state laws concerning waste management were coming into play at this time.

PROBLEMS OF TRAINING, COMMUNICATION, AND PUBLIC RELATIONS

The new emphasis on cleanups, waste management, and the disposal of toxic substances meant that few professionals had much knowledge of the topic, but substantial trained manpower was needed. EPA and DER were both faced with a situation in which they could not afford to keep trained people on their payroll. Trained professionals were in great demand for private waste management consulting firms. The former DER official stated that, as soon as EPA would train someone adequately, private firms would hire him away at three times the salary. The first EPA supervisor on-site had had only 6 months' training. EPA saw tremendous turnover in personnel during the early phases of cleanup at Hilltown Chemical. The DER official attributes some of the mistakes made by EPA to this turnover, emphasizing that "there was no institutional memory at all."

Although EPA involved DER in the emergency phase, it did not consult either city or county officials for the first 2 weeks. Nor did EPA initially inform the public about what was occurring. City officials first learned of the cleanup when a state legislator called them to find out whether something was going on in his district.

Several community residents and workers were candid and concerned. One worker said, "One day I drove past the plant and saw guys in moon suits walking around where I had been working in a T-shirt and shorts a few months ago. The area had barbed wire around it. What was so different about the place now?"

In March 1982, local government officials met in Hilltown and were notified of the emergency cleanup. They learned that the site was not safe, that EPA was allocating Superfund money to reduce the danger of explosions and fire, and that lagoons containing toxic materials were leaking into a stream that ran through a playground into the river. Officials of nearby towns were instructed to develop emergency plans that were implemented the same week. However, the cleanup continued with no participation by local officials.

Residents felt both alarmed and curious. The meeting with officials had been closed to the public. Only 2 days later did EPA officials discuss the issues with the public through a talk show. There were complaints that the public information was "over people's heads." The city's Director of Public Works expressed great frustration over EPA's practice of not sharing information or consulting with local government. He noted that people would call him for information about what was going on. When he said he did not know, "They thought I was hiding something." Finally, after several weeks had passed, he was permitted to visit the site daily to learn the day's plan.

Turnover at EPA meant that there was little continuity in communications. The individuals who released press items and handled public relations changed often and never stayed in town very long. When EPA personnel changed, local officials were neither notified nor introduced to new staff. Media representatives had difficulty identifying the appropriate individual to obtain information. Finally, EPA permitted press briefings by the official in charge on-site, rather than routing information through offices in other cities.

The communications problems placed the DER on-site coordinator in a difficult position. He was primarily responsible for the security of the emergency area perimeter and air monitoring of the site. Because they were not being consulted, local officials were constantly trying to obtain access to the site to find out what was going on. Also, the incident received considerable national attention in the media, and reporters and cameras were everywhere, trying to get an inside story. The on-site coordinator had to physically throw the mayor off the premises. He also mentioned that all kinds of public figures wanted to be seen as involved in oversight, charging, "They all wanted their picture taken in front of the Hilltown site." An environmental health specialist who witnessed these events later said, "I wish we would have had some training in crowd control."

The DER on-site coordinator attributed much of the communication difficulty to "territoriality" by the government agencies involved. He pointed out that the city was also the county seat, so both had jurisdiction. Also, the surrounding communities had responsibilities in the event of an emergency. Yet, there was no initial consultation of the fire departments nor any joint emergency planning. Only after several incidents in the emergency cleanup phase did the EPA require the city of Hilltown to develop an emergency plan, which was published in the local newspaper. Meanwhile, the DER coordinator had to satisfy federal and local concerns, but his superiors were accountable only to EPA.

The actual emergency cleanup took 6 to 8 weeks. The crews worked from 7 a.m. to 7 p.m. and stopped only one day, for Easter. During this time, the crews removed barrels of acids and bases and completed a survey of the chemicals above ground. There was no competitive bidding for these jobs. An out-of-state company that was considered expert was brought in to do the work. This situation caused some resentment in the Hilltown community because men who had worked for Hilltown Chemical believed that they knew more about the site than outsiders. Furthermore, in an area with high unemployment, it was not considered fair that outsiders were hired for these jobs. Even the job of putting a fence around the site was given to an outside contractor.

The DER on-site coordinator pointed out that, in the early days of the Superfund, it was slow going for the EPA because each situation was considered unique. Many procedures were learned at Hilltown, including what not to do. The on-site coordinator characterized the Hilltown chemicals as a "witches' brew." Any given drum or tank might contain anything.

The DER coordinator was also responsible for monitoring emissions into the air, and guarding the welfare of DER employees on-site. EPA placed emergency phones on-site but did not tell anyone their purpose until after several incidents that might have required their use.

INCIDENTS DURING
THE EMERGENCY CLEANUP

Several events alarmed the community during the emergency phase of the cleanup. In two incidents in March, clouds of fuming sulfuric acid were released over the community. The workers had been checking the structural integrity of an old rusting railroad car oil tank that contained oleum, a super-concentrated sulfuric acid under pressure. The crew could not tell how much oleum was in the tank because there was a crust on the top. When they placed a small amount of water in the tank, the oleum exploded in the form of a small acid cloud that dissipated rapidly. No one knew whether to report it, so no one did. In a second release, less than 2 weeks later, the crew added water too rapidly to the oleum. It was concentrated in pockets under the crust and exploded in a large cloud of acid droplets. Workers on-site put on their masks in time, but road workers on the nearby superhighway suffered from inhaling the droplets. Furthermore, EPA had to pay for repainting numerous cars around town that were corroded by the droplets.

One former worker, reflecting much of the community's attitude, was scathing about this accident: "Everyone knows you don't mix oleum and water."

Hilltown Chemical Company shared a gas line with the Central State Company. When the gas company shut off gas to Hilltown Chemical, it also shut off gas to Central State. To restore gas to this company, the line had to be moved. Shortly before the second oleum cloud was released, a bulldozer accidentally cut through the gas line. As the bulldozer worked, a 2-inch high-pressure gas line wrapped around the cleats of the machine. A high-pressure explosion was prevented only by good luck: The gas line was plastic, and the weather was cold and rainy.

In the public uproar over this accident, the red phone's purpose finally was explained. Also, by this time, a local emergency management plan was implemented, allowing local organizations to respond to any further incidents.

Twice during the course of the emergency cleanup, an army bomb disposal unit was brought on-site. On the first occasion, EPA had located a large amount of crystallized picric acid inside the plant building. Picric acid in crystallized form is highly explosive, and there was enough on-site to do serious damage to the town. On the second occasion, the army removed several unmarked storage cylinders that were too corroded to analyze. Rumors circulated that these cylinders might contain nerve gas.

SUBSEQUENT CLEANUP

After the emergency phase, a three-phase cleanup began. Phase I of the longer-term cleanup began in 1982. The cyclone fence was locked, and the site was considered "stabilized" and ready for remedial action. Phase II, which occurred in 1988 and 1989, included the removal of all contaminated buildings and structures. The site is currently in Phase III, which involves removal or treatment of contaminated soil and groundwater. Several carefully researched options for this phase were studied, but the long-term cleanup is expected to take at least 30 years.

The cleanup activities became a routine job after the initial alarm that triggered the emergency phase. Officials did a complete survey of the grounds and buildings, proceeding with the removal of all stored materials. Officially, the EPA was concerned only with migrating hazardous waste, not with what was actually on the site. There was concern that Hilltown's contamination was moving off-site by polluting the groundwater. Subsequently, the city performed a study and found no contamination of groundwater, but this is not to say that such contamination might not occur in the future.

Although individual towns had emergency plans, these were not coordinated at the time of the emergency cleanup. By late 1982 and early 1983, the EPA required that a formal community emergency plan be in place before the Superfund cleanup phases could be initiated. One worker said,

> Before that, everyone thought there would be no real problems concerning the site, that Hilltown was a joke, and that all of this was just a training exercise. Now everyone at the city, county, and state level had to work furiously to get the plan together.

Dissatisfaction persisted about EPA's perceived failure to communicate. As late as May 1983, local officials still had to write to the regional director to ask for information about EPA plans that directly affected local jurisdictions. Also, EPA's initial proposed timeline for subsequent cleanup was, in the words of the mayor, "preposterous." The mayor credits federal and state legislators with pushing the cleanup ahead. However, no one is happy with the current timeline.

SECTION II

COMMUNITY CONFLICT ABOUT EXPOSURES

A CLOSER LOOK AT HEALTH EFFECTS

People in Hilltown were alarmed about the health experience of some former workers. Two brothers who had worked at Hilltown Chemical for years died of bladder cancer, and another worker who had management responsibility had to have his bladder removed in the late 1970s.

The town's experience forced a new look at the scientific information about Hilltown Chemical and BNA exposure. Periodic health surveys indicated that the surrounding county had the highest cancer rate in the state. The author of the report said that the excess cancers were "probably due to occupational exposures." Such statements meant little to the residents in neighborhoods around these dirty chemical plants because BNA is inhaled while on the job. Other carcinogens and suspected carcinogens, however, were another matter.

In the late 1970s, the union at the Central State Chemical Company, the plant adjacent to the Hilltown Chemical site, demanded a health surveillance program because Central State workers had been exposed to BNA and other toxic agents. At this time, a large petrochemical company had acquired Central State and proposed a health surveillance program in which its medical department would provide services. The union rejected the proposal and, instead, agreed to a compromise in which a local physician would provide medical surveillance. However, resources for this program were limited, and the physician had to make difficult choices among workers for priority for medical care and surveillance.

CITIZEN LEAGUE FOR ENVIRONMENTAL ACTION NOW (CLEAN)

The former production manager of the Hilltown Chemical plant returned to town about 1 year after the emergency situation. Although he had once had management responsibility in the plant, he had also managed to organize a union at the plant and notified the federal Occupational, Safety, and Health Administration (OSHA) about safety violations in an effort to improve plant conditions. On his return, he heard "rumblings" about fears over health effects of the plant, but he believed the cleanup issue was "almost dead." Although EPA was beginning Phase I of the long-term cleanup, many questions were not being answered about worker and resident health or about the sites for dumping chemical waste. He realized that the various government agencies would need more pressure to continue the cleanup at Hilltown Chemical and to deal with health issues. He has applied such pressure—but he continues to pay a personal price for his work. One respondent called him "the idiot who started all this."

During the initial cleanup phase, a new reporter at the local newspaper began to investigate the Hilltown Chemical situation. He raised many questions, such as why wasn't anything more happening to clean up the site and what possible health effects could be evident in the workers. Learning about each other's concerns, the reporter and production manager formed the Citizens League for Environmental Action Now (CLEAN) in April 1983. The organization, initially formed by and for the workers, later expanded to include concerned community members.

One of the first issues the group addressed was whether Hilltown Chemical had used BNA after the 1962 ban. The Hilltown plant had been inspected in the 1960s and had been declared free of BNA. Nevertheless, employees suspected correctly that BNA was stored or manufactured on the premises after that time. The EPA had no method to test for BNA because it was a banned substance, but the crew improvised and used a black light at night to help locate the contamination. Many people were shocked by the BNA findings.

How could traces of BNA have appeared in the plant after the ban and the inspection? Workers with some training in chemistry studied the manufacturing processes at Hilltown Chemical. They consulted with a professor of environmental health at a nearby university and discovered that BNA could be inadvertently produced as a side product of Broenner's acid if the process was not carried out correctly. A 1981 NIOSH report had reached the same conclusion. The workers were very proud that they educated themselves about their exposure. Would anyone listen, however?

CLEAN'S STRATEGY

The CLEAN organization proceeded on four fronts. First, they pushed the EPA on further cleanup of the site because the general feeling was that EPA was not moving quickly enough. Second, they pushed DER to identify and clean up the possible dump sites around the city for wastes from the chemical plants. They then initiated lawsuits against the assets of the company and against major chemical companies that had commissioned jobs from Hilltown Chemical. Finally, they pushed for a health screening program to be funded by either the chemical companies involved in the lawsuit or the government.

Participants in CLEAN believe they were well received by the average person in the community. After all, they pointed out, they were not "tree-hugging hippies"; they were long-term Hilltown citizens. Several of the leaders were supervisors at Hilltown Chemical, and their health problems gave them scientific credibility. Several officials and citizens agree that CLEAN was a positive force. However, CLEAN also had major resistance from some elements of the Hilltown community.

The recession of the early 1980s hit Hilltown hard. Central State closed in June 1983 after facing a threat of forced closure under federal regulations. Another company left Hilltown soon after. Businesspeople, faced with publicity over environmental and health problems in the town, feared new investors might be driven away. They did not want to be known as the "cancer capital of the state." In addition, CLEAN members pointed out that some town leaders had a long, involved relationship with the Hilltown Chemical Company. Many people, however, just wanted the health problem to go away.

One CLEAN leader described the way that the group conducted itself in dealing with public officials. Members started with very polite inquiries about the issue at hand (cleanups and health screening). When they experienced delays in getting a straight answer, or when the answer was that nothing could be done, the group went to the superiors of those officials, to elected representatives, or to the media.

CLEAN found that experts were skeptical that BNA could have been produced on-site after the ban. Officials also resisted the idea that the workers might be at high risk of occupational disease. CLEAN got scientific assistance from a well-known expert in occupational health from a nearby university. One unemployed member of CLEAN (it was rumored that after he started his activism, no one in the area would hire him, even 30 miles away) became totally dedicated to the organization and testified about Hilltown's problems before the U.S. Congress. Additionally, CLEAN always knew which news crews were in town and used them to present their side of the story.

State legislators openly supported CLEAN because, as the former production manager said, they had to present the stance that "we don't want workers to die." However, CLEAN had considerable difficulty getting local government or the local medical society to address the problems at Hilltown Chemical.

PRESSURE ON DER

A former DER official saw CLEAN's actions somewhat differently, because he was the one under pressure to investigate waste sites. He agreed that CLEAN probably needed to use the tactics it did because government agencies involved in the cleanup tended to underestimate the intelligence of the public. But for 3 years, DER was "at the beck and call" of CLEAN to investigate possible dump sites for chemical wastes, he said. For example, CLEAN wanted an investigation of the senior citizen apartments that were built adjacent to the Hilltown Chemical site; some feared that the area had been used as a hazardous waste dump site. Although the DER ran a full investigation, this official did not think it was justified to spend so much money on vague memories of dump sites. The investigation found no evidence of contamination.

For the most part, CLEAN contacted the district DER director, who then forwarded their concerns to this official for investigation. However, the official had to deal with many other advocacy groups, agencies, and local government representatives concerning the Hilltown issue. Furthermore, DER had relatively few staff to deal with many area sites that were well-known dangers. When staff have to work overtime on an investigation, that overtime has to be carefully justified to superiors. Currently, there are 42 hazardous waste sites under investigation in Hilltown or the surrounding county, many of them brought to DER's attention by CLEAN.

THE LAWSUITS

In 1983, individual plaintiffs filed lawsuits concerning occupational exposures and failure to notify workers and townspeople of those exposures. Initially, the claims totaled $800 million and were filed against assets of the Hilltown Chemical Company, the Central State Chemical Company, and 14 third-party defendants, including some of the largest chemical companies in the nation. This total was later reduced to $500 million, then to $200 million; the amounts recovered to date are much less.

One CLEAN representative said that the group's intention was to settle out of court with the chemical companies to create a health screening program for the workers, but that they asked for such a large sum of money so that they could bargain more effectively for what they wanted.

Initially, CLEAN worked with the plaintiffs to hire a nationally known law firm to represent them in possible legal action. CLEAN attempted to contact all involved workers who were still in the area. The firm they retained was described as being very good at working with the townspeople and getting the people to open up.

The plaintiffs filed suit in the state court system. CLEAN members described this as a big mistake because the county's judge was intimidated by the chemical companies' fast-track, big-city attorneys. These attorneys have asked for many continuances with no resistance from the judge. The suit is still pending. The plaintiffs tried to refile in federal court, but the chemical company attorneys would not allow them to do so.

Some media representatives said that the public viewed the lawsuits as appropriate because the company had always had shady practices, and people's health had been injured. The lawsuits increased local tensions, however. Some businesspeople feared that no new businesses would locate in the town with such big lawsuits pending and with a labor force of "troublemakers."

RISING COMMUNITY FRUSTRATION

Increasing local frustration over government actions culminated in May 1983 in a public meeting convened by EPA and attended by representatives of the federal EPA, NIOSH, Centers for Disease Control (CDC), DER and DOH. There was an overflow crowd and considerable attention from the national media. The meeting lasted from 7:30 p.m. until midnight. Tempers flared and tensions ran high as community members perceived a condescending and cavalier attitude in the government representatives.

The agencies' presentations were not well received. Community members and workers demanded a screening program and help from the government agencies, but requests were denied on the basis that the plant no longer existed. Also, the CDC representative stated that the screening program was not warranted because nothing was found in environmental surveys to justify it. However, CLEAN was able to cite the high incidence of bladder cancer in chemical workers, as well as the statewide data showing a high cancer incidence in the county. One official angered people when he suggested that, until a government program could be launched, they should see their family doctor. One elderly woman stood up and said, "If you're not working and barely have enough money for food, how can you pay doctor bills?"

CLEAN presented CDC with a petition from 1,500 residents asking for a health screening. Federal officials would make no promises but did not rule out the possibility of federal funding.

DEALING WITH GOVERNMENT
ON HEALTH ISSUES

Under state law, workers had no recourse to Workmen's Compensation for exposure. First, the law covered only existing disease, not increased risk or early detection programs. In addition, Hilltown chemical was self-insured under Workmen's Compensation; when the company went bankrupt, its insurance ceased to exist.

In May 1983, the area's state legislators introduced a bill in the House to institute health screening for the Hilltown Chemical workers and residents around the plant at a cost of $120,000. The bill passed both the House and the Senate, but, according to legislative aides, staff did not inform the governor of the importance of the bill, or the chemical involved. The governor did not approve the appropriation. In a press release in June 1983, he stated that EPA had found no "dioxins" on-site and that federal funding for a screening program might become available in the future. The governor received considerable bad press for this move. An editorial in the town paper noted,

> Just when citizens felt they had broken the bureaucratic barrier and were receiving some help, [the governor] wiped out the $120,000 in a deficiency bill for health screening. . . . This action is consistent with the style of the . . . administration: act on something without consulting the people involved. . . . In one capricious action, the governor has further damaged the confidence of an entire town.

CLEAN kept the pressure on DOH to provide services to residents and workers. The governor stated that DOH had plenty of money to do the screening. During this same period, however, the DOH experienced massive cuts in its resources. Personnel and programs were being eliminated. DOH spokespeople repeatedly told the press that there was no money to do health screenings. Finally, the state's Secretary of Health announced that there was enough evidence to begin screening. According to his press announcement, 1 week after the governor's veto of the appropriation, $2,000 would be made available for urinalysis, a "preliminary figure" that "might change as the situation progressed." DOH planned to start with testing of employees, then expand to nearby residents if problems were found.

Only one public health nurse was available to the screening program at the Hilltown office. Attrition in the state's regional office meant that special staff would have to be brought in for the program.

DOH finally gathered a local task force, including CLEAN members, local physicians, and the local hospital administrator, and determined that, in addition to worker screening, a community survey was necessary. The survey, aimed at determining whether there were more cancers among the residents around the Hilltown Chemical site than in the population as a whole, found no adverse health effects. The protocol DOH developed, however, was "full of holes," according to one CLEAN member. Community residents mainly objected that DOH surveyed only existing neighborhoods around the site. In 1972, however, flooding forced residents from one neighborhood, and their homes were subsequently demolished to make way for the superhighway. DOH officials claimed that they did not have the funds to find these former neighborhood residents. In response, CLEAN took it upon themselves to name and locate these people, but they were never surveyed.

Even some DOH staff people acknowledged department delays in mounting an effort. Furthermore, staff acknowledged a general failure to include community members in planning surveys and health screening efforts. They pointed out that citizens tried to tell the DOH what they knew about the effect of Hilltown Chemical on workers, "but the DOH was not interested." One DOH employee stated that "most agencies put too much emphasis on the credibility of their own people and assume a lack of credibility in everyone else."

THE DOH SCREENING PROGRAM

Occupational health experts advocate bladder cancer screening as a means of early detection. Although there is still some controversy over its effectiveness, screening efforts include urinalysis to detect blood in the urine, and examination of cells from the bladder wall that have been sloughed off in urine. A Pap test can reveal whether these cells are changing. In some occupational programs, cystoscopies are performed periodically. However, this is an expensive (and painful) procedure.

New experimental methods also hold promise for detecting bladder cancer much earlier than the Pap test. One of these was presented at a meeting on bladder cancer funded by NIOSH. At the time of this meeting, CLEAN was still pushing for health screening for Hilltown Chemical workers. A grant from a local church enabled two CLEAN members to attend this meeting, but the DOH staff in environmental and occupational health lacked the necessary funds to attend. CLEAN members, convinced that this new experimental method would help to protect the Hilltown Chemical workers, successfully lobbied to include this method in the DOH screening effort.

Although screening began in 1983 and continued through 1985, funding was very slim. A single public health nurse and a secretary, under the direction of one physician from the state headquarters, conducted health screening for workers. Additional nurses visited periodically from the regional office. However, all the staff involved had many other duties to perform in connection with their usual work for DOH.

To be eligible for screening, DOH stipulated that a worker had to have been employed at least 3 months at Hilltown Chemical. Furthermore, only residents within a 50-mile radius of Hilltown were included. To contain costs, workers who lived beyond this radius were not notified. DOH obtained workers' names from CLEAN and employer records. Records prior to 1972, however, had been lost in the flood. According to DOH staff people, these eligibility rules created problems. Some people who had worked at Hilltown for a shorter time were concerned about their health and could not participate; likewise, some residents near the plant could not understand why they were ineligible for screening.

At the same time, many workers who were eligible would not take part. Some of the workers had no health complaints and could not understand why they had to be screened. Other workers, already involved with the lawsuit, were afraid they would jeopardize their case by participating in the study.

In addition, community tension caused many workers to avoid the screening program. Media attention to the exposure problem stressed the dramatic victimization issues, as well as the political and legal aspects. This harmed the screening program's positive message that something could be done about the problem. Also, the social stigma attached to working at Hilltown Chemical, compounded by the adverse publicity, kept many former employees from participating in the screening for fear that they might be identified as Hilltown Chemical workers. For example, television news clips showed easily identified workers entering the screening site in a small community where most people were acquainted with each other. Although confidentiality was guaranteed, this publicity worried workers about possible consequences for their current employment and health insurance.

Community tension, lawsuits, a negative media slant, and social stigma, as well as pressing personal problems and an economic recession, limited participation in the screening to 47% of the eligible workers who were notified. Under the circumstances, it is highly unlikely that a better participation rate could have been gained by any group, anywhere.

SUMMARY

The DOH program was a one-time effort, even though the latency period for bladder cancer after BNA exposure averages 20 years. CLEAN continued to press for resources for a permanent health program for workers and succeeded in having a new program mounted in 1986. If you were in charge of this new program, how would you overcome community tensions? How would you get workers to take part? Who should run such a program, and how should it be run?

SECTION III

ACTIONS TO ADDRESS THE PUBLIC HEALTH RISK

THE NEW SCREENING PROGRAM

The 1980 Superfund law created the Agency for Toxic Substances Disease Registry (ATSDR) to develop health registries of populations exposed to toxic substances. However, the Reagan administration failed to fund and implement the program until a lawsuit by the Environmental Defense Fund forced the government to implement the law through a consent decree. Under this national program, the state DOH was funded to create a new screening, notification, and health registry program in 1985 for Hilltown Chemical workers. The registry was to focus exclusively on BNA exposure because the health effects of other potential carcinogens were not as certain.

DOH decided to contract with another organization for the registry, because the Hilltown office did not have the staff to develop one. A university research group obtained the contract in 1986. This group had read about a screening program for chemical workers in another state (see Chapter 4) and decided to incorporate some of its features in their plan.

SCREENING PROTOCOL

Workers were to be notified by letter about their risk for bladder cancer, interviewed about their health and work history, and asked to provide a urine specimen. The tests were the same as in the DOH screening effort: urinalysis to test for blood in the urine, Pap test on cells in the urine, and the experimental method that aimed at detecting incipient bladder cancer. A positive test could mean any number of things besides bladder cancer, such as a bladder infection. If workers tested positive on any of these screens, they were counseled by a urologist on the project, and, if they were within the 50-mile radius of Hilltown, they were offered free diagnostic tests at the subcontractor hospital. Payment for treatment was not covered by the program.

Initially, higher-risk workers were to be tested annually for 5 years, whereas lower-risk workers were to be tested once. Higher-risk workers were those who worked more than 5 years at Hilltown Chemical or who worked there prior to 1966. However, the first year's data showed a higher than expected number of positive tests among the group believed to be at lower risk. The protocol was, therefore, changed to provide a yearly screening to all former workers, regardless of their length of employment.

PLANNING ACTIVITIES

The university contractors neglected to visit the community to learn its culture and history ahead of time. Additionally, the competitive bidding process prohibited DOH from sharing information about their experiences in advance. Consequently, as one team member said, "We blundered right into the middle of a tense situation we did not understand." The team delayed implementation of the screening program for 2 months so that they could gain further information.

The program developers consulted with DOH and federal sponsors, visited the nearby Larsen asbestos program, and learned from NIOSH experience. They also discussed the situation with many kinds of community leaders, learning the history of the Hilltown problem and the current feeling of community members. By talking with such leaders, the program was able to avoid some disastrous mistakes that could have destroyed credibility before a single worker was screened.

By 1986, community tension had declined somewhat, with most parties frustrated and exhausted over past efforts to address the Hilltown problem. The DOH studies of residents and workers had been completed, and at least some answers concerning health risks were in hand. Also, the focus on BNA exposure meant that the town could actually do something through early detection of bladder cancer. Finally, as neutral third parties from out of town, the registry researchers were, to some degree, protected from community tensions.

STEPS TO OVERCOME
COMMUNITY TENSION

The program immediately established a community advisory board that included representation from affected parties, such as CLEAN, as well as respected leaders, such as the Chamber of Commerce (which had taken the lead in seeking positive resolution of the Hilltown problems before), the president of a defunct union local, the hospital's pathologist, and a representative of local religious leaders. This step was possible only because tension had diminished. Initially, some of these individuals refused to sit on the same committee as others. These leaders realized, to some extent, that they needed to solve a mutual problem. Although almost everyone in town grumbled about at least some of the people on the committee, publishing the advisory committee membership in the local paper sent a signal that the screening program was not allied to any one faction.

Another important step was the creation of a worker's advisory committee to enable former Hilltown Chemical workers to participate in the system design and creation of notification materials. The committee also consented to pretest the notification materials to ensure that they were understandable and would motivate workers without producing dysfunctional fear. In addition, the worker committee contacted the former Hilltown Chemical workers whom they knew and reported any materials or operations that created dissatisfaction among workers.

The program notified the medical community, well in advance of any publicity, about the nature of the screening activity. Two goals were addressed by this communication: The physicians were notified about the bladder cancer problem to alert them of signs and symptoms, and the physicians were assured that the program would not be practicing medicine. Although free diagnostic services were provided if workers tested positive, the screening itself was aimed strictly at early detection and health education activities that were not within the scope of usual medical care.

Conversations with townspeople showed the program staff that it would be necessary to hold the lawsuit issue at arm's length while disposing of worker inquiries about the suits in a responsible manner. When screening staff encountered questions from workers or their families about lawsuits, they stated that the screening program had nothing to do with the lawsuits, and questions should be directed to workers' attorneys. This policy was explicit from the beginning, so that no staff member became embroiled in an extraneous issue or offered misleading advice. Program staff add that this was the responsible course as well, because workers and their families have been known to confuse legal and medical sources of assistance. In some instances, this misunderstanding hindered workers' ability to seek legal recourse for legitimate problems.

Law firms involved in other toxic exposure lawsuits have often advised their clients not to participate in screening. The Hilltown program was fortunate in that a single law firm handled the suits. While avoiding co-optation, the Hilltown program established low-key communication with this firm. The firm mailed a letter to all its Hilltown clients, stating that the screening program had nothing to do with their lawsuits and that clients should participate to protect their health. A dedicated paralegal professional was primarily responsible for convincing the firm to make this decision.

NOTIFICATION AND RECRUITMENT SYSTEM

The registry team planned a system of notification and recruitment in which former employees would receive information through many channels. Three major strategies for recruitment were used: a media campaign, two mailed notification letters, and personal contact by the clinic coordinator.

Within a 50-mile radius of Hilltown, an intensive media campaign announced the availability of the free screening program during the fall and winter of 1986; subsequent media messages have been less intensive. Public service announcements stressed the benefit, as well as the ease, of screening, preparing workers for the notification and recruitment efforts that followed. By this point, the more sensational aspects of the Hilltown story were no longer news.

In media messages, an explicit appeal was made to family members and friends of workers, under the assumption that someone in the family would get the person into screening. Interviews with participants later revealed that this strategy was useful. Sixty-three percent had discussed the screening with someone, generally family members (36% of participants), friends (12%), or other Hilltown Chemical workers (11%). Of those discussing screening, 79% received encouragement to participate, and 39% said they would not have come for screening without such encouragement.

In addition, community members were now ready to support the screening program. Local religious leaders agreed to urge their parishioners to participate, and all local businesses (except for a national chain with a policy against such practices) agreed to place copies of the program pamphlet at the front of their offices and buildings. It was evident that working with community leaders reduced the community polarization.

Notification letters were mailed 3 weeks apart to the person's last known address. Letters were mailed in batches each week, so that worker questions could be answered, fears alleviated, and appointments made on a timely basis. The ethics of this decision is clear—if the screening coordinator had been overwhelmed with inquiries, people would have waited for service while their fear and helplessness increased, and participation would have suffered.

Notification letters and all other materials were written at the lowest possible reading level and were pretested on volunteer workers. Enclosed with the letter was a pamphlet that provided an official description of the program and addressed many questions, fears, and concerns.

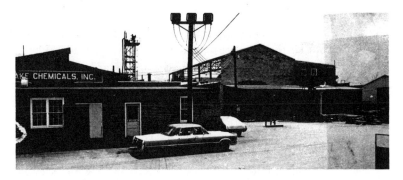

**IF YOU EVER WORKED AT   CHEMICAL COMPANY
OR   CHEMICAL COMPANY
*PLEASE READ THIS LETTER!***

IT COULD SAVE YOUR LIFE.
**This letter can tell you what you can do to
protect your health.**

Figure 2.1. Insert Accompanying Notification Flyer to Workers

Also enclosed was a flyer with an old picture of the plant (see Figure 2.1). Even illiterate workers could see this flyer and the letter, realize that something important had come in the mail, and ask someone to read it. The clinic coordinator initiated personal contact if workers did not respond to either letter. Screenings were conducted in a private location at hours convenient to participants, and some screenings were conducted through home visits.

EFFECTS OF THE
SCREENING PROGRAM

Four years after the initiation of the program, all but 33 of the workers had been located. It is extremely rare that so high a number of workers would be located after all these years. In addition, the participation rate among those notified is 80%. Of those remaining, most have delayed participation for one reason or another. Some are too ill to take part, whereas others are going through a variety of life crises. Some simply have put it off. Rather than closing the books on these individuals, the screening coordinator, who is persistent and calls periodically, leaves the option open that they can participate when they are ready. When she believes that the official notification letters are discarded without being opened, she mails a handwritten letter that she feels they would not believe "was a bill." The screening coordinator has interviewed and tested men throughout the 50 states. When workers will not come to the hospital, she has visited them on isolated farms. She has collected urine specimens in fast-food restaurants and prisons.

The screening coordinator worked hard to make workers comfortable with her. Because they frequently visit the screening office after a hard day's work, dressed in overalls or work clothes, she dresses casually to make them feel comfortable in her office. The hospital in which she is located protests her attire, but she insists that professional clothing would make these men much less likely to share important information or stay in touch.

To date, two cases of bladder cancer have been found in participants. In addition, quite a few people continue to test positive at screening and must be monitored with cystoscopy for the likely development of bladder cancer at some future date.

Surveys of the Hilltown community and surrounding area show that community tensions about the Hilltown Chemical situation have diminished substantially over time. For several years, however, members of the CLEAN organization continued to pay a personal price for their involvement. The former production manager had particular difficulty getting employment. As time went on, the public generally saw the screening program as having some success. In the words of the screening coordinator, the town now respects the CLEAN members for their work in getting the screening program. Some members of this organization continue to be involved in environmental problems elsewhere in the state and offer their experience to other communities on a voluntary basis.

As one CLEAN member put it, the organization took a low profile after the screening program started. However, they were not totally satisfied with the scope of the screening program, primarily because it screens only for bladder cancer rather than a range of possible exposures. It does not screen for leukemia or other health effects caused by arsenic or lead; in essence, the program may have distracted from the need to monitor other health effects. However, federal funders might well reply that other exposures are unknown. How can health conditions be monitored when the exposures are not known, when the health effects of exposures are not known, or when there are no records? Another source of unhappiness is the fact that the program is funded for only 8 years, yet many of the workers can be expected to contract bladder cancer an average of 20 years after exposure. CLEAN members fully intend to press for new funding for the program, using their earlier tactics.

A CLEAN member described Hilltown as rural and stagnating, not easily progressing with the times. New industry would gain a great deal of community trust and respect by developing innovative ideas, such as screening programs. The current program, in this man's view, shows that the community can deal constructively with its problems.

KEY ISSUE

THE SOCIAL CONSTRUCTION OF RISK

We began with this case study because: (a) it is relatively small in scope, so the problems should be manageable; (b) objectively, the health risk seems straightforward; medicine knows a lot about this carcinogen, and there is little controversy over what it does, which should make dealing with it a fairly simple task; (c) in spite of the small scope and well-understood risk, the problems were neither manageable nor straightforward—they were a mess. To understand what happened, the reader needs to consider three general questions:

▲ What does it mean for a risk to have a social reality as well as a physical reality?

▲ Why does the layperson not perceive risk in the same way as the scientist?

▲ Why does the social reality of risk so often induce conflict and stress?

Risk is socially constructed. Social scientists maintain that concerns about risks cannot be explained completely by objective reality or scientific evidence. Rather, societies choose some risks for attention and ignore others. In a pioneering analysis, Douglas and Wildavsky (1982) used this premise to explain why people emphasize some risks and not others. They pointed out that it is not possible to focus attention on all the potential dangers that exist in a society; instead, each culture selects a subset of perceived risks upon which to focus. Douglas and Wildavsky maintained that the choices about which risks to emphasize reflect a culture's values, moral code, and institutions. The final choice may not reflect objective scientific evidence.

In the Hilltown case, public health professionals made the initial choice to focus on an occupational health risk. However, the health risk was always associated in townspeople's minds with jobs and low social status. Later, it was colored by the community's dissatisfaction with government, by lawsuits, and by fears for the area's prosperity. Review the picture in Figure 2.1. A worker receiving this picture in the mail did not simply receive notification about danger from bladder cancer; instead, the picture brought back a whole host of associations, experiences, fears, and hopes.

The social construction of risk does not deny that risks truly exist. However, some have interpreted the social construction argument this way.

> Risks do not exist "out there." Instead, there are only subjective perceptions of risks . . . taken to such an extreme, the social construction of risk viewpoint appears to violate common sense and calls into question the logical and rational foundations of societal risk management. (Johnson & Covello, 1987, p. 3)

Recent discussions helpful to policy and practice focus on an interplay between the social construction of risk, the choice of risks to investigate scientifically, and data on risk that may or may not enlighten the choice of societal concerns (Rayner, 1987). Fischhoff (1989) put it succinctly:

> Although there are actual risks, nobody knows what they are. All that anyone does know about risks can be classified as perceptions. Those assertions that are typically called actual risks (or facts or objective

information) inevitably contain some element of judgment on the part of the scientists who produce them. (p. 270)

Scientists bring their own preferences and values to perception of risk. This is true because scientists decide what is valuable to study, what to bring to the public's attention, and how. Understanding the biases that both experts and laypeople bring to risk perception is critical to improving risk communication.

Work on the social construction of risk helps the practitioner to anticipate some important dynamics around any risk issue. The social construction framework is especially helpful to understand why some groups appear more concerned about particular risks than others. In complex societies, not everyone shares the same values and beliefs (Douglas & Wildavsky, 1982). Without minimizing the concerns that an activist group might have over a pollutant or an occupational exposure, this framework can help to explain why an activist group might form in the first place. It can also explain why the group formed around one risk issue rather than another potential danger.

The case study illustrates one strategy that might be employed constructively in confronting risks. That is, the program did its best to focus attention on the physical risk about which something was known and about which something could be done. In other words, the screening program that was eventually mounted by the university group did its best to separate itself in the public mind from the lawsuits, as well as past political and environmental messes. Although the social issues around the risk were acknowledged, and the program was tailored to those considerations, the university group succeeded in placing the focus back on the medical and technical issues. This made it possible for people to participate in the screening program without distraction by these other agendas.

Perceptions of risk are flawed. An important body of literature indicates that humans perceive risks with some systematic biases. Baruch Fischhoff recently summarized this work in two key sources for the practitioner: "Risk: A Guide to Controversy," which appears as Appendix C in the National Research Council (1989) publication *Improving Risk Communication*; and "Risk Perception and Communication," a chapter in the 1993 volume of the *Annual Review of Public Health*

(Fischhoff et al., 1993). Although a complete review is not feasible here, some highlights will illustrate the usefulness of this work for the professional confronting risks.

In making choices about whether to take action to protect themselves from a risk, people develop options about what to do. Their choice depends on the size of the risk, its seriousness, and potential benefits that might arise from various choices. Fischhoff (1989) notes that for their individual actions, people weigh options differently than do risk managers or policy makers. People's estimates of the size of a risk depend on a variety of factors, including the way the questions are framed (positive or negative) and availability bias (overestimation based on how easy an event is to remember or imagine). People do not automatically calculate the cumulative probability of an event either, as seen in their estimates of the risk of car crashes. People also tend consistently to underestimate their own personal risk for a variety of dangers (Fischhoff et al., 1993). The literature clearly indicates that the way a risk is framed, in terms of the positive (protection) and negative (danger) matters greatly to people's overall perceptions of the efficacy of protective action (Slovic et al., 1987).

In addition to these biases in estimating the size of risk, people may or may not have accurate intuitive theories of how risks work. For example, workers in the present case generally did not know how bladder cancer developed as a result of BNA exposure, or how the danger could be minimized through early detection. To make informed choices about risk, Fischhoff and his colleagues maintain that it is important to provide laypeople with accurate intuitive theories, or mental models, of the way in which the risk works. This method rests on the consistent finding that "people process new information within the context of their existing beliefs. If they know nothing about a topic, then a new message will be incomprehensible. If they have erroneous beliefs, then they may misconstrue the message" (Morgan, Fischhoff, Bostrom, Lave, & Atman, 1992, p. 2050). The authors recommend a four-step process for development of improved risk communications:

1. Elicit people's beliefs about a hazard (both accurate and inaccurate) through open-ended questions.

2. Measure prevalence of these beliefs through structured questionnaires.
3. Develop communications based on what people need to know to make informed choices.
4. Evaluate communications in several testing modes, before, during, and after the receipt of messages.

This brief review cannot possibly do justice to the scope of these authors' work. Review of the original sources is important both to understand fully the biases in both expert and laypeople's perceptions of risk and to use fully the tools these researchers are developing to aid the practitioner.

The social construction of risk can induce conflict and stress. We have come to expect stress and strain as a feature of any controversy over exposure to possible carcinogens, the celebrated examples being Love Canal and Three Mile Island (Fowlkes & Miller, 1987; Walsh, 1987). The social construction of a health risk, rather than individual risk perception, can explain some of the negative consequences associated with the risk. For example, Renn, Burns, Kasperson, Kasperson, and Slovic (1992) describe the *social amplification of risk* as a process in which health risks interact with the social milieu to produce new economic and political consequences and social strife. For example, many workers fear that worker notification, if publicized, would cause the loss of health benefits or current employment—employers might not want to pay for the health consequences of past exposures.

Wandersman and his colleagues (Edelstein & Wandersman, 1987; Wandersman & Hallman, 1993, 1994) have noted that some attempts to cope with environmental threats to health may themselves induce stress. For example, when people turn for help to the sources we often think of (elected leaders, government agencies, helping professions), these may react by stigmatizing and victim blaming. The concept of *victim blaming* was introduced by social work and social policy; it is the tendency to find individuals responsible for their own problems, despite the social, political, or economic forces that preceded these problems (Ryan, 1971). Victim blaming for disease operates most clearly in the present day in the case of AIDS (Oppenheimer, 1988). Historically, people have sought an explanation of illness in the actions of afflicted individuals. For example, the populace regularly blamed plague, small-pox, and other epidemics on the poor, on immigrants, or on other groups who were most hard-hit, seeing their behavior or characteristics as the cause of illness (Oppenheimer, 1988; Risse, 1988).

It is perhaps surprising to see victim blaming in occupational or environmental disease. Yet, it happens regularly, integral to the social construction of risk. In fact, the single instance of a negative reaction to worker notification fits this pattern (see Chapter 4 for a review of psychological reactions to worker notification). Sands and colleagues (1981) describe a worker notification in which the social context promoted victim blaming to such an extent that supporting "facts" were fabricated out of thin air. Their study focused on about 30 B. F. Goodrich employees, screened as part of a vinyl chloride project, who were found to have liver abnormalities. Discussing their findings, Needleman (1993) notes,

> The company's nursing staff had complained that the workers designated as high risk were coming into the dispensary with great frequency, creating the widespread impression that these workers were either unduly anxious or malingering. However, analysis of dispensary records [and personal physician visits] showed that . . . their illness behavior was more or less the same as everyone else's. . . . Rather, it was a misperception of the workers' behavior by a social audience strongly expecting to see a negative reaction. (p. 19)

Stress may be the special price of activism. Wandersman and his colleagues have made the point that community members' attempts to solve the problems around environmental exposures can often work to increase emotional strain and distress. They note two reasons for this: frustration with government and group polarization induced by activism.

Frustration with government. Communities tend to turn to government and other institutions to help them cope with the effects of exposures. Yet, these institutions are limited in terms of what they can do (National Research Council, 1989). They may not be capable of offering relief to new problems. No one may ever have envisioned such problems. In other cases, they may be legally prohibited from offering help in any but the most rigidly prescribed fashion.

In the Hilltown case study, the work of state and federal agencies illustrates the limitations imposed by environmental and occupational law. Communities may not generally understand what government officials are permitted to do when confronted with urgent community demands. Restrictions or no restrictions, however, there is little doubt that this early Superfund experience was not the best in terms of community relations.

Polarization induced by activism. Wandersman and colleagues point out that activism is a two-edged sword. Activists on behalf of occupational or environmental problems need to draw attention to their problems. At the same time, their methods, including increased publicity about the problems themselves, can threaten other interests in the community.

The landmark National Research Council (1989) publication, *Improving Risk Communication,* lists other reasons for increasing conflict over risks, including recent changes in the nature of hazards we experience and our knowledge about these hazards; changes in U.S. society including an increased reliance on technology, distrust of our institutions, and the emergence of new institutions and organizations; and politicization of the technological debates around risk, through regulation, tort law, and other institutional changes.

None of these forces has to prevent community leaders or public health professionals from working constructively to address health problems. To anticipate problems and opportunities, it helps to know that risk is socially constructed, that one can ascertain people's views of the risk, and that stress and conflict can be predictable, if not avoidable.

NOTE

1. In this case study, stakeholders were guaranteed anonymity. As a result, we changed names of places and withheld our documentation for quotation and sources.

CHAPTER **3**

SCIENCE VERSUS SERVICE IN A COMMUNITY-BASED LEAD SCREENING

CAROLYN E. NEEDLEMAN

MARTIN L. NEEDLEMAN

INTRODUCTION[1]

In principle, public health professionals are committed to both sound epidemiological research and effective public health intervention. What happens when the two goals conflict? This case study describes just such a collision, in a community designated here as Port Royal. In this case, scientific research concerns shaped a community-based health screening in ways that were poorly matched to the health concerns of community residents. Tensions between

AUTHORS' NOTE: An abbreviated version of this case has been submitted to *Environmental Review*.

the goals of *science* and *service* went unforeseen, unrecognized, and unresolved throughout the lifetime of the project. As a result, neither goal was satisfactorily achieved.

 ## KEY ISSUE AND GENERAL QUESTIONS

This case illustrates *the central importance of community support* in confronting health risks. Without such support, even the most elaborate and expensive interventions may fail, as this one did. The discussion section following the case suggests some ways that outside professionals can build local support and also highlights some common mistakes to avoid. Specifically, the discussion addresses these questions:

▲ What kind of *social reconnaissance* information is needed before undertaking a community health study?

▲ How can outside professionals identify the appropriate community leaders to work with?

▲ Given that their agendas and priorities may differ, how can outside professionals and community residents develop enough genuine exchange and reciprocity so that both parties see the project as worthy of support?

 ## STAKEHOLDERS

Port Royal community
Polish residents
Irish residents
Catholic Church
Munkville community
White working-class residents
Young urban professional (Yuppie) residents
Federal funding agency
City health department
University researchers
Hired interviewers

TIMELINE

1970s, 1980s   Documented lead exposure in Port Royal
1987-1988   Port Royal lead screenings by city health
               department
1989   Federally funded lead exposure study
               begins and encounters noncooperation
1990   Secondary study carried out to find
               explanation for low participation by
               community residents

SECTION I

BACKGROUND: A RESEARCH EFFORT FAILS

The screening in question, carried out on the outskirts of a large city in the northeastern United States, focused on environmental exposures to lead. Lead has been recognized for centuries as a serious health hazard. Workers exposed to high levels of lead dust or fumes suffer elevated risks for a number of debilitating and potentially fatal diseases, including kidney disease, hypertension, and damage to the peripheral and central nervous systems. The families of exposed workers can also be put at health risk when lead dust is accidentally brought home from work on clothes and hair. In addition, community residents—especially those in older homes and those living near highways or manufacturing areas—can be exposed from flaking lead-based paint in their homes; from dirt in streets and gardens, contaminated by airborne lead pollution; and from ongoing air emissions of lead by factories.

Although work settings provide the most dramatic examples of lead poisoning, community health risks from lead are of special concern for several reasons. First, the symptoms caused by lead exposure are often vague: fatigue, weakness, aches and pains, cramps, and diminished mental capacity. Without the connection to a clear exposure source such as a work hazard, and without the classic indicators of acute lead toxicity, such illnesses are likely to go unrecognized as lead poisoning and may not get proper medical treatment.

Second, a large proportion of those affected in a lead-contaminated community will be children. This is a serious concern because children, especially those under 6 years of age, suffer health damage at lower levels of lead exposure than do adults. They are at particular risk for lead-related impairment of their mental capacities, suffering brain damage that may be interpreted as congenital mental retardation or as a psychiatric problem. In the public health scientific community, there is a growing consensus that for children, exposures can be dangerous if they cause a blood lead level of even 10 micrograms per deciliter—a level treated as acceptable in some existing government regulations.

Finally, the sheer magnitude of the population affected makes community lead contamination a major public health problem. Even if further contamination were to cease immediately, lead deposited in the past would remain a health threat in communities across the nation (Public Health Service, 1990).

The problem of community lead contamination is now beginning to be viewed with the urgency it deserves. A number of cities, usually working through state and local health departments, have already established service programs for citizens at risk—for example, community screening programs to identify cases of lead poisoning needing medical treatment, programs to provide home inspections and lead abatement assistance to home owners, and programs requiring mandatory reporting and follow-up of positive findings in blood-lead tests performed by medical diagnostic laboratories. At the same time, in order to examine the problem more systematically, government research agencies have shown increasing interest in sponsoring studies that advance scientific understanding of community lead exposure—for example, rigorous epidemiological studies of the biological lead burdens among community residents in areas likely to contain lead hazards. Both types of effort are critical to the problem's solution.

Unfortunately, expectations about how service and science are to be balanced can become very confused in community-based lead screenings. This is what occurred in the case of Port Royal, to which we now turn.

THE LEAD EXPOSURE STUDY

In September 1989, supported by a $250,000 grant from a federal agency, the city health department of "old city" undertook a lead exposure study in three communities. The primary objective of the research was to characterize the distribution of blood lead levels in the lower Port Royal area, the site of an industrial source of lead contamination. Port Royal also contains many older row houses, which pose potential lead hazards from paint and plumbing. Therefore, as a control for residential exposure, similar blood lead measurements were planned on parallel samples in two comparable neighborhoods, upper Port Royal and Munkville. These two areas were considered unexposed except for the background lead contamination from old housing and other non-point sources—those not attributable to the industrial source—presumed to be common to all three neighborhoods.

Community lead exposure problems, particularly among children, had been documented in Port Royal since the 1970s. In response to requests from community residents, the city health department had already sponsored two voluntary blood screening programs in the area, one in April 1987, which yielded capillary blood samples from 397 residents (an estimated 8% of the area's population) and a second in September 1988, which yielded venous blood samples from 525 residents (22% of the area's population). Both screenings were specially targeted at children under 6 years of age, with the first including 119 and the second including 116 children. However, the data from these voluntary screenings were of limited epidemiological value due to the relatively small sample sizes, potential biases from self-selection, and uncertainty about background lead levels. Moreover, it was felt that the use of capillary blood sampling in the first screening may have yielded unsatisfactory data; capillary blood sampling is convenient because it involves only a finger prick, but the technique gives less reliable results than venous blood sampling, in which a larger amount of blood is drawn by syringe. For these reasons, the health department felt the existing data did not provide a good scientific base for policy decisions or full explanations to the community.

To resolve this unsatisfactory state of affairs, the federally sponsored lead exposure study aimed to go beyond the currently available information, once and for all generating definitive scientific data on the exact nature and distribution of the community's biological lead burden. With technical support from two of the area's universities, a rigorous research design was developed to provide sound population-based findings for lower Port Royal, based on venous blood measurements in a representative sample large enough to permit detailed analysis.

The research plan involved a preliminary door-to-door census in all three of the study neighborhoods to ensure inclusion of all residents in the sampling frame. Based on this census, the sample would be drawn to include 100% of children under 6 years of age and 15% random samples of other residents stratified by age—older children, adults, and the elderly. Those selected for the sample would be requested to come to convenient central locations, where their blood would be drawn by qualified phlebotomists and interview data would be collected by trained interviewers. Subjects who failed to appear at the central sites (expected to be a relatively small number) would be recontacted and visited at home by a data collection team made up of a phlebotomist and an interviewer.

Timing was felt to be critical in the study. Because the research focused on lead exposure from external rather than indoor sources, all blood sampling and interviewing had to occur within the month of September, so as to reflect the effects of outdoor recreation over the summer. The research plan projected completion of most of the data collection within the first 2 weeks of September at the central sites, with follow-up home visits to nonparticipants during the last 2 weeks of the month.

During the summer preceding the study, the community census was completed with apparent success. Steps were taken to reinforce community cooperation, such as creation of an advisory board made up of influential community residents. The study samples were drawn, letters mailed, interviewers trained, and phlebotomists selected to receive the study subjects at the central locations in early September. Unfortunately, as the project entered the data collection stage, it became apparent that despite all the well-laid plans, something had gone badly awry.

In terms of community participation, the results of the lead exposure study were, to say the least, disappointing. Residents who appeared as requested at the central data collection locations numbered approximately 400, out of a total contacted sample of 2,900. Follow-up home visits with those who failed to appear, originally envisioned as a small "mopping up" operation, became by necessity the primary means of data collection. Although concentrated effort through the home visits yielded an additional 336 subjects, this was still far fewer than anticipated. Overall, the study achieved a participation rate of only 25% of the planned sample (29.5% including participants who completed the questionnaire but refused blood testing). This low level of participation seriously undermined the study's goal of providing an accurate and reliable characterization of the biological lead burden carried by Port Royal residents.

What went wrong? Could lessons learned from this experience help avoid a similar outcome in future research of this kind? Sound exposure research is badly needed in low-income urban neighborhoods that have suffered lead contamination, so it is important to understand the problems this study encountered.

THE SECONDARY STUDY

The researchers directing the lead exposure study felt quite baffled in interpreting the community's resistance to their research. Convinced that they had been as sensitive and careful as humanly possible in planning the study, they felt that some mysterious characteristics of the neighborhoods themselves must be to blame. A project postmortem was clearly in order. Accordingly, the principal investigator secured the funding agency's approval to commission a small-scale supplementary study, called here the *secondary study*. Two sociologists, both with backgrounds in environmental health, community planning, and field research methods, were contracted to do this work.

The purpose of the secondary study was frankly exploratory, aimed at casting a research net wide enough and sensitive enough to interpret the vaguely defined problem of low community participation without knowing in advance what its salient features might be. The study relied on qualitative techniques commonly used in social science community studies and ethnographies, drawing most of its data from key informant interviews with community residents and project staff. This methodological approach, perhaps less familiar to most public health professionals than quantitative and experimental methodology, has been found useful for public policy research in a variety of different contexts (Miles & Huberman, 1994; Needleman & Needleman).

The lead exposure study's researchers and funding sponsors expected the secondary study to reveal some cultural peculiarities of the three target neighborhoods that might explain why residents had been so resistant to the screening. There are indeed some special features of these three communities that needed to be taken into account better than they were. But as we shall see, the reasons for residents' noncooperation were only partly a function of community characteristics. In a much more fundamental sense, the problem arose from unexamined assumptions and unacknowledged value choices built into the project itself.

SECTION II
REASONS FOR COMMUNITY NONPARTICIPATION

Even under the best of circumstances, the target neighborhoods would have posed a challenge in terms of cooperation with scientific research. Socially, all three resemble what urban anthropologists call "urban villages" (Gans, 1982)—tightly knit, conservative, working-class urban communities, usually with an ethnic base, that tend to be highly suspicious of outsiders.

In upper and lower Port Royal, residents are mainly of Irish and Polish descent. Many of the area's older Polish residents do not speak English. Most residents have grown up in the area and have numerous relatives living nearby, forming close kinship-based social networks. They display a great deal of pride in their homes, typically owner-occupied row housing that is old but well maintained. Catholic churches and parochial schools figure heavily in the area's social organization, with fairly sharp lines drawn between Polish Catholic and Irish Catholic. Family roles appear to be traditional and patriarchal. The residents feel the neighborhood is on the defensive, and they harbor deep fears about invasion from the impoverished minority communities that abut the area.

The third study community has quite a different history and social organization, despite its superficial resemblance to upper and lower Port Royal. Located west of the city's business district on the bank of a river, Munkville was once a small mill town with its own distinct identity. It is still considered by its residents not really to be part of the city. The area has recently begun to attract young professionals bent on gentrifying its old row houses to enjoy the neighborhood's quaintness, spectacular views, and easy commute to downtown. This different kind of invasion has created growing polarization and considerable tension between the new middle-class professional residents and the white ethnic, working-class, predominantly Catholic residents who originally populated the area. The importance of religious institutions and parochial schools appears to be declining somewhat, making the community less cohesive than Port Royal. There are several active community improvement organizations, mainly oriented toward the interests of the new residents.

In all three communities, it was (in retrospect) clear that the approach the researchers used to enlist community cooperation had been poorly matched to the values and current concerns of the residents. For example, in upper and lower Port Royal, where social organization revolves mainly around home, family, and church, community life tends to be what Gans (1982) calls *person oriented.* Risk communications through letters, posted notices, or radio spots are likely to be ineffective because they lack the element of human interaction. Even on an issue of clear community concern, risk messages need direct, personal reinforcement by a familiar, known, and trusted authority within the community. Without such reinforcement, a written request to appear at a central site to give blood for a research study, emphasizing abstract appeals to the public interest and the advancement of science, simply will not seem important. The same value framework suggests that home visits to collect data will meet with resistance because of residents' strong sense of privacy and sanctity of the home.

As for Munkville, the residents there are currently preoccupied with the rising tide of gentrification. Old residents worry about tax increases and property values being inflated by Yuppie outsiders with money to throw around. New residents worry about neighborhood youth harassing merchants and customers of the boutiques and cheese shops that are beginning to spring up. Neither the old nor the new residents see themselves as being associated with the city or any of its problems, including lead poisoning. In the minds of the Munkville residents, there is no background of awareness about lead-related health problems in the community, no sense of being threatened by a point source of lead exposure such as the factory in Port Royal, and no consciousness that lead screening could be of any benefit. A written request to appear at a central location to give blood for a community screening falls low in residents' priorities, and home visits are likely to be seen as an unwelcome and unnecessary inconvenience.

Another relevant social factor not well appreciated in the primary study's research plan was these communities' perception of blood sampling. In all three communities, drawing blood is an extremely sensitive issue, because of both general dislike of needles and erroneous but fear-producing ideas about contracting AIDS by giving blood. A number of community informants mentioned that it is asking a lot to have blood drawn, especially by strangers in a nonmedical setting. One key informant, a teacher, remarked, "They just must not have realized what needles mean to these people." Very strong incentives would be needed to justify what many residents apparently interpreted as a frightening and risky procedure, whether at the central sites or at home.

PITFALLS IN USING SOCIAL NETWORKS

Clearly, working through Port Royal's existing social networks was advisable, and some attempts were made to do so. Identifying and enlisting the help of community social networks, however, calls for considerable finesse. Mistakes are easy to make. For example, among the Polish residents of Port Royal, the Catholic monsignor occupies a position of great respect, expressed through extreme formality and ceremony. Requesting his help is not a matter of making a businesslike call; it demands an elaborate show of courtesy and deference, with the initial contact being made through an intermediary from the monsignor's inner circle. Through the secondary study, it became clear that a particular Republican representative in the community would be the best person to play the intermediary role. But the lead screening project had contained no assessment of how social networks are arranged in this particular community, and the proper etiquette was not understood. Therefore, unfortunately, the initial contact with the monsignor's office was made in a very inappropriate way—by telephone through a secretary, unintentionally communicating disrespect. Worse yet, the caller mistakenly referred to Port Royal as Bridgeburg, a nearby neighborhood held in contempt by Port Royal community leaders. These initial errors seem to have undermined church support for the project, which badly hurt its chances of gaining community support.

An added complexity is that, in an ethnically mixed community like Port Royal, community institutions such as the Catholic Church are likely to have their own internal factions. Support from an Irish priest was little help with Polish Catholic residents, and vice versa. Secular community leaders presented similar complexities. For instance, the local councilman who lent his support to the lead exposure study was not universally liked by residents in Port Royal, so his sponsorship was a mixed blessing. Because the researchers assumed that the councilman spoke for the whole community, other local political figures with wider community support were not contacted.

Mistakes in working with the community can also occur by omission. In Port Royal, the parochial schools represent a major focal point of community social activity and information sharing. There are regular meetings of the area's parochial school administrators, which, with the church hierarchy's permission, could have been used to explain the project to the area's school principals. With the principals' support, it would have been possible to publicize and legitimize the project through teachers' notes to parents, homework assignments, and parents' home and school meetings. Neighborhood friendship and family networks would have then spread information and receptive attitudes about the study even to those without school-age children. However, this opportunity was missed both in the initial planning of the lead exposure study and as a possible support when the data collection ran into trouble.

In the exploratory secondary study, community residents listed several additional types of community opinion leaders whose support would have helped the original study, including bankers, funeral directors, and bar owners. Without prior investigation, it would have been hard to predict that these were positions of high influence in the community.

Obviously, tapping into social networks is not a mechanical process. There is no formula that fits all communities. Each community requires its own assessment—*prior* to the intervention itself—of whom to contact and how to go about it.

PROBLEMS IN COLLECTING DATA

The problem of community noncooperation came into sharpest focus around the door-to-door data collection. The project's hired interviewers reported wide variations in cooperation. Some usually met their assigned number of interviews; others found extraordinary resistance.

All, however, experienced considerable frustration. One interviewer reported going to 100 houses and getting only five interviews. Almost all reported many instances of getting no answer at the door when there was clearly someone home, refusals to give blood samples after interview data were collected, and numerous perfunctory or evasive answers to interview questions. Some ran into language problems with non-English-speaking residents. Some African American interviewers were subjected to what they interpreted as racial slurs. Some interviewers even reported that dogs were let out of the house to chase them away.

The secondary study gave special attention to the role that racial prejudice might have played in the poor response to home visits. Most of the phlebotomists and some of the interviewers doing the door-to-door data collection were African American. In planning the interviews, the original study's researchers had anticipated a possible problem with racial prejudice because of Port Royal's general sensitivity about race and because a recent racial incident had inflamed community feelings (a local white teenager had been beaten by minority teens from outside the neighborhood). However, the principal investigator in the lead exposure study made a value-based decision in favor of nondiscriminatory hiring for the interviewers, regardless of the possible impact on community participation.

The secondary study found that, in this case at least, a firm stand for equal opportunity did not appear to have the costs that were feared. Using minority interviewers in a white ethnic community was not interpreted by the key informants as a significant factor explaining community nonparticipation. However, the perception of racism did cause serious problems of interviewer staff morale. Although some of the African American interviewers had no problem, others reported feeling very uncomfortable or unsafe because of looks and remarks directed at them by community residents. Some handled their anxiety by dressing "extra funky" to show that they were not afraid, which may have intensified the problem. One interviewer quit because she found the data-gathering process too stressful.

Although race hostility was not apparently a key factor in nonresponse for the door-to-door interviewing, two somewhat related issues proved more significant. Residents in these communities have reality-based worries about the safety of letting strangers into the house, especially after dark. Crime is a strong community concern in all three areas. In Port Royal, by unfortunate coincidence, a well-publicized wave of house burglaries was occurring at the time of the home interviews. The burglars' mode of operation was for one to engage the resident in conversation at the front door while a confederate entered through the back door and looted the house. The fear of crime reportedly made some residents afraid to open the door to the interviewers, denying staff the chance to show the identification they carried.

In addition, Port Royal is an area where religious groups frequently canvass the neighborhood seeking donations and converts. Residents have learned from experience that when groups of people knock on the door, they are likely to be religious solicitors who "talk and talk and waste your time." Because the interview teams fit the dreaded description, some residents preferred not to open the door.

The secondary study examined several other issues that the principal investigator and project director of the lead screening thought might have contributed to nonparticipation. First, residents of lower Port Royal might feel reluctant to cooperate because the factory presumed to be the source of lead contamination provides employment in the community. Interviews with residents and key informants suggest that this was not a common sentiment. In terms of actual numbers, not many (fewer than 100) of the area's residents work at the suspect facility. The factory is not highly visible in the community, and most residents are probably unaware of its existence and location. If they do know about the factory, they associate it not with lead hazards but with a fire that occurred at the site in 1988.

Second, residents might fear that blood tests would reveal the presence of lead-based paint inside their homes. Because this might expose them to abatement pressure from the city, a development potentially costly to them as home owners, they might prefer not to know. Resident and key informant interviews gave no support to this speculation. Residents are reportedly unconcerned about the city's lead abatement requirement— mainly, it seems, because they do not know about it.

Third, the results of previous community lead screenings, although inconclusive, might have allayed the residents' fears and made them less inclined to participate in a new study. Our interviews lent some credence to this possibility. Although few Port Royal residents know much about the past studies in any detail, there was reportedly a general feeling that if the results had been alarming, something would have been done about the problem. The issue of community lead exposure seemed to have lost some of the urgency that residents had expressed at an earlier point.

PROBLEMS IN THE RESEARCH DESIGN

The research design itself contributed to the problem of nonresponse. In some ways, the researchers in the project fell victim to their own enthusiasm. The basic research question could potentially have been addressed with a fairly simple design, say a sample or even a 100% survey of children under 6. This approach would presumably have yielded a response rate higher than that achievable with a more diverse sample, because mothers of young children proved to be the most cooperative part of the project sample in all three communities. The project's unusually strong professional resources and generous funding, however, presented the researchers with a golden opportunity to go beyond just a modest study. It was seen as a chance to produce the most complete, rigorous, definitive exposure characterization possible. In the words of one of the researchers, the project was "swept away by globalism."

The ambitious research design that resulted from this impulse for completeness went well beyond documenting the fact of community lead exposure, addressing a number of subsidiary questions about the exact patterns of exposure. Each embellishment implied an extra burden of social complexity in collecting the data. Including subsamples of teens, adult males, and the elderly greatly increased the number of interviews needed and caused confusion and resentment among community residents, who wondered why the researchers were testing some family members and not others. In addition, some of the questions on side issues alienated respondents. For example, the interviewers asked about alcohol use, a sensitive subject that people felt embarrassed to discuss, especially in front of other family members.

The problem is not that the design was wrong but that its sociological implications were ignored. If the buildup of social complexity had been recognized and taken into account, and given adequate time and planning resources, all might have gone well. As it was, with scant time and attention given to the social side of planning the research, the elaborateness of the design overbalanced the whole effort.

The researchers were aiming to obtain interview data and blood samples from 2,900 residents within a period of several weeks at an anticipated 80% rate of participation. This breathtakingly optimistic expectation implied very high levels of community motivation to cooperate—yet, the known participation rates in past voluntary screenings had been low (8% and 22%). Community participation had to be higher this time than for past screenings, because at the level of intricacy planned, the project's data analysis could not be carried out effectively without relatively complete data. But despite the critical importance of high participation to support the analysis plans, strategies for ensuring complete data were neglected.

It is important to note that the issue here is not ineptitude or insensitivity. On the contrary, the researchers were well trained scientifically, strongly committed to public health values, and quite sensitive to the rights of human subjects. The problem may lie in the nature of science training itself, with its emphasis on research methods appropriate for highly controlled laboratory settings. These techniques tend to work poorly in field settings, where conditions are uncontrolled and the research subjects have minds of their own.

One way that this misapplication of laboratory-style methods showed up was in the high value that the researchers placed on the preliminary census. In their proposal to the federal funding agency, the university researchers had written,

> In any community study such as this, achieving high participation rates is a major methodological challenge. Complex factors affect each family's decision regarding participation. Even with an intensive outreach effort, our 1988 survey only achieved participation by about one in five area residents. Consequently, we propose an innovative approach: a neighborhood census. We will contract with an experienced local research organization to enumerate all residents living in the study area. Our sample will be drawn from this roster.

They added, "Of course, simply conducting a census does not guarantee that reluctant individuals will participate." However, the actual research planning proceeded under that assumption. Implicitly, the previous low participation was attributed to lack of complete information about the study population, rather than to insufficient motivation for community residents to volunteer. Implicitly, the potential problem of low participation was assumed to be remedied by the census itself. Complete population information for sampling purposes was seen as the most vital need, as if voluntary cooperation were not an issue.

Unfortunately, the fragility of community motivation to cooperate went unacknowledged, unplanned for, and perhaps even unrecognized. Impressive resources were poured into the census, but no corresponding effort went into serious investigation of the community's culture and social organization. The need for special planning around social networks, influential community residents, and cultural values was simply eclipsed by "hard science" faith in a sound sampling plan.

It was assumed that the methods for getting people to cooperate were standard and obvious, requiring no special preliminary research. The researchers followed a commonsense approach: get some advance publicity through the census; have the study announced in mass media and through local institutions, such as churches; form a board of influential community residents to lend legitimacy; and send request letters to homes. Unfortunately, these methods did not work—at least, not well enough to get people out by the thousands, at night, in the rain, without clear personal benefit. The census contacts were not used to motivate participation, public announcements were low-key, and the community advisory board appears to have been more ceremonial than participatory. The letter sent to residents, drafted and used without pretesting, was written at an inappropriately high (college) reading level. It appealed to abstract ideals, such as public spiritedness and contribution to scientific knowledge—certain to be weak motivators for these urban villagers.

Interestingly, more effective motivational strategies were hastily devised after community noncooperation started becoming evident (i.e., when there were more interviewers than residents showing up at the central sites). A wave of telephoning, initiated in desperation by a health department official and carried out by dragooned health department volunteers, was successful in significantly raising the participation rate at one of the central sites. Residents turned out in much higher numbers than before and responded very positively to the calls, saying things like "I'm glad you called. I wanted to come, but would have forgotten." Extra telephone calls were subsequently used to boost participation at central sites in all three study communities.

However, because telephone calls had not been built into the original research design, they proved difficult to make. The sample lists had been ordered without telephone information because the need for phone numbers was not anticipated, so looking up the numbers was cumbersome. The health department callers were untrained ("some of us were great, some were definitely not") and uncertain whether a highly personal tone in the call was appropriate or not ("getting personal took too long and some residents got impatient"). Also, despite their demonstrated effectiveness, phone calls were not used in connection with the door-to-door contacts. Because such extensive telephoning had not been planned, there were no resources for it in the grant.

ROLE OF THE FUNDING AGENCY

Certain features of the project's federal funding compounded these problems. For example, it was assumed that the timing of the project could be adapted to the usual bureaucratic funding processes without harming the study. This may be the case for laboratory research, where the motivation and cooperation of research subjects are not issues. However, in community-based research, where the participation of research subjects is voluntary, timing is everything. There is a need for a period of community investigation and negotiation prior to the actual data collection. There is often a "golden moment" of community receptivity that cannot be re-created if it is missed. And sometimes there is a critical time point that cannot be postponed—as in the case of Port Royal, where data had to be collected in September to reflect outdoor lead exposure during the summer.

In the Port Royal project, as is often the case with federal funding, many months elapsed between the approval of the research proposal and the actual authorization for using the funds. The authorization finally came through shortly before the September "window of opportunity." Even if the researchers had wanted to do a more adequate community reconnaissance and to work more interactively with the community advisory board prior to the data collection, the administrative delay in grant processing left no time for these efforts. As for the hired interviewers, they felt alienated from the project and never jelled as a team, in large part because there was not enough time for the necessary training and support meetings prior to and during the short data collection period. According to the interview staff themselves, their low morale led them to accept superficial and probably invalid answers to some of the interview questions.

The federal funding agency does not appear to have included any social scientists on its review panel or to have scrutinized the plans for working with the community anywhere near as thoroughly as it scrutinized the hard science aspects of the plan. In the secondary study, agency staff explained that these matters are left up to the grantees. However, there was apparently no discussion with the grantees about their past experience with community-based research (which was minimal) or about their plans to get technical assistance from social scientists if necessary. Essentially, medical and technical research skills were put to work on social science tasks, without much oversight from the funding agency. It was apparently assumed by both the funding agency and the grantees that securing community cooperation was a relatively simple assignment, one that intelligent people could do without any special training, experience, or research guidance. This may be an understandable belief among professionals skilled in technical fields but unfamiliar with sociology, anthropology, and social work. Unfortunately, as in this case, it can be a blind spot that wrecks the entire project.

LACK OF A SERVICE COMPONENT

In the final analysis, the most fundamental problem in securing community cooperation was a clash between the scientific priorities of the lead exposure study and the service priorities of the community. Although the ultimate justification for the study was public health, it was seen by project staff and by the funding source as a research effort, definitely not a community service intervention. Indeed, the researchers were strongly committed to avoiding the self-selection biases of earlier, more service-oriented screenings in Port Royal, in order finally to achieve definitive findings for the area. For purposes of scientific rigor, they wanted to follow the sampling plan faithfully, collecting data on only those residents selected for the sample. By contrast, the residents assumed that a community study sponsored by the local health department and supported by federal tax dollars would be planned to help all of those at risk for lead exposure. They expected the screening to help the community understand and deal with its lead-related health problems.

In principle, mutually beneficial ways to reconcile the twin goals of science and service could have been developed. For example, the research design could have incorporated a service component by *embedding* the sample—selecting the sample first, then offering screening as a service to the whole community, and finally, cleaning up the methodology by excluding data from nonsample participants and collecting data on sample members who had not yet participated. However, this approach posed problems in terms of cost. The federal funding supported collection of data on the sample, not blood testing in the community at large. A mass screening would have been expensive, and the health department could not make funds available for this purpose from its own budget.

This situation put the researchers in a Catch-22. If they raised community concern by a full-fledged public information campaign, they would create pressure for a voluntary mass screening that they did not want and could not afford. So they kept publicity low-key and relied primarily on individual letters to motivate participation by only those particular individuals they wanted as participants. However, in communities like the three being studied, low-key, impersonal, individualized publicity methods were not effective motivators. The formula simply didn't compute.

Attempts to walk this tightrope put the researchers in an awkward position that sometimes bordered on the absurd. For example, they felt compelled to turn down offers from community groups interested in helping them publicize the study. Also, although they planned to inform residents of their individual test results and to follow up medically with anyone found to have high blood lead, they deliberately did not use the research for public health education. They kept the letters and interviews scrupulously free of information that would have helped residents understand hazards, symptoms, and abatement techniques related to lead. They did not stress the individual health benefits of testing, and they did not promise or plan any general community action follow-up to the research.

The result of such caution, the secondary study found, was that many residents simply did not see the point in inconveniencing themselves to participate in the project, when there was no explanation of a community problem and no clear personal or community benefit from participation. Ultimately, the community "failed to cooperate" because the researchers failed to make a convincing case for why they should.

This science-versus-service problem is not limited to the specific case discussed here. On the contrary, it occurs frequently in community-based health research projects. In return for participating in the project, community residents expect to get something from the study that meets their own needs and concerns. If they find that the main goal is collecting data on their health for someone else's research purposes, they tend to feel used, or even exploited. Whether fair or not, community residents—especially in minority neighborhoods—sometimes see parallels to the notorious Tuskegee syphilis experiments, where human research subjects were studied like laboratory animals with no concern at all for their service needs (Jones, 1981). Meanwhile, professional researchers and their institutional sponsors may feel equally frustrated, because their studies are well intentioned, and they generally have no mandate or resources to provide local services.

Effective resolution of this dilemma may require a fundamental rethinking by researchers and research funding agencies of how to reframe the priorities of community-based research so that both goals can be addressed at once. In the meantime, professionals engaged in community-based health studies need, at the very least, to be aware that their research may be asking much of community participants, and giving little back to them. Wherever possible, those who study the health of communities should look for opportunities to include some kind of service to their participants—if not actual access to health care, then at least health education, useful information, and referral to existing local services.

KEY ISSUE

THE CENTRAL IMPORTANCE
OF COMMUNITY SUPPORT

LAURA C. LEVITON

CAROLYN E. NEEDLEMAN

With the growing emphasis on confronting community health risks, professionals in public health and related fields have become increasingly involved in "working with" the communities affected. To do this effectively, professionals need to take a step back and consider

▲ What kind of social reconnaissance information is needed to plan a community health study?

▲ How can outside professionals identify the appropriate community leaders to work with?

▲ Given that their agendas and priorities may differ, how can outside professionals and community residents develop enough genuine exchange and reciprocity so that both parties see the project as worthy of support?

Understanding the community. One clear conclusion from the Port Royal case study is the folly of undertaking community-based health research that assumes voluntary participation by residents without first committing time and effort to develop more than a superficial understanding of the community's social structure and values. A preliminary social reconnaissance of the community is needed—one that not only notes the existence of potential problems but also identifies the most effective strategies for gaining the residents' cooperation.

An important starting point is to consider exactly what is meant by the term *community*. Given the complexity of the concept, no single definition can be all-encompassing. As John McKnight (1991), a well-known community organizer, observes, "If you ask the sociology depart-

ment what a community is, you will never leave the sociology department."
Amitai Etzioni (1993), in his seminal book on the communitarian movement in American politics, refers to community as "the conditions and
elements we all share" (p. 15). But then, which levels of community are
we talking about? As Etzioni notes,

> Communities are best viewed as if they were Chinese boxes, in which
> less encompassing communities (families, neighborhoods) are nestled
> within more encompassing ones (local villages and towns), which in turn
> are situated within still more encompassing communities, the national
> and cross-national ones (such as the budding European Community).
> Moreover, there is room for nongeographic communities that criss-cross
> the others, such as professional or work-based communities. When they
> are intact, they are all relevant, and all lay moral claims on us by
> appealing to and reinforcing our values. (p. 32)

Social scientists have analyzed communities using many different
conceptual frameworks—typological perspectives that classify different kinds of territorial groupings that share values, cohesion, and
continuity; ecological perspectives, in which spatial, economic, and
health indicators are mapped; conflict perspectives, in which communities are the location for struggles over resources; and functional perspectives, in which networks and linkages among people are analyzed as a
social system (e.g., Warren, 1978). Each of these approaches is helpful
to develop a plan to work effectively with communities experiencing
health risks. For example, understanding the linkages among people can
be turned into an asset for programming to get a health education
message across (McAlister, Puska, Salonen, Tuomilehto, & Koskela,
1982) or to access volunteers (e.g., Kong, Miler, & Smoot, 1982).
Understanding the economic divisions, ethnic diversity, and contradic-
tory political interests present within a community can serve as an
antidote to a simplistic, overly homogeneous view of community sentiment. Knowing the spatial and economic organization of the community—for example, the transportation system, current health service
resources, and health insurance profile of the population—helps in
understanding community residents' ability (or inability) to act on
information about health risk. It is especially important to understand

the community's organizational resources for solving problems, often termed *community capacity*; this point is addressed in greater detail in Chapter 5.

Community members often share identifiable values; but as the Port Royal case study makes clear, professionals need to test their assumptions about community values. Port Royal, potentially a candidate for inclusion in the Superfund program because of its lead problems, had been the focus of considerable official attention from the Environmental Protection Agency and the city health department in the years prior to the ill-fated lead study discussed in this chapter. Given this background and the pressure from environmental groups and some highly vocal residents in Port Royal, the researchers assumed that the community as a whole was informed and concerned about lead exposure. As it turned out, however, general community consciousness on the issue was in fact low in Port Royal. Many residents knew little about lead as a health hazard. Others viewed this latest lead screening cynically, soured by the history of past official activity without visible results in terms of services or hazard abatement. *The lesson is: The community leaders most visible to outside professionals do not necessarily speak for the whole community.*

At a minimum, professionals planning community-based projects need to assess the following, prior to the intervention:

a. Some basic facts about the community's sociodemographic characteristics. This part of the social reconnaissance should include a profile of *residents' personal characteristics* such as ethnicity, education, literacy, income levels, employment patterns, family status, and so on. It should also include another level of information too often neglected, the community's *characteristics as a social system*: facts about the local economy and social structure, available health services, organizational resources, and the community's central values and concerns. Both kinds of information are usually obtainable from secondary sources such as census data or preexisting community descriptions; local public librarians and planning department staff may be useful resources.

b. Some basic facts about the local history of the health risk itself—past publicity, the surrounding politics, competing local concerns, and the level of trust or distrust associated with past interventions or research related to the health risk. This information can be gleaned from the archives of local newspapers, the local health department, and/or from key informants knowledgeable about the community's history.

c. Some basic facts about who functions as the community's opin-ion leaders, whose aid might be enlisted in support of the project, and how best to approach them. This information is best obtained through informal interviews with key informants.

Ways to work with community. How can outside professionals find out who speaks for a community? There are a number of strategies, some of which were used by the sociologists who performed the secondary study in Port Royal: interviewing key informants identified through word of mouth; selection of community representatives based on formal leadership positions; and *snowball sampling,* in which each informant is asked to name additional community opinion leaders who should be interviewed.

Community organizers employ similar strategies to map community assets and interest groups (Bracht, 1990). For example, in his work on community organization, McKnight (1995) makes use of a special feature of communities, community associations. Communities gener-ally contain groups of people who come together for mutual benefit, to solve shared problems, for enjoyment, for social status, and so on. Community associations can be as informal as a church lunch group or as formalized as the American Legion post. These associations are wellsprings of capacity to address community needs. They can get out the vote. They can start neighborhood watches. They can cooperate in public health campaigns. In one project, McKnight (1988) and his students set out to identify as many associations as possible within a single Chicago neighborhood of about 85,000 people. Within a fairly brief time, they located 575 different local associations, plus 121 organizations that operated actively within the neighborhood although they were based in the larger metropolitan area.

Their most productive strategy in finding these associations was to contact individuals whose formal roles made them well informed about the community (for example, ministers and librarians). They also found it useful to consult local newspapers, directories such as the phone book and self-help directories, and other print materials. In addition, using word-of-mouth information, they identified a small number of individual residents who qualified as key informants simply because they were well connected to local associations and were very knowledgeable about the neighborhood. Figure 3.1 reproduces a map of the different categories of associations that McKnight and his students discovered. Although their emphasis was on locating local organizations, they clearly gained much broader information as well. Their report notes,

> Not reflected [in the map] . . . was the wealth of information we learned, especially from personal calls and conversations with pastors [in another neighborhood the best source might be different]. . . . We also came across some people who are clearly very involved in the neighborhood and who would be excellent contacts for getting acquainted with other local residents. (McKnight, 1988, p. 9)

The discovery of so many community organizations in this project illustrates another important point: It is not necessary for a practitioner or leader to depend on one or two organizations exclusively to work effectively with a community. If the issue is a good one, there are many associations that might be receptive to addressing the risk problem and might bring important capacities to the table.

In the Port Royal case study, two obstacles prevented a clear understanding of community social structure and concerns. The first was that time did not allow for adequate investigation. Because the research schedule was very compressed in its initial stage, groundwork in the community and orientation/training of the interviewers had to be simplified to the point of being mainly symbolic. Although agency staff point out that the investigators expended more energy for community outreach than is usual in a study of this kind, it was obviously still not sufficient to avoid poor participation rates. *The lesson is: At all costs, plan sufficient time for doing the community groundwork and defend it from getting short-changed in implementation.*

The second obstacle to working effectively in the Port Royal study communities was that the complexity of "working with the community" was not appreciated. The primary study's research staff had little past experience with large-scale data collection in a community context.

Artistic Organization:	choral, theatrical, writing
Business Organizations:	Chamber of Commerce, neighborhood business associations, trade groups
Charitable Groups & Drives:	Red Cross, Cancer Society, United Way
Church Groups:	service, prayer, maintenance, stewardship, acolytes, men's, women's, youth, seniors
Civic Events:	July 4th, art fair, Halloween
Collectors Groups:	stamp collectors, flower dryers, antiques
Community Support Groups:	"friends" of the library, nursing home, hospital
Elderly Groups:	Senior Citizens
Ethnic Associations:	Sons of Norway, Black Heritage Club, Hibernians
Health & Fitness Groups:	bicycling, jogging, exercise
Interest Clubs:	poodle owners, antique car owners
Local Government:	town, township, electoral units, fire department, emergency units
Local Media:	radio, newspaper, local access cable TV
Men's Groups:	cultural, political, social, educational, vocational
Mutual Support (Self-Help) Groups:	Alcoholics Anonymous, Epilepsy Self-Help, La Leche League
Neighborhood & Block Clubs:	crime watch, beautification, Christmas decorations
Outdoor Groups:	garden clubs, Audubon Society, conservation clubs
Political Organizations:	Democrats, Republicans, caucuses
School Groups:	printing club, PTA, child care
Service Clubs:	Zonta, Kiwanis, Rotary, American Association of University Women
Social Cause Groups:	peace, rights, advocacy, service
Sports Leagues:	bowling, swimming, baseball, fishing, volleyball
Study Groups:	literary clubs, bible study groups
Veterans Groups:	American Legion, Amvets, Veterans of Foreign Wars & Auxiliaries
Women's Groups:	cultural, political, social, educational, vocational
Youth Groups:	4H, Future Farmers, Scouts, YWCA

Figure 3.1. A Map of Associations

Source: John McKnight, *Getting Connected: How to Find Out about Groups and Organizations in Your Neighborhood.* Evanston, IL: Center for Urban Affairs and Policy Research, Northwestern University, 1988. Reprinted by permission.

Unaware of the enormous challenges inherent in such research, they (and the federal funders) did not consider bringing in social scientists or experienced community field-workers at an early stage. Existing guides on how to work with the community in a risk communication intervention, which might have been helpful, were apparently not used. As a result, opportunities for community involvement were missed, and some well-intentioned efforts at community contact backfired without the researchers' being aware of it. *The lesson is: Do not reinvent (or worse, fail to use) the wheel. Enlist appropriate social science expertise when the research task calls for it.*

Why do communities get alienated? Professionals entering communities to work on health risks are almost certain, sooner or later, to encounter hostility from at least some community members. At first blush, this may seem very unfair. After all, the professional is taking leadership on the risk issue to help, not hurt, communities.

A simple thought experiment often helps professionals understand such community reactions. Assume for the moment that you are sitting in your living room in the evening, opening the mail. An official letter from the health department falls in your lap. You are informed that health department data indicate a greater than average rate of mental illness in your zip code. The health department intends to organize a screening campaign to help your community deal with its problem and requests that you come in to be tested. What are you feeling at this moment?

In reality, such a letter would probably never appear at your home; however, health agencies do initiate campaigns about less overtly sensitive topics all the time. At a minimum, your reaction might be indignation: How dare they malign my neighborhood in ways that might hurt its economy and public image? How dare they tell me that I need screening to see if I'm mentally ill? The *way* these problems are handled may be just as important as the decision to address them in the first place, because community cooperation is necessary to solve them.

Simply put, experts run the danger of appearing arrogant about their special authority to deal with public health problems. As mentioned in Chapter 1, the play *An Enemy of the People* has become a general metaphor for public indignation over peremptory professional actions concerning health risks. In this play, Ibsen's protagonist suffered from both naivete and arrogance about his right to define the community's health risk, commenting,

> A man should never put on his best trousers when he goes out to battle for freedom and truth. . . . That the mob, the rabble, should dare to attack me as if they were my equals—that is what I can't, for the life of me, stomach! . . . One half of the population is stark mad, and if the other half hasn't lost its wits, that's only because they are brute beasts who haven't any wits to lose. (pp. 90-91)

To some extent, Ibsen's ironic play reflects the reality of early public health history. Edwin Chadwick, the physician who first championed sanitation in London, is justly celebrated for his contributions to public health. However, according to one historian's account (Gray, 1979), Chadwick was completely impatient with any objections to his proposals, and his personal manner was viewed by many of his contemporaries as so insufferable that more politically astute physicians had to advocate sanitation before progress could be made. These examples are extreme, but they do illustrate professional assumptions that tend to deprecate community authority and subordinate it to professional authority. Public health professionals interested in confronting risk need to watch this tendency, because ultimately they must rely on communities to implement many of their recommendations.

The communitarian movement, as represented by writers such as John Gardener (1991), Amitai Etzioni (1993), and John McKnight (1995), regards the disparagement of communities as a fundamental problem in American society. These authors point to a long-term increase in the influence and power of professionals, hierarchical institutions, and government at the expense of community resources and authority. They see an erosion of

> the social webs that communities provide, in neighborhoods, at work, and in ethnic clubs and associations, the webs that bind individuals, who would otherwise be on their own, into groups of people who care for one another and who help maintain a civic, social, and moral order. (Etzioni, 1993, p. 248)

Etzioni (1993) attributes the decline in the value placed on local communities to changes in our expectations about society, as traditional obligations and bonds among people have given way to a mass society in which relationships among neighbors, relatives, and community organizations are eclipsed by those based on industry, formal organizations, and the state. According to Etzioni, as the importance of traditional community declined, faith in institutionalized science gradually increased:

> Other major forms of progress were believed to accompany the movement from a world of villages to one of cities. Magic, superstition, alchemy, and religion—"backward beliefs"—would be replaced by bright, shining science and technology. . . . Old-fashioned values and a sense of obligation were expected to yield to logic and calculation. . . . By the same token, the network of reciprocal obligations and care that is at the heart of communities would give way to individual rights protected by the state. (p. 117)

These expectations have shaped current professional assumptions about who has the right to define and to solve health problems. The Institute of Medicine (1988) notes,

> As public health became a scientific enterprise . . . prevention and control of disease were no longer tasks of common sense and social compassion, but of knowledge and expertise. . . . It became clear that not only public and individual restraint were needed to control infectious disease, but also state agency epidemiologists and their laboratories were needed to direct the way. (p. 65)

The same forces may also have helped fuel community skepticism about, and alienation from, public health professionals and their institutions. As the Institute of Medicine's 1988 report on the *Future of Public Health* observes, people value the public health mission, but they generally harbor negative feelings about specific public health agencies. The feeling is that public health agencies have not been responsive to the communities' perceived problems. Indeed, much of the conflict in confronting environmental health risk at the community level can be traced to the way the problems are framed by professional experts—as being technological and objective and value neutral, when in fact there are underlying values involved that deeply affect and divide communities (Becker, 1996; Dake, 1992; Freudenburg & Pastor, 1992; National Research Council, 1989).

In the Port Royal case study, the community expertise that might have broadened the researchers' perspective was overlooked. Specifically, although a community advisory board was created, it was assigned a passive role. Set up in the primary study's planning phase, the board served mainly to provide legitimacy to the study. It was not tapped for substantive input into the research design, and some of its members felt used as window dressing. In retrospect, a more interactive review of the research plans with board members—either as a body or as individual key informants—might have alerted the researchers in advance to at least some of the project's participation problems. *The lesson is: To get the most value out of community advisory boards in field research, take them seriously as knowledgeable consultants.*

Some community organizers would fault the way in which lead exposure was selected as the focus of effort in Port Royal in the first place. Even though some community voices had raised concern over lead from time to time, the initiative for the lead exposure study came from professionals, not the community. Professionals, not the community, chose the terms in which to address the problem. This expert-driven approach was used in order to maintain the rigor of the lead exposure research for the purposes of reporting to an external scientific audience. But it is an approach unsuited to confrontation of community health risks in the local setting itself, which necessarily requires a more democratic give and take of information among many different interest groups. The National Research Council (1989) sums up the issue this way:

> In the past, the term risk communication has commonly been thought of as consisting only of one-way messages from experts to nonexperts. . . . We see risk communication as an interactive process of exchange of information and opinion among individuals, groups, and institutions. When risk communication is viewed in this way, significant, though perhaps less obvious, underlying problems can be better discerned and treated. (p. 2)

NOTE

1. In this case study, stakeholders were guaranteed anonymity. As a result, we changed names of places and withheld our documentation for quotations and sources.

CHAPTER 4

WORKER HEALTH IN BLACK AND WHITE

LAURA C. LEVITON

INTRODUCTION[1]

This case study describes events in a federally funded
project to notify people of a health risk based on their past
occupational exposure to a toxic substance. For many
reasons, the various parties perceived what happened in
remarkably different ways. The case illustrates why community history and culture must be taken into account in
dealing with health risks. Because two thirds of the workers
were African Americans, their past exposure and subsequent treatment came to be seen by them as a civil rights
issue—literally in black and white terms. For occupational
health professionals, the past worker exposure and the
need to address exposure were also clear-cut, right and
wrong issues. The workers' health risk became the symbol

of a national debate over a worker's right to know about occupational health risks. For those who spoke for the larger community, however, the federal worker notification project was also a black and white issue—but in reverse. Community leaders say federal officials came into their town, caused trouble, and left without solving the problem. Their viewpoint is valid, too.

It must be said that, in the course of doing this case study, we occasionally encountered inaccuracies in statements. However, the major events occurred nearly 10 years before the case was created. It should not come as a surprise that some people may have selectively recalled information. In fact, it is the great difference in impressions that matters most in this case study.

 ## KEY ISSUE AND GENERAL QUESTIONS

This case study illustrates, more than any of the others, the importance of understanding the ethical positions underlying public health work. The discussion presents four ethical principles that may come into conflict, which may explain differences in stakeholder perspectives about the "right" course of action. Specifically, the discussion addresses these questions:

▲ What are the various ethical positions that crop up when decisions must be taken about risks?

▲ How can decisions about these risks be evaluated according to these ethical principles?

▲ How can the implementation of those decisions be evaluated by the key ethical principles?

 ## STAKEHOLDERS

Former workers at Classic Chemical Company
Neighborhood organization

Lawsuit participants
Classic Chemical Company and parent company
NIOSH scientists (both for and against worker notification)
Labor advocates
News media in city of Classic
State and local health departments
Classic city establishment community leaders

TIMELINE

1940-1955	Classic Chemical Company uses BNA in dye production
1949	Chemical Manufacturers Association states that BNA is a dangerous carcinogen
1955	Large manufacturers cease BNA production
	Classic Chemical begins production of BNA
1967	Chemical corporation purchases Classic Chemical
1968	*Classic Chronicle* prints article on BNA hazards
Early 1970s	NIOSH is created
1972-1973	NIOSH studies Classic Chemical workers
1972	Classic Chemical ceases manufacture of BNA at urging of NIOSH
1970s	Federal debate over role of NIOSH in notification efforts
1978	Discussion begins on Classic screening
1979	First academic article on Classic Chemical workers
1981	News story breaks in *Classic Chronicle*
	Lawsuits filed
1981-1984	NIOSH-funded screening
1984	Lawsuits settled
1985-present	Company-funded screening effort is part of settlement

BACKGROUND: A HEALTH RISK UNDER WRAPS

DESCRIPTION OF THE COMMUNITY

Classic City is an urban community of the Deep South, bordering an important commercial waterway. It has grown from an agricultural to a manufacturing economy, specializing in textiles, chemicals, and paper products. Tourism is also a major industry because of the natural beauty of the setting. Classic City has one of the state's largest medical complexes and is home to a medical school.

Classic City is a typical small Southern city, as reflected in demographics and lifestyles. The majority of the 50,000 residents are African American. The median per capita income at the end of the 1980s was around $8,100, and more than 30% of the population lived below the poverty level. Unemployment ranged between 9% and 10%. As in most southern states, a right-to-work law discouraged unions and encouraged transient manual labor, often in poor working conditions.

The majority of African Americans still have relatively little education, although younger black people have had greater educational opportunities. African American and other minority populations live in segregated areas of the city, and life appears socially divided. Wealthier, seasonal residents, as well as those in government and industrial power in the city, are white. White people say that government—especially the federal government—should not intervene in people's lives. Even the workers' attorney mentioned that he did not believe in federal intervention: "We fought a war with the north over that."

THE CLASSIC CHEMICAL COMPANY

Taking advantage of a nearby river and abundant natural gas, the Classic City area has one of the largest concentrations of chemical industries in the South. Although several large area chemical manufacturers are highly respected for their approach to worker safety and health, one smaller firm caused concern.

Between 1940 and 1972, the Classic Chemical Company both used and manufactured beta-naphthylamine (BNA). BNA is one of the most widely known and powerful chemical carcinogens known to occupational medicine, increasing the risk of bladder cancer by as much as 90-fold. Workers develop bladder cancer on average 20 years after exposure. Workers absorb BNA through inhalation, touch, and eating in areas contaminated with BNA dust.

By the mid-1950s, BNA was widely known, in the words of occupational health professionals, as a "notorious" chemical bladder carcinogen. In 1949, the Chemical Manufacturers Association developed a Materials Data Handling Sheet that listed BNA as a known carcinogen for which no degree of exposure was safe. Prior to 1950, larger chemical companies had made BNA, and the Classic Chemical Company had processed it into other substances. However, the larger companies stopped manufacture in 1955, citing their conclusion that there was no safe level of exposure. (See Chapter 2 for more on BNA.)

Classic Chemical had used BNA in the manufacture of dye, but, in 1955, the same year that the larger companies stopped production, it began to manufacture BNA itself. Dyes using BNA could be made for less money than alternative processes. Why did the company start making BNA when the larger companies stopped due to worker health risks? In the words of one community leader, the company had always been seen as an "outsider" and a "rogue company" by the local power elite.

A chemical conglomerate bought the plant in 1967. It was a fairly large chemical company, and its corporate leadership was reasonably sophisticated about chemistry and occupational safety and health. Several of those interviewed said the new owners must have been aware of the dangers of BNA. Despite a debate within the company about BNA, however, Classic Chemical continued to manufacture it. In 1968, the *Classic Chronicle* printed an article about the banning of BNA in another state and its continued use at the Classic Chemical plant. The article called it "extremely hazardous" and said it "produces bladder cancer." In response, the plant manager sent a letter to the editor in which he said the danger from BNA for bladder cancer was "less than smoking one cigarette." This incident was the only public discussion of the BNA issue until 1972.

Most workers at the Classic plant had little education but were relatively well paid. Jobs at Classic Chemical were fairly desirable in the 1950s and 1960s. According to some people, the plant hired black workers because it was located in a predominantly black section of town. Also, relatives and friends of workers were the first to hear about new openings at the plant. Community leaders say that, for this reason, and not by some intentional plot, the workforce was primarily black.

One former worker described his job. He worked part-time at the plant through high school and college. He said it seemed a dirty and dangerous place to work. However, pay was good. He got his job through the son of one of the supervisors, who was his friend. He started working there as a laborer, and, after a while, he was promoted to a chemical operator earning an extra 50 cents an hour. Eventually, he had responsibility for vats that were part of the BNA production process. He had to have special sheets and bedclothes because he would excrete the BNA through his pores at night.

He said that the men could not help getting BNA on themselves because they had to haul it in its liquid form and some BNA would spill. Except for college-age youths like himself, most of the workers were middle-aged and not well-educated. According to this former worker, from time to time, all sorts of safety problems occurred at the plant, such as barrels of chemicals exploding. The dangers were just accepted and, according to this worker, "were part of a macho attitude to the job."

Prior to 1981, several workers developed bladder cancer, but they were never told about its possible relationship to their work. Workers were required to be examined by the company physician to be eligible for company payment of medical care. One worker said he visited the company physician with symptoms of bladder cancer and was told he had an ulcer. The worker then visited a private physician who told him that he had bladder cancer and needed to get it treated. However, he did not challenge the company doctor's diagnosis at the time and did not receive treatment. When he finally became really sick, he sought care. By then, his bladder cancer was in an advanced stage, and he lost both his bladder and one kidney.

Until the 1981 notification effort took place, this worker said no one told him anything about the cause of his bladder cancer. They just removed his bladder and kidney. He felt bitter about the course of events.

He mentioned that he had only worked at the company to support his family because there were no other opportunities in town. He said that if he had known what the company was doing, he never would have worked there. He also was amazed that the company knew it was using a substance that causes bladder cancer. This man later testified before the Senate Subcommittee on Labor concerning the High Risk Worker Notification Bill, an effort to mandate federal notification of workers found to be at high risk of occupational diseases.

Another former employee claimed that management was well aware of the harmfulness of BNA because it was the only chemical not stored in the warehouse. Management's offices were located over the warehouse. One large chemical company shipped BNA to Classic Chemical Company in the late 1940s and early 1950s and specified that warning labels were to be used on the containers. However, workers say they never saw a label on any of the chemicals.

NIOSH BECOMES INVOLVED

The National Institute for Occupational Safety and Health (NIOSH) was created in the early 1970s. Part of the Institute's mission was to study the effects of occupational exposure to potential carcinogens. The organization's leaders decided that NIOSH should begin by studying the known carcinogens and clearest cases of exposure because these were best understood and easiest to quantify. Because BNA had been clearly identified as one of the most powerful workplace carcinogens, NIOSH chose to study worker groups exposed to BNA.

In 1972 and 1973, the deputy director of NIOSH field studies, Dr. Bill Jones, decided to study the worker population at Classic Chemical because it was one of only two companies in the United States known to still manufacture or use BNA. In 1972, he contacted local health department officials and the medical school about the study on BNA. He talked to a general practitioner who was serving as the physician for Classic Chemical about BNA and possible worker health problems. The company doctor had no idea what BNA was. Dr. Jones obtained the names of the employees' physicians and notified them that workers had been exposed to BNA and that the chemical had a potential to cause bladder cancer. The letter urged physicians to check workers for signs of bladder illness.

In 1972 and 1973, NIOSH conducted urine studies for detection of bladder cancers in workers then employed at Classic Chemical Company. The studies found no sign of overt cancer, but Dr. Jones felt that there was enough evidence to warrant a screening and notification program for the workers. Screening for bladder cancer is fairly simple, and if bladder cancers are detected and removed in their early stage, patients have highly favorable outcomes. NIOSH notified workers at the plant in 1972 and 1973 of their exposure to BNA and set up a pilot screening program for them. However, according to the director of the Classic City health department, hardly anyone participated. He explained that "no one wanted to know if they were sick. These people were poor, uneducated, and scared."

A problem, from Dr. Jones's point of view, was that no former workers were notified. BNA causes bladder cancer an average of 20 years after exposure, so many former workers were at greater risk than current workers. The only way NIOSH could contact former workers was through personnel files at the company. It was not clear who was legally required to notify former workers—NIOSH or the company. At that time, there were no regulatory controls or government standards for BNA, but there was definite industry concern. In the early 1970s, federal action on occupational health and worker notification about exposures was still in its early stages.

Dr. Jones urged Classic Chemical to cease production of BNA. Company representatives point out that within 7 days, the company stopped making BNA and bulldozed the plant that manufactured it. The company also agreed to pay medical bills and lost wages for any workers who were ill because of exposure to BNA. Dr. Jones also sent letters to both the local and state health departments, urging them to notify and screen former workers. However, he never received a response to these letters. The director of the Classic City health department, a traditional, older Southern man, later claimed he never saw the letter. He was only beginning to reorganize the health department at the time and claimed he would have had to forward such a letter to the state health department before any county level response could take place.

Dr. Jones left NIOSH in 1973 to complete his medical training. He believed that NIOSH had an obligation to notify any workers that it studied about health risks. He believed that Classic Chemical was a renegade operation hidden in the South to use a poor, uneducated worker population. He felt that the only reason the parent company stopped manufacturing BNA was that NIOSH exerted pressure; Classic Chemical knew that "the jig was up." Although the parent company had debated whether to make BNA during the entire 5-year period in which they had owned the Classic Chemical plant, Dr. Jones charged that this was a sophisticated company, and one that should have known what they were getting into when they started making BNA. He also questioned why neither the local nor the state health departments did anything to address the health concerns of the former workers. Finally, he criticized NIOSH's lack of action to notify workers at that time.

The parent company's version of events is somewhat different. The vice president said in the press that the company inherited the problem of BNA contamination when it acquired the Classic Chemical Company and did not feel any responsibility as far as the exposure was concerned. However, they felt sympathetic to the workers' problem, stopped BNA production immediately, and later supported the federal screening effort.

FEDERAL DEBATE OVER NOTIFICATION

When NIOSH studied the Classic Chemical workers, it had no authority and no resources to inform former employees of their risk. Letters from NIOSH to the state and local health departments, informing them of the problem, were ignored. From that point, the Classic Chemical workers were at the center of a national debate about the federal role in worker notification. Was NIOSH strictly an epidemiological research organization, or should it also take an activist role to inform workers it was studying when they had an increased risk of health problems? Although all concerned subscribed to workers' rights to know about exposure to substances that could affect their health, relatively few in positions of power shared the view that NIOSH should actively assume the role of telling them.

Dr. Jones felt that the federal government had resources to notify former workers immediately in 1972; however, this was not done. He presented a program plan to NIOSH to do such notification in 1973; it was rejected. Dr. Jones tried to stimulate interest in the Classic Chemical situation by publishing the first academic article on the worker cohort in 1979.

National labor and other worker health advocacy groups pointed to the Classic Chemical workers' situation as an extreme example of the need for a more activist approach to worker notification. They felt it was outrageous that the state and local agencies charged with public health in Classic City were ignoring one of the clearest cancer control issues in their state. Notification and early detection of bladder cancer could well save workers' lives.

The Classic Chemical situation became a symbol of the consequences of federal noninvolvement in worker health. It was described in hearings that resulted in the creation of the Occupational Safety and Health Administration. In May 1977, an article concerning worker health appeared in a national publication. The article described the Classic Chemical situation and asked why the government was sitting on all the information about high-risk worker groups around the country. Also appearing at this time was an influential book on worker health and cancer, which discussed the Classic Chemical situation.

At the prompting of the AFL-CIO, the House Subcommittee on Human Resources of the Committee on Labor held hearings in 1977, during which NIOSH officials were pointedly asked why they studied workers but did not notify them about risk. More than 75,000 workers had been found to be at increased health risk due to occupational exposures in NIOSH studies. NIOSH officials pointed out that they did not have the express authority to notify workers and that the resources for notification were limited. Furthermore, if notification were handled poorly, these officials felt it could do more harm than good by inducing anxiety in workers. Nevertheless, the officials promised to investigate the matter and produced a position paper on worker notification.

A 1986 article on the politics of NIOSH indicated that the agency's survival was also threatened by the prospect of an activist stance on notification. Decision makers questioned whether companies might be threatened by worsening industrial relations and by lawsuits as a result of notification. They might, therefore, pressure government for the dismantling of the organization and harm NIOSH's primary mission of determining the real risks to worker health. Certainly, the organization has never received generous funding from the federal government; the overall priority for worker health was fairly low in most presidential administrations of the 1970s and 1980s.

Even when NIOSH later funded a screening program in Classic City, it was conducted against a backdrop of policy activity at NIOSH. The director asked legal counsel whether NIOSH had an obligation under statutes or regulation to notify people. The answer was no. However, several influential staff people argued that NIOSH had an ethical obligation to notify workers about health risks and past exposures.

SECTION II

FEDERAL INTERVENTION AND ITS EFFECTS

NOTIFICATION STUDY

At the height of the NIOSH internal debate, a NIOSH official, Dr. Smith, was searching for a doctoral dissertation topic that would provide useful information to the organization while also satisfying his professional needs. Like Dr. Jones, he was an advocate for worker notification, but he advocated from within NIOSH. He examined the literature on notification of high-risk groups and found that there were many unanswered questions about how to do it well. He decided to study the effects of worker notification for his dissertation, in part to give NIOSH some firsthand experience in what would be required if NIOSH were to notify all the worker cohorts they determined were at increased risk of occupational disease.

Workers of the Classic Chemical Company who had been employed prior to 1972 had never been notified of the risk presented by BNA. They were ideal for a study of notification because the absence of a union meant that they were highly unlikely to hear about their increased risk from sources other than NIOSH. Furthermore, the carcinogen to which they had been exposed, the progress of bladder cancer, and the importance of early detection were well understood.

In 1978, Dr. Smith met with the director of the Classic City health department, with representatives of the state medical school, and with Dr. Jones, who had by that time moved back to Classic City to work as an occupational physician at a local defense facility. Dr. Smith believed that the project required more than merely notifying workers and providing screening services for early detection of bladder cancer. The workers could not simply be left hanging after notification without knowing more about bladder cancer and protective measures. However, there were no local funds and only limited NIOSH funding for this study. Also, NIOSH had very limited experience in implementing worker notification.

Dr. Smith then became aware of an opportunity through the Workers' Institute for Safety and Health (WISH). WISH is an occupational health research organization located in Washington and affiliated with the labor movement. WISH had resources for worker notification and screening programs, and a linkage to this effort might improve the effectiveness of a program for the Classic Chemical workers. Therefore, Dr. Smith convinced WISH to apply resources to the Classic Chemical workers demonstration and developed a relationship with WISH.

Dr. Smith then met with the company, workers, and health commissioner. He encouraged the health commissioner to set up a committee at the health department, the Committee on Hazardous Substances, where all the stakeholders (former workers, the company, the health department, and community members) could express their concerns. However, it rapidly became clear that this committee did not adequately represent workers' concerns. Therefore, a second committee was formed to provide this viewpoint, the Committee of Concerned Citizens. WISH funded the committee to answer workers' questions, encourage their participation in screening, and advocate for their needs. Because NIOSH funding was time-limited, the committee also worked closely with workers to obtain longer-term financial support of the medical surveillance effort.

TECHNICAL ASSISTANCE
AND "OUTSIDE AGITATORS"

NIOSH needed cooperation from local community agencies and organizations in order to do a successful study. The company's cooperation was needed because they had updated records on former workers and could encourage workers to participate in screening that would detect bladder cancer at an early stage. NIOSH also needed a local contractor to help in tracing, contacting, and screening workers. NIOSH chose the local health department to be the fiscal intermediary for payment of medical services and to keep the registry of bladder cancer cases. NIOSH contracted with the state's medical school to do screening and diagnosis because, in the Classic City area, this organization had the best staff, space, accessibility, and willingness to participate.

According to Dr. Jones, as well as newspaper articles from 1981, the medical school resisted involvement in the screening program. The associate dean of the medical school was very reluctant to get involved because he questioned whether the program was appropriate to the mission of the school. He also worried that the medical school's involvement might offend private physicians in town. The WISH staff involved with the screening program perceived that the medical school staff had concerns about serving black people in the clinic.

Once planning commenced, it ground to a halt. Classic City community leaders became fearful that the notification program was a thinly disguised effort to unionize local workers. The debate centered around WISH. WISH was not funded by the labor movement but was closely affiliated with it. In Deep South circles, however, such distinctions do not amount to much. Several people involved in the study, from north and south alike, agreed that the introduction of a labor-affiliated organization caused the health department, community leaders, the company, and the medical school to balk at participating. In the words of one individual, "They could barely tolerate the idea of the federal government being involved with affairs in Classic City, let alone organized labor."

WISH aimed to create a community group that could offer personal and emotional support to workers. WISH contacted church leaders to obtain their support for the project, as well as specific individuals identified as key participants in civil rights and other community betterment activities.

One local community activist became a leader of the Committee of Concerned Citizens. He was affiliated with labor and had been involved in various movements and protests in Classic City in the 1960s. Unfortunately, the white community and, especially, the Classic Chemical Company viewed this individual as "an admitted communist and convicted felon" who had burned the American flag. In actuality, he had only been convicted of misdemeanors during protests. Later, the company representatives and others were able to point to WISH's support to portray the Committee of Concerned Citizens as a "front for organized labor." WISH had provided a relatively small amount of money to the Committee of Concerned Citizens in 1982 and 1983 to cover the costs of the organization. In 1984, the local activist received limited financial support from WISH while he trained committee members to advocate for an ongoing screening program once NIOSH funds ran out.

To this day, opinions about the Committee of Concerned Citizens differ radically. To the staff of WISH, the idea that notification was a disguise for organizing a union was ridiculous. For one thing, it would have obscured the purpose of screening, and, for another, very few people were currently employed at the plant. According to Dr. Jones, the company overreacted to WISH's presence in the project. He also pointed out that the Committee of Concerned Citizens was not organized or sophisticated enough to unionize Classic Chemical. He thought that the group made an honest attempt to bring workers in for screening. Although community meetings organized by the Committee of Concerned Citizens had fairly good attendance, Dr. Jones could see no activity he would term union organizing. In fact, Dr. Jones felt that given their problems, the workers should have had better orientation on union issues and that the Committee of Concerned Citizens would have been a good vehicle for that.

Representatives of the Oil, Chemical, and Atomic Workers Union came to Classic City to study the issue once or twice. Dr. Jones felt their true goal was to discover whether they could organize a large nuclear power facility nearby. Nothing ever came of it, and he did not think they were really serious about organizing the Classic Chemical Company.

In contrast to these views, some in Classic City are convinced that unionization was the true aim. WISH was described in the local newspaper as "the research arm of organized labor," with a board of labor leaders. The plant manager said that the unions had convinced NIOSH to start the notification program in the first place and that Dr. Jones had told former employees they should sue the company. The director of the

Classic City health department also shared this view, stating that the federal notification effort was "a blatant labor movement drive. . . . These people came in here, and they had the workers believing they were all going to die from cancer."

A former reporter for the *Classic Chronicle* put the reactions in perspective. She believed the Northerners did not realize the great fear of unions that Southern community leaders share. She called it "a real phobia" in Classic City. When WISH first arrived on the scene, she noted, they were very obvious about organizing. The reporter summarized, "I don't think it was possible to steer clear of this issue."

WISH representatives noted that they were fully aware of the attitudes toward labor but believed there was no other resource to develop a support network for the former workers. They noted what they called

> attempts . . . to avoid any efforts to inform, educate, or promote group action among the workers that this program was designed to assist . . . by focusing on the menace of organized labor, this community has achieved exactly the opposite of what it wanted.

WISH staff also mentioned that it was rather difficult to structure the screening effort and supporting activities. Many of the workers were older African American men with little education who were unaccustomed to questioning authority and unaware of how to organize a support group. Also, the city's business community was sensitive to anything that would put the chemical industry in a bad light or affect the many other chemical companies in the area. WISH staff felt there were definite underlying racial attitudes that led Classic City to treat the workers' health problem lightly. Finally, WISH staff believed that the city's leaders wished the problem would just go away. In spite of these obstacles, however, the project finally obtained the necessary cooperation. People's attitudes were mixed; they did not like the idea of a federal program in their town, and they did not like their tax dollars being spent on worker notification. In the end, however, they had to agree that screening for early detection of cancer was the only humane thing to do. The company executives finally led the way and encouraged the health department and medical school to participate.

NOTIFICATION BY NEWSPAPER

During the planning process, Dr. Smith and WISH briefed the media about the proposed study. The intent was to avoid adverse or partial information being leaked to the press because community leaders were extensively involved in planning. The planning team needed to prepare an adequate support system before announcing the start of screening. However, the *Classic Chronicle* broke the story early, which constituted de facto notification of the former workers.

A reporter described why she broke the story. Most people in Classic City did not know that workers had been exposed and nothing had been done for 10 years—it was a revelation. Nobody had realized that a company in their town had done something this bad, and it was "a shock" to the community. The reporter pointed out that her publisher had been invited to the initial meeting with community leaders, invited her along, and notified NIOSH of that fact. She saw the announcement of the program as a story. When she announced that she was going to write a story about this, "all hell broke loose."

The reporter interviewed experts at the state medical school for more information about BNA and bladder cancer. At that point, she got calls from NIOSH, the state medical school, and other "powerful people" in town. The message she received was "don't do this yet . . . we're not ready to serve people yet . . . you'll start a panic." The reporter held off for a week, then went ahead with the story. She felt that it was good that she broke the story because it took months for notification and screening to start. She pointed out that once an official holds a meeting that 50 people attend and certain facts are announced, this becomes public information. She feels, however, that many people never forgave her.

The reporter also felt that union fears may have contributed to people's reaction to her stories. Because the local community viewed Classic Chemical Company as an outsider and a villain, it would be easier for unions to appeal to workers. She believes the newspaper publisher thought that writing the story could stop union organizing. Both the community and the paper were very anti-union and would "do anything to keep unions out."

Delays because of the union issue were, unfortunately, compounded when NIOSH funding for the project was delayed for 8 to 10 months. This is not an unusual state of affairs in federal government, and it was beyond Dr. Smith's control. An editorial was published in the *Classic Chronicle,* entitled "Ghastly Delay," in which a cartoon of Dr. Smith appeared and NIOSH was severely criticized for not implementing the notification on a timely basis. However, Dr. Smith was able to use this publicity as internal ammunition to get NIOSH to move more quickly in funding the notification program.

The reporter did not understand why the federal government had so much trouble getting started with its screening program. She felt it was not good to announce that an agency would do something and then take a year to get it implemented, especially when people were being told that something might kill them. The people at NIOSH told the press that no one was going to die in the next 6 months. Because of this life-threatening potential, however, the reporter felt obligated to break the story in a way that the workers could understand. In every story, she reiterated that it had been 10 years from the time the federal government discovered the situation to the time that it was willing to implement a screening program. The reporter noted, "Community leaders absolutely hated the fact that I brought this up."

She put in many cautions and qualifications about the health risks involved. She wanted to make sure that people were fully informed; people could not know for sure that they would get bladder cancer, but they might need the information. At first, she had good information from officials of the medical school and from NIOSH about the chemical and what could happen. Later, these officals stopped cooperating with her. She believes they felt that she had sensationalized the story. Her response was,

> How are you not going to have a sensational story when you've got 9 out of 10 workers that may eventually get bladder cancer? When you invite a reporter to a meeting, it's going to get covered, no matter what. If you try to stop a story from being published, it won't work. But they really felt like I was out to get them.

The reporter became closely involved with the story and with people on all sides of the issue. She did not have any personal stories at first because she did not know the people at that point. As the project got started, however, she could talk to workers and report personal experiences. She worked through WISH to identify workers because the state medical school would not give names; Dr. Jones provided a lot of background and contacts.

From the beginning, the reporter talked with the company executives about her stories. She warned them that, no matter what they said, people were going to see "a big company beating up on the little guy," and they would feel the workers were victimized. This attitude troubled company officials because they had encouraged the screening effort.

Of the 50 articles published in 1981 and 1982, the primary focus was on the exposure and the availability of the screening program. However, few of the articles focused on the fact that BNA exposure only increased the chances of getting bladder cancer but did not make this outcome a certainty. Also, less than one quarter of the articles stressed the fact that treatment for bladder cancer is usually successful if the cancer is detected early in its development. The newspaper did not stress the positive.

Views are mixed about whether the newspaper stories induced panic or other emotional reactions. The reporter does not think so. However, the workers' attorney felt the stories, especially the first ones, were very emotional: "You'd be convinced you were going to get bladder cancer any day if you read this." People who had lost a bladder to cancer, and those who had lost loved ones, first read about the causes in the *Classic Chronicle*; one worker mentioned that it was traumatic to hear about the problem this way. At a minimum, he believes it did not inspire confidence in the federal notification effort to read that the government had kept the information quiet for 10 years.

Mrs. Charles is married to one of the workers. As an active member of the Committee of Concerned Citizens, she later reflected on the media attention and community reactions. She felt that before 1981, no one in town wanted to be bothered with the fact that some African American chemical workers had been exposed to a carcinogen. She says that the people in town viewed the whole situation as "a joke." When the federal government arrived and created an official program, it suddenly became a serious situation. In her view, however, it immediately became a very political situation. She does not think this was necessary.

Mrs. Charles was also upset about the way she felt that the white community tried to blame the workers who smoked. Smoking contributes to risk for bladder cancer, and this issue was raised during the notification program. The company representatives announced that so many workers smoked that it would be impossible to accurately attribute the blame for bladder cancers. Mrs. Charles responds that many people stereotyped the problem and believed that "all black people drink and smoke a lot, and that's why they get bladder cancer." She feels this was incredibly unfair. Her husband very rarely smoked or drank alcohol, yet he got bladder cancer.

The reporter for the *Classic Chronicle* corroborates the belief that most of Classic City cared little about the workers. They were a small group, and they were African Americans. The reporter believes the community would have reacted differently if a larger company and its workforce had been involved. However, the white community did not know the people, so they did not care.

An attorney who represented many of the workers presented another side of the wider community's apparent indifference or suspicion. He said the workers just did not have a popular cause. The general attitude opposed expenditure of taxpayers' money for notification or for most other social causes.

MEETINGS AND LAWSUITS

Mr. Lee, a former worker, described the initial meetings to organize the Committee of Concerned Citizens. After his father told him about the problem, he attended the public meeting at which the screening was first discussed. At later meetings, Mr. Lee learned that BNA would cause people to have bladder cancer. He did not attend all of the meetings because he felt that a lot of people talked, but very little happened. He said that at that time, there was no notification or advice about what to do. WISH and the local community activist were pushing for screening and notification to begin. People experienced the most anxiety from 1978 to 1980, when they did not know how things were going to go. Once the screening program started, anxiety was somewhat alleviated.

Dr. Jones kept a low profile during the planning stage, at which time it was not clear how the notification and screening effort would be structured. When the union issue hit, the effort was delayed, and in fact, it looked as though it would not start at all. When stories began appearing in the newspaper, Dr. Jones felt free to help workers who were worried about their situation. He talked with workers individually and at organizational meetings and told them they needed to seek legal counsel for help in properly diagnosing and treating any illness associated with BNA.

Based on the initial meetings of the Committee of Concerned Citizens, workers started looking at the possibility of suing the company for failure to notify them about exposure to BNA and for possible injury to their health. One attorney said he attended public meetings organized by the Committee of Concerned Citizens at the request of Dr. Jones to reassure people that something was being done. One worker felt this was an important step because he felt the workers were intimidated by authority and would not consult a lawyer unless they were pushed to do so; they needed someone to argue for their rights.

Lawsuits amounting to more than $334 million in damages were filed against Classic Chemical Company by 167 workers. One attorney began his involvement in the case at the same time the first newspaper stories appeared. Two or three workers visited who had been his clients before. Through word of mouth among workers, he got many other clients and ended up with 200 individual cases. He joined forces with another attorney to handle most of the lawsuits together. When the attorneys discovered that BNA did not have the same effect on everyone, however, they decided to file suits in groups of five people.

The attorneys filed most of the suits in federal court; some were filed in the state superior court. One of the most serious questions was whether, in fact, they could sue the company at all. The exclusive remedy for worker health problems in the state was Workmen's Compensation. The problem was that a worker had to contract an illness within 1 year after leaving the job in order to receive Workmen's Compensation. Because BNA exposure takes an average of 20 years to result in cancer, this excluded most of the plaintiffs. However, in the 1940s, the state legislature listed the specific diseases covered by Workmen's Compensation. The law said any occupational disease that was not listed could be addressed through a common law action or tort against the offending company. The plaintiffs maintained that this law applied to BNA and to bladder cancer.

One of the workers' attorneys, who is white, feels that in 1980 and 1981, activism over the lawsuits and the screening program "turned this into a civil rights issue" in the minds of many workers. Two thirds of the workers were black. Some activists got angry at the attorney for not seeing the problem as a white-black issue.

Many workers were reluctant to get involved in the committee, although they did eventually participate in screening. The Committee of Concerned Citizens believes that several vocal members were black-listed for protesting the Classic Chemical Company's practices. Worker involvement was further reduced when word spread that these individuals could not find jobs. One active participant, no longer able to get loans from the bank for his business, was told that his credit rating was lowered due to his exposure to BNA. Prior to this time, it had never been a problem to get loans, however, and the Committee of Concerned Citizens interpreted this as more evidence of blacklisting.

The community activist who organized the Committee of Concerned Citizens eventually left Classic City because he could not get another job. One of those interviewed mentioned that this "trouble-maker" was "run out of town." When informed that he was now employed in another city, this individual caustically remarked, "The SOB is finally working."

SECTION III

FEDERAL NOTIFICATION EFFORT

COMPONENTS OF THE PROGRAM

The NIOSH effort included a mortality study of deceased workers, a screening program for living workers, and a surveillance program for the entire cohort. Of about 1,400 former employees, almost 300 had died of various causes by the time of the notification. NIOSH micro-filmed all employment records in 1972 and funded screening for bladder cancer from 1981 to 1984. Because important information about the people was missing in many cases, it became a major effort to trace the former workers for notification.

In preparation, letters were sent to about 900 area physicians, explaining the purpose of the notification program and epidemiological study of BNA. These letters identified the Classic City health department as the registrar of all identified cases. Throughout this period, officials of the parent company gave their verbal support to the screening effort. "We don't want to be known as heartless people who don't care about the welfare of people," said the chairman of the board. The company endorsed the efforts of the Committee of Concerned Citizens and actively encouraged workers to participate.

Notification letters were sent to more than 1,000 former workers in mid-1980. Follow-up letters and personal contact followed for workers who did not respond to the first letter. For former workers who lived in a 50-mile radius of Classic City, screenings and diagnostic care were free of charge at the medical school. NIOSH contracted with individual physicians for screenings outside of this area. The screenings were to have two phases: analysis of urine to identify workers suspicious for bladder cancer, and, for suspicious cases, a diagnostic phase for a definitive determination. Screening also included an interview concerning medical and occupational history. The diagnostic phase included cystoscopy, a fairly painful procedure.

Screenings at the medical school began in September, with clinic sessions two times a week. Soon, participation started to drop. However, more workers started attending after personal contacts, community meetings, ministerial announcements, news media coverage, and Committee of Concerned Citizens outreach. The newspaper reported some of the reasons former workers gave for not participating. One man almost did not get screened because he heard that it was painful (it was not); other workers feared being subjects in cancer research.

Participation in screening was successful. About 80% of the workers participated in spite of fears and dissatisfactions. In 1982, more workers had been screened than expected, and the program started to run out of money. Although NIOSH allocated additional funds, a request by the Committee of Concerned Citizens for city or county revenue sharing funds to supplement this funding was denied. NIOSH researchers made do with what they had.

WORKERS' EXPERIENCE
OF THE PROGRAM

Dr. Jones and Dr. Smith met with the workers and gave them the history and background of their exposure. In addition, organizers told the workers what to look for in terms of symptoms of bladder cancer. Workers expressed a lot of anger at this meeting. People had questions about why NIOSH sat on these data for 10 years without notifying people, especially former workers.

Workers later expressed dissatisfaction over their treatment by the state medical school. This facility had an excellent technical reputation, but few of the workers had any prior experience with the facility. Furthermore, in the words of one respondent, it was "the place that black people went to die." It is not clear whether it had this reputation because it was a tertiary care facility and medical school, or for other reasons.

The workers' experience in this facility was mixed; although the family medicine group treated them fairly well, the urologist apparently was very curt and gruff, although technically very competent. Ten years after their initial screening, several workers remember being dissatisfied with the amount of information provided to them about their condition. One former worker, who had worked at Veterans Administration hospitals during his military service was not happy about what he felt was omission of important medical tests for the cohort. Those tests were not relevant to bladder cancer screening, but either no one had explained this to him or he was not willing to believe it.

The Committee of Concerned Citizens considered that keeping an eye on the state medical school was part of its job. The group spoke up if they felt there were any problems with the medical care provided to workers. Several workers mentioned that they felt they had not been treated well by the state medical school during the screening process. Mrs. Charles certainly felt that the medical school staff did not explain the issues well. Suspicious of their findings, she visited a private physician in another city to get an independent opinion. One worker charged that the interview in the federally funded screening was too personal. It troubled people that these questions were being asked without explanations. People at that time were convinced they were going to die, and they wanted to provide for their families. Many just did not understand what an "increased risk" really meant.

The reporter who broke the Classic Chemical story disagrees that blacks were treated differently from whites by the medical school. She thinks that many people did not know what to expect when they were going into testing because black women primarily visited the medical school for well-baby clinics or for pediatric care, and there was no context for black men to go there. Moreover, she said, "it looks like a castle," and people were uncomfortable there.

The workers' attorney believed people's dissatisfaction was due to a failure to explain the situation in terms they could understand. One of his clients was screened time after time over the years and found not to have bladder cancer. Yet, he was convinced that he had bladder cancer and was "killing himself with worry." In the urology department, the doctors were upset that they even had to deal with such a poor and uneducated group of patients. After a while, the medical school hired a white woman urologist, which made the men very uncomfortable.

The workers perceived that they were being treated as second-class citizens at the medical school. If people had other jobs and were covered by insurance, they preferred private physicians for consultation on their health risk. This created difficulty in getting people back for screenings.

The medical school's mixed record on the lawsuits engendered more suspicion. One contention in the lawsuit was that people had experienced mental pain and suffering because they had been exposed to BNA. Fear that something was going to happen to them was causing a lot of stress. Psychiatrists testified as expert witnesses on this subject. Unfortunately, the company's expert was the chief of psychiatry at the state medical school. Immediately, workers suspected a conflict between the screening program, which was supposed to be for them, and the psychiatry department, which was working against them. Eventually, the chief of psychiatry withdrew as an expert witness. According to the workers' attorney, it was "just a case of the head not knowing what the feet were doing."

African American workers became convinced that their treatment by whites in the notification and screening program was racially motivated. Their attorney believes that this raised doubts about the credibility of the program. One client who had a biopsy told the attorney, "If I had been a white man, it would not have hurt as much." The attorney replied, "Well, if I had been on that table, I would have hurt just as much as you." Several people complained to the attorney about mistreatment in the screening program, and they refused rescreening. The attorney eventually talked some of them into getting treatment elsewhere. His clients then discovered that biopsies and cystoscopies hurt everyone, so they returned to the NIOSH-funded program. The attorney also suggested that they talk to Dr. Jones about getting rescreened. In spite of these problems, the second screening's participation rate was again about 80% of notified workers.

SETTLEMENT OF THE LAWSUITS

Preliminary NIOSH results were admitted as evidence in the lawsuits. The NIOSH study revealed a total of 13 confirmed cases of bladder cancer. In court, the company alleged that 13 cases was not a significant number. However, the worker cohort as a whole has about a fourfold excess risk of bladder cancer compared to national estimates of incidence. Some worker groups were running a much greater risk—African American workers with more than 10 years of employment at Classic Chemical had 111-fold increase in risk for bladder cancer.

In the federal district court, the workers got a favorable ruling against the company. While their case was under appeal, they settled out of court. Although settlement amounts were kept out of the public record, the average amount was said to be fairly low. All told, they cost the company about $1 million, although initial suits exceeded $300 million. The settlements included compensation for workers who develop cancer in the future. However, more compensation was to be given to workers who develop cancer in the near future, rather than later in their lives. The reason for the graduated cutback was that as time passed, it would not be possible to decide whether a cancer was due to exposure to BNA or other sources. Several people developed bladder cancer later and received such a settlement, according to one attorney.

Some of the workers and their families expressed suspicion of the settlements. In the words of one worker's wife, "The judge sat the people down and explained to us that a bird in the hand was worth two in the bush, and we should take the settlement that we were given." Their lawyers agreed. Some workers became convinced that the lawyers had "sold out." One of the attorneys, who had represented workers' families for a long time, was hurt by this accusation. He described one occasion in which workers and their families picketed outside his office, claiming discrimination.

Several dissatisfied workers then took their cases to the state supreme court. The court ruled that the cases could not be presented because the exclusive remedy for such exposures was through the Workmen's Compensation laws of the state. However, the period during which such cases could be filed under Workmen's Compensation had long since lapsed for most workers. The supreme court said that it would be willing to hear a new case, presented as a Workmen's Compensation case, to entertain the idea of extending this period for filing a case. However, workers have not pursued this option.

COMPANY-FUNDED SCREENING PROGRAM

The company representatives refrained from comment on the lawsuits while they were pending. On the eve of the state supreme court decision, however, they broke their silence. They complained that the company was being vilified by the press, although they had encouraged workers to obtain screening. They also complained that the Committee of Concerned Citizens was not operating in good faith. As part of the lawsuit settlement, the company had agreed to continue notification and medical surveillance. Yet after the defeat of plaintiffs in the state supreme court, the company representatives claimed they were funding screening because of a sense of duty to the workers, not because they were compelled to do so. Screening is performed at the county health department. When the company's screening program was set up in 1985, the Committee of Concerned Citizens said it was inadequate.

The parties disagreed about oversight of the company program. Workers were uneasy about the health department conducting screening because the health department director was the same official who had allegedly ignored NIOSH's 1973 letter warning about BNA exposure. Workers were also uneasy over the company's role in informing workers about their screening results. Given that the company would have to pay damages for any new bladder cancer cases, workers doubted whether they would go to great lengths to inform workers of test results. No oversight committee was ever formed, and the health department turned down federal money to enhance the program. Although the parent company was willing to pay about 30% of the money for a screening program, public and private sources were not approached for the remaining funding.

LONG-TERM CONSEQUENCES

It is believed that few workers have continued to get screened for bladder cancer. According to respondents, a small ad appears periodically in a corner of the local newspaper announcing the availability of medical surveillance. However, many of the former workers are illiterate. There is no one with responsibility to remind the workers to get rescreened for bladder cancer, and most of the workers cannot afford screening on their own.

Mrs. Charles became very bitter and disillusioned about the medical profession in general. She would like to consult a urologist outside of the area because she wonders whether all the local urologists have been paid off by the company. Her husband still has his bladder, but, in her view, they are both sitting on a "time bomb," just waiting for something to happen. She says no one has ever given her a straight answer about what her husband can expect. He has not been to the doctor in 2 years, and she does not know how often he should get checked for bladder cancer. He has to get a cystoscopy, which is a very painful procedure. Her husband does not use the company program, and she doubts that very many workers do. Why should they use it when the BNA exposures were hidden from workers, people were operated on without being told why, settlements were small, and the people were not treated well when they did seek medical care?

Another former worker feels that workers were initially frightened by the notification but now feel a bit more confident: "So far, so good." He feels, however, that more personal contact would have alleviated fears that people were not willing to express in public.

Although NIOSH has policies in place for doing notification, it still lacks many resources for this purpose. In the late 1980s, interest mounted to have NIOSH provide notification. NIOSH is now in the course of notifying the worker cohorts it has found to be at increased risk of occupational disease. The community in Chapter 2 benefited directly from Dr. Smith's experiences.

At the state level, the Classic Chemical workers' case helped to pass the worker "right to know" law in the mid-1980s. However, some workers pointed out that this state law is limited compared to many, and it does not cover city and county employees.

One of the WISH staff who helped to launch the project was asked what she would do differently if she were to start the project over. She noted that, because she could not change the color of the workers, the region in which they lived, or the attitudes of the townspeople, she would not change a thing. She felt that it was important for the federal government to step in to correct an injustice if the local and state health departments would not do so.

KEY ISSUE

POINTS OF VIEW REFLECT ETHICS AND VALUES

There is more going on in this case than a simple struggle over stakeholder interests. When we probe into the values that support these points of view, we discover differing ethical positions. Certainly, resolving or minimizing conflicts will depend on understanding stakeholders' points of view, their values, and their assumptions about the facts. Strategies to do so are presented in Chapter 7. However, the Classic Chemical case more than any other challenges us to justify actions on the basis of ethics. Various legitimate ethical positions are reflected in the case.

This book cannot assure that the reader will resolve every conflict in confronting risk; but it can assist the reader to articulate the ethical principles that justified action. This discussion therefore addresses three general questions:

▲ What are the various ethical positions that crop up when decisions must be taken about risks?

▲ How can decisions about these risks be evaluated according to these ethical principles?

▲ How can the implementation of those decisions be evaluated by the key ethical principles?

Competing ethical principles in confronting risk. Some conflicts cannot be resolved. Some injustices will not be erased. The Classic Chemical case epitomizes these problems. As one stakeholder pointed out, she could not change the color of the workers, the region in which they lived, or the attitudes of the townspeople. However, she could look in the mirror the next day. By her own code, she had done what she could do. Health professionals and community members may conclude that a conflict cannot be resolved completely. So often, resources to resolve it are inadequate, the infrastructure cannot rise to the challenge, or staff are not prepared to deal with new aspects of the problem. Nevertheless, they will want to justify how they handled the conflict, both to themselves and to the public.

The Classic Chemical case illustrates a related problem in confronting risk: The stakeholders saw events from such radically different viewpoints that we start to wonder whether people were all talking about the same things. In fact, they were not talking about the same events—they were talking about their interpretation of events. In the case study, the assumptions that stakeholders made about each other almost killed the screening and notification effort at several points. It has drastically affected workers' willingness to seek medical care ever since.

Stakeholders in many of these case studies can be differentiated by how they value four ethical concerns: efficiency, justice, beneficence, and autonomy. Ruth Faden (1987, 1990) has described in sensitive terms how these values can sometimes come into conflict in public health policy and practice. Legitimate differences of opinion can arise in confronting risk because people set different priorities among these ethical principles. Understanding the principles will assist the reader both to evaluate the options that are proposed for confronting risk, and to respond intelligently to challenges from stakeholders.

Among health professionals, beneficence is the obligation to do good and avoid harm for patients. Good and harm are defined strictly in medical terms, such as health, disease, pain, and suffering. Under the principle of beneficence, public health professionals have a duty to notify communities about health risks and to help individuals to minimize or cope with risks. Autonomy sets priority on respecting individual preferences, privacy, and values. Autonomy is a central principle in democracies, where high value is placed on maintaining individual liberty and choice. For this reason, it is asserted that a primary justification of public health activity is to inform the public, so that people are able to make choices about health (Cole, 1994).

Many public health measures balance these two considerations. For example, prevention of epidemics and control of environmental exposures emphasize beneficence over autonomy; this activity has always been part of the government's police powers, because the sources of disease pose a clear and present danger to the community (Risse, 1988; Rosen, 1958). In other areas, such as the control of cigarettes, regulation of seat belts, or persuasive campaigns for lifestyle change, the line might be drawn differently, and this continues to be a matter of active debate. It is noteworthy that the National Research Council's 1989 sourcebook, *Improving Risk Communication,* advocated fully and openly informing the public as the aim of risk communication. Attempts to persuade, manipulate, or otherwise influence the behavior of the public were not a distinct aim, and not always a valid one. They may be required, but they are not automatically justified.

In balancing beneficence and autonomy, it is critical to distinguish the need to know and the right to know. In the case of HIV infection, for example, beneficence dictates that we not generally disclose people's HIV infection. The person's need for privacy, concerns about discrimination, and other negative consequences of disclosure outweigh the autonomy needs of the public. An excellent sourcebook on the ethics of disclosure and nondisclosure is *Secrets: On the Ethics of Concealment and Revelation,* by Sissela Bok (1983). *Secrets* is particularly helpful for social workers or for anyone who needs to judge the needs of individuals against the rights of the public.

Justice becomes a public health consideration when activity aims to increase equal access to resources that would increase health, such as medical care, screening programs or other technology, and information. It also becomes an important justification when public health aims to protect innocent parties from harm or to ameliorate risks where exposure has already occurred. Efficiency becomes important when certain protections that the majority of citizens desires can be achieved only through collective action. For example, the state, and all of us through our insurance premiums, has an interest in containing the cost of medical care. People often justify public health activity to prevent costly illness on the grounds of efficiency. Also, the cost effectiveness of various prevention activities is more and more coming under scrutiny because of concern over efficiency (Haddix, Teutsch, Shaffer, & Dunet, 1996). Justice and efficiency concerns sometimes warrant actions that also encroach on the principle of autonomy. For example, many would say that in a free market economy, we ought to minimize regulation of industry; however, regulation of a safe and healthy food supply is essential for efficiency—the collective interests of the public. In the same vein, hospital personnel may not wish to come into contact with people living with AIDS. However, in the name of justice, hospitals need to minimize discrimination against people living with AIDS, with consequent effects on employees' autonomy.

Do we encroach on the autonomy principle in confronting risks? We do it all the time, in the sense that we restrict the freedoms of those who create a risk to communities (Beauchamp, 1985). However, it is important to recognize legitimate differences of opinion in where we draw the line—what value is given to autonomy compared to other ethical concerns. The debate becomes particularly active when we confront risks that arise from personal lifestyle choices such as smoking or physical inactivity. An important exchange in the magazine *Reason* of January 1996, reprinted in *Priorities,* the publication of the American Council on Science and Health, outlined this debate. Sullum (1996) and Cole (1994) strongly support traditional public health activities when these endanger the community. For example, they would strongly support air pollution controls, even when these impinge on the personal freedom of the polluters. However, they are concerned about efforts to modify risks when these depend on individual lifestyle choices. Restriction of freedom to exercise a choice is, in their view, a violation of the principle of autonomy. According to Sullum,

> Most public health practitioners would presumably recoil at the full implications of the argument that government should override individual decisions affecting health because such decisions have an impact on "society as a whole." They are no doubt surprised and offended to be called "health fascists," when their goal is to extend and improve

> people's lives. But some defenders of the public health movement recognize that its aims are fundamentally collectivist and cannot be reconciled with the American tradition of limited government. (p. 16)

Others would argue that "free will" has already been violated when advertising manipulates young people into smoking, when pushers of illegal drugs seduce children into addiction, and when automobile design and road conditions can kill us when we "choose" to ride on the highways. In the case studies presented in this volume, freedom of choice is definitely restricted when people cannot afford private medical care to detect early cancers, or when they fear the loss of employment for joining a protest movement.

Under such conditions, confronting risk may require more than the simple provision of information. Although many public health professionals argue for greater governmental involvement on issues that affect autonomy, they set the boundaries firmly. Faden (1987), for example, distinguishes between information that merely persuades and information that manipulates, coerces, or deceives. Persuasive appeals still appeal to information and reason, and therefore the choices a person makes are still autonomous choices. An effective persuasion campaign is an example of a strategy that has potential to satisfy several principles, increasing the good that is done (beneficence) and maintaining liberty (autonomy). In the same vein, the National Academy of Sciences publication *Improving Risk Communication* sets as a goal the provision of information to make informed choices about risks, not the improvement or protection of health per se.

The title of this book is *Confronting Public Health Risks* because it implies more activity than simply communicating or providing information. In confronting risk, we try to solve problems, enter an exchange of ideas about the problem, and encourage collective action where needed. To that extent, public health practitioners may sometimes open themselves up to the criticism that they violate the autonomy principle. However, the National Academy of Sciences (1989) notes that as long as the options for dealing with a risk are debated in a democratic process, our national values are likely to be preserved.

Evaluating decisions by the key ethical principles. Each of these cases can be evaluated in terms of how they balance the four principles of beneficence, autonomy, justice, and efficiency. There are two levels of evaluation. The first level deals with the original decisions to confront the risk and take action. Whose decisions rest on a solid ethical foundation? What arguments can be made for the various positions that stakeholders take, and are they justified? The second level is just as important, if not more so: how were these ethical principles respected or violated as events unfolded? After all, implementing a decision is not the same as making a decision; things never work out exactly as we intended. It is said that the road to hell is paved with good intentions. Did some decisions create a hell for people confronting risks?

The Classic Chemical case study serves as an example of how we might evaluate decisions. The role of the federal government, for example, was a matter for appropriate debate. State and local stakeholders sensed that the federal government was intruding on their authority: They valued the division of governmental powers in part to maintain autonomy and prevent federal encroachment on liberty. They also did not feel that a local public health issue warranted federal intrusion. However, the division of public health responsibility assumes that state and local agencies will address public health problems. Neither industry nor state and local agencies had ever informed the workers that they needed medical attention, once they had left the company's employ. Therefore the federal effort was required to satisfy the principles of justice and beneficence.

Of course, federal stakeholders were not of one mind in the debate over whether to notify workers of risk. Advocates had lost an effort to include worker notification in the original OSHA law of 1970 (Needleman, 1993). Instead, NIOSH notified companies, unions, and state health departments, often with the aim of abating the exposure that caused disease (Schulte et al., 1993). One can make the argument that public health authority should be delegated in this way in the interest of liberty/autonomy; furthermore, state and local governments possess permanent infrastructure to cope with public health problems; it is more efficient for these bodies to confront the risk than for the federal government to do so directly.

In the late 1970s, however, NIOSH leaders articulated another concern about notifying workers. Their concerns involved a special interpretation of the beneficence principle, as well as a respect for the division of government. NIOSH officials hesitated to notify workers about their health risks because they had no mandate, no resources, and they did not know what the consequences would be. Would notification do more harm than good?

Needleman (1993) describes the debate, which reflects the principles of autonomy, beneficence, efficiency, and justice.

> Supporters of notification held that exposed workers have a fundamental right to know the facts, regardless of the consequences. They usually went on to point out notification's potential benefits in terms of earlier disease detection, health-promoting lifestyle changes, and improved recovery for legitimate workers' compensation claims. Opponents of notification, however, predicted widespread overreaction. They feared that notification might create anxiety and psychogenic illness in large populations, undermining the mental health of many individuals who, although exposed, would never actually develop the occupational disease in question. In addition, opponents maintained, notification would impose high social costs by stimulating large numbers of unwarranted lawsuits. (p. 12)

At the time, NIOSH officials were justified in their concern about overreaction and therefore beneficence. Large initiatives on hypertension control were under way, and these indicated that simply telling people they had high blood pressure could lead to anxiety and increased absences from work (Haynes, Sackett, Taylor, Gibson, & Johnson, 1978; Russell, 1986). Some form of follow-up care and counseling was required, for which resources had to be allocated. Would the same problems emerge in worker risk notification?

Later studies examined these worries, and they generally seem to have no foundation. In and of themselves, neither worker notification nor screening for occupational disease causes any family dysfunction, psychopathology, or maladaptive stress reaction (Hornsby et al., 1985; Houts & McDougall, 1988; Meyerowitz, 1993; Meyerowitz, Sullivan, & Premeau, 1989). Once these worries were tested and no foundation was discovered, the ethical justification in favor of notification became increasingly strong. Indeed, NIOSH now requires that the study of worker disease that it supports must include a plan for notification.

Evaluating the implementation of decisions by the ethical principles. Evaluating the process of notification is different from evaluating the decision to notify workers. Unfortunately, the way that the Classic Chemical workers were notified raised new concerns, specifically about justice, efficiency, and beneficence. It is important to emphasize that these events may not have been avoidable. Nevertheless, we can point to specific consequences for workers that were less than ideal.

The principles of justice and autonomy appear to have been satisfied when workers became aware of their risk. On the face of it, this permitted them to exercise an informed choice about what to do. However, providing information assumes that people are capable of using it. Certainly, workers used the information in choosing whether to participate in lawsuits and in medical screening.

But recall a key concept from Chapter 2: People interpret new information in the context of their existing beliefs. Information presented outside this context will be incomprehensible or will be misinterpreted. The case study suggests that workers were not satisfied with explanations that were given to them. In spite of the community supports that were built into the notification process, it is fairly clear that workers were not given enough of the context to understand what was happening. At least one person misinterpreted a risk for cancer as having cancer.

Does this anecdotal information imply that studies are wrong when they conclude that notification and screening do no harm? Not really. Those studies assumed adequate preparation and understanding of the risk communication. The newspaper broke the story without advance preparation. Without such preparation, the process can violate both the principle of beneficence (harm may have been done) and the principle of autonomy (information enables a free choice). One might add that the process was hardly an efficient way to enable health, when one considers that the newspaper never emphasized the benefits of early detection and caused workers to distrust the federal funders.

The process affected beneficence (and therefore efficiency) in other ways. The way in which the newspaper broke the workers' story was traumatic for many. Also, the newspaper emphasized negative aspects, such as betrayal of trust, vulnerability to disease, and delays in action. Recall from *Key Issues* of Chapter 2 that the framing of positive and negative in a risk communication is a powerful way to affect people's overall assessment of the value of action. Also, people believed, rightly or wrongly, that they were not treated with respect at the medical school. Respect for people is another central ethical principle and is encoded in standards for health educators (cf. Simons-Morton, Greene, & Gottlieb, 1995).

Summary. Some conflicts cannot be resolved. However, those who confront risks will be adequately prepared to justify their actions by understanding the ethical principles upon which public health activity rests. Respecting the ethical positions of others who may disagree is the first step toward conflict resolution, which calls for negotiation on the basis of principle (see Chapter 7). Confronting risks is also a learning experience. By frankly appraising the results of decisions by the ethical criteria of beneficence, autonomy, justice, and efficiency, professionals and communities can learn to do better next time.

NOTE

1. In this case study, stakeholders were guaranteed anonymity. As a result, we changed names of places and withheld our documentation for quotations and sources.

CHAPTER **5**

HIV AND THE SCHOOLS IN A HIGH PREVALENCE COMMUNITY

LAURA C. LEVITON

REGINA R. REITMEYER

INTRODUCTION[1]

This case describes community concerns about Human Immunodeficiency Virus (HIV) and AIDS as it affected the inner-city public schools of a community with many AIDS cases. This was not Kokomo, Indiana, where the presence of one child with HIV set off a panic. The school system and the community had far more serious and realistic concerns. The chances were fairly good that teachers would encounter a child with HIV or a child whose parents are dying of AIDS. Confidentiality protection, support services for kids and parents, and a need for staff training about HIV loomed large. Compared to communities with a lower incidence of AIDS, Garden City presented very different dilemmas for health professionals and teachers. The formal leadership of Garden City really did not do very well in confronting this risk. In spite of these leaders, some committed educators and health experts eventually got the chance to develop some positive and creative solutions. Those solutions depended critically on organizing teachers, students, and parents as resources for education and AIDS care. The grim picture of Garden City improved when people were redefined as having capabilities as well as needs.

KEY ISSUE AND GENERAL QUESTIONS

In the 1980s, fear of HIV infection through casual contact was so prevalent that service systems all over the country were in an uproar. But what happened in service systems where HIV-positive individuals were not just a possibility, but almost a certainty? This case illustrates how the fear of HIV was conditioned by the presence of many other pressing problems. More important, it illustrates how identification of community strengths finally permitted service delivery to get beyond an irrational fear of HIV to tackle its real HIV problem more effectively. In the discussion that follows, three general questions are posed:

▲	How do professional worldviews affect the definition of communities: as bundles of deficits or areas of strength?

▲	How can community strengths be identified to confront health risks?

▲	How can community strengths be built upon to confront health risks?

STAKEHOLDERS

City government
City health department
City AIDS task force
Area hospital AIDS consortium

City school board
City school administration
City teachers and nurses
City students and parents
State Pediatric AIDS Advisory Committee
State health department
State department of education
Centers for Disease Control (CDC)

 TIMELINE

1930s-1950s	Immigration of Southern blacks to Garden City
l960s	Election of first African American officials
Early 1980s	AIDS found in young children
1984	State begins to allocate AIDS care funds
1987	Community AIDS education begins
1988	Consortium of providers is created
1989	Garden City hospital provides care to about 200 HIV-infected children
	CDC awards AIDS education grant to Garden City schools
1990	State deficit leads to retrenchment on AIDS funding
	Garden City schools finally appoint AIDS coordinator
	Coordinator trains teacher volunteers

 SECTION I

BACKGROUND

DESCRIPTION OF THE COMMUNITY

With a metropolitan area population of almost 2 million, the pseudonymous Garden City accounts for roughly 400,000 people. Over 50% of its population identify themselves as African American; Italians and Hispanic groups are also concentrated in Garden City. An early center for manufacturing and transportation in the United States, Garden City saw many of its factories close and its neighborhoods turn shabby during the Great Depression. Southern blacks seeking jobs in defense plants during World War II crowded into these rundown areas, while middle-income families moved to the suburbs. By the 1960s, the population was largely poor, and the city lacked financial resources for adequate services. Nearly half the voters were African Americans with little political power, contributing to racial tensions and charges of widespread dishonesty in city government. Investigations led to convictions of many politicians and resulted in the election of the community's first African American officials.

By the late 1980s, Garden City's economy gave rise to much unemployment, excessive poverty, and high crime rates. With a $550 million shortfall in the state budget and a low community tax base, government funding was simply not available to solve most community problems. Residents were described as struggling through a daily existence too fraught with hardship to focus on health risks that lay in some theoretical future.

The center city presented a picture of boarded-up stores and threatening security systems. High-rise public housing projects were finally demolished and were being replaced by a half-hearted attempt at gentrification with the construction of condominiums. Crack cocaine hit the city hard, but other drugs were always common. One could smell marijuana smoke on the street, even in front of the school district offices.

AIDS IN GARDEN CITY

State records revealed that annual AIDS cases among Garden City residents climbed to over 400 by 1989, bringing the 10-year total close to 2,000 reported cases. Overall, the number of reported AIDS cases in Garden City is about equal to that of several much larger metropolitan areas in the nation. Although many residents acknowledged having relatives or acquaintances with AIDS or HIV infections, few discussed the disease openly. Many attributed AIDS-related deaths and illnesses to pneumonia, disguising and denying the real cause in an effort to avoid any connection to AIDS. Even relatively well-educated people were ready to voice continuing suspicions that AIDS was developed as a conspiracy to wipe out the African American population.

Garden City ranks high among cities having the most AIDS cases for children ages 5 to 19. An in-depth study uncovered nearly 200 cases of pediatric AIDS (not just HIV infection) in the state through mid-1989. A 1988 blinded statewide seroprevalence study of newborns suggested an annual birthrate of roughly 250 HIV-infected infants, primarily among the state's poor urban minorities.

When HIV infection was discovered in infants, "the problem came to us," explained a spokesperson for a Garden City hospital. "We worked on it from a number of fronts, and the hospital was very supportive." By mid-1989, area hospitals were providing services to about 200 HIV infected children. More than half of these children lived with caretakers other than their biological parents.

In 1989, the state AIDS advisory committee reported mounting evidence of a substantial increase in adolescent AIDS cases. High rates of teenage pregnancy and sexually transmitted diseases among adolescents, as well as the prevalence of drugs, indicated great danger. The state's AIDS advisory committee learned some alarming information about nonrepresentative samples of this age group. One Garden City clinic found that .5% of clients 15 to 19 years old were infected, but 4% were infected in the 20 to 24 age group. Officials feared that many of these young adults were infected in their teens.

LOCAL AND STATE GOVERNMENT

The city was governed by a mayor and council. A city-based health department provided diversified services ranging from prenatal care to environmental and product safeguards. Because of poverty, many of the residents used the health department instead of personal physicians for all medical needs. Leadership was slow to materialize, however, for providing services for patients with AIDS or HIV infections. In 1988, the state provided more than $100,000 in AIDS funding to the city's health department. The already overburdened Sexually Transmitted Disease (STD) Clinic served only as a referral service for AIDS and HIV cases. Private grants provided an additional $40,000 in 1988 for the city's AIDS efforts. A city task force, established by these funds, took over the referral service and helped people with AIDS to find case managers.

When the state began to address the AIDS issue in 1984, about half a million dollars was allocated for statewide efforts. The figure jumped to about $30 million in 1989, but a huge deficit forced the state to retrench on AIDS and other issues in 1990. A large portion of the early state funds for AIDS services went to Garden City. Officials contended, however, that this funding was intended to help the city establish, not maintain, AIDS programs. The state required city officials to pursue other avenues of financial support if they wanted to introduce or continue AIDS programs.

During his political campaign, the new governor pledged to find new financing for the state's AIDS crisis. With a new party in power in 1990, however, new state administrators took over. The resulting "learning and adjustment" period created additional difficulties for ongoing state-wide initiatives. Although the state was often criticized for being slow to deal with AIDS, it was also credited with being proactive and compared favorably with other states on AIDS services and programs.

Although the governor promised a statewide plan to combat AIDS, no specific measures had emerged by 1990. The department of education, however, upheld its intention to mandate AIDS education in all grade levels throughout the state. Although each school district retained authority over its curriculum, the state department of education offered a suggested curriculum and provided training and workshops through the office of the department's AIDS coordinator. Yet, all was not well in education, either—in 4 years of operation, the coordinator's position had been held by three different people.

COMMUNITY LEADERS IN DENIAL

City officials, nonprofit organizations, and corporations had combined their efforts to renew Garden City through construction projects and efforts to attract new businesses to the area. Little of this cooperative spirit was evident on AIDS, however. For years, city officials refused to acknowledge the problem despite early evidence of an AIDS epidemic in Garden City. State officials charged that as late as 1988, the city continued to ignore AIDS. According to some interviews, city leadership insisted that residents from surrounding communities were coming to Garden City for care and creating a false impression that the city was hard hit. Also, officials viewed AIDS as an illness experienced only by drug users. The community at large was not concerned about its health, and therefore, people with AIDS posed little threat to political careers. Political leaders also worried that efforts to attract industry to revitalize the community would be hindered by a reputation for excessive AIDS cases. Finally, in the view of the state, the Garden City health department was not strong enough to get the city's attention on the problem.

So anxious were city officials to distance Garden City from the AIDS issue that they refused to allow the state to establish an acute care facility for AIDS and AIDS Related Complex (ARC) patients within the city limits. The state's AIDS advisory committee had recommended building a 60-bed facility to fill some of the more urgent service gaps in Garden City. "Politics and economics were responsible" for Garden City's opposition, according to a state health department spokesperson. An alternate site outside the city was eventually selected for the facility, but it "meant 18 months of wasted effort," the spokesperson added. Incredibly, one city official expressed curiosity about why the state had not built an AIDS facility for Garden City—almost a full year after the facility started operating at its forced location outside the city limits.

A prominent foundation offered grants for AIDS case management, to secure the range of services that were needed. The state urged city officials to apply. "It was painfully clear to us," said a state spokesperson, "that unless the state applied, the money wouldn't come in. The local authorities gave us their blessing, but they weren't going to do anything else."

COMPETITION FOR RESOURCES

As demand grew for AIDS services, the number of AIDS service organizations increased. However, available funding was on the decline, intensifying competition for financial support and promoting a "house divided against itself." Service providers alleged that agencies withheld information from each other to protect their own interests. A statewide report noted that the approach to the AIDS crisis was not coordinated. Some agencies duplicated services, such as education and training efforts, while no one provided other services, such as outreach and intervention with teen dropouts.

The city's task force tried to remedy this situation. Representatives from various service agencies and community groups agreed to serve on the task force. They tried to cooperate and coordinate their services, but the situation was still far from perfect. A county executive held a public meeting on AIDS, but none of the city's task force members was invited or even notified. This, despite the fact that Garden City was the county seat and numbered among cities with the highest percentage of AIDS cases in the state. City task force members were angered by published reports of the meeting in which one participant was quoted as saying that "AIDS is a disease of choice."

HIV/AIDS IN THE GARDEN CITY PUBLIC SCHOOLS

The Garden City school board determined policy on HIV, as well as many other school policies. The board was elected, and some factions were at war with the mayor. He was said to resent the public's tendency to hold him accountable for the school board's actions, even though he could not appoint them. Politics reportedly entered into the school system operations regularly. Although some school administrators described the board as caring and sensitive to the HIV issue, some faculty and community members viewed it as politically motivated and unrealistic in its approach to problems.

The district consisted of about 90 public schools, 55 of which were elementary schools and 10 of which were specialized schools devoted to the chronically ill, physically impaired, or learning disabled and to other youngsters who were unable to attend self-contained classes. The board oversaw an annual budget of approximately $350 million. About 70% of the 49,000-member student body was African American, with Spanish-speaking students making up another 15%.

The school administration building was rundown, unkempt, and extremely busy with visiting parents, students, and teachers. One administrator contrasted work in Garden City with work in the suburbs, "the land of milk and honey." He pointed out that teachers could always choose not to work with inner-city kids if they could not take it. He went on to describe how almost 300 students had recently been discovered in hotels for the homeless. They were then reenrolled in the schools.

He pointed to the growth of special schools in the city, caused by the increase in birth defects among children whose mothers used drugs when pregnant or did not get prenatal care.

The courts initially set the state policy on education of HIV-infected children. By state mandate, infected children, as well as infected staff, had the right to be in school. Even before the state mandate, the school board required that the identities of infected children remain confidential. A limited number of central administration staff had access to the health records. However, many teachers and other staff had unrealistic fears of contracting the disease, like so many human service providers throughout the 1980s. Because of their fear they occasionally tried to circumvent the mandate for confidential access to school. By contrast, the teachers' union actively supported infected staff in their right to continued employment.

Because education and prevention were the only defense against HIV infection, the state also required AIDS instruction from kindergarten through the 12th grade. Unlike the yearlong controversy that preceded the state's mandate on sex education a decade earlier, the AIDS education mandate was quietly and unanimously adopted. Parents were assured they would have an opportunity to review materials prior to distribution.

Educators blamed the Garden City school board for focusing too much on attendance and test results and not enough on AIDS education. Administrators staunchly countered these charges by pointing to the overwhelming number of concerns addressed by the board. "I think the board members are very concerned," remarked one supporter. "One of the initial open forums on AIDS was called together by the board president. I don't think there's any lack of interest in this city or that anybody is trying to hide (AIDS) under wraps." Administrators described residents as being "happy with what we're doing, but everybody wants us to do more." The state health department director reacted skeptically to this comment: "It's laughable to expect an inner-city school district to do much about AIDS."

PARENTS AND CHILDREN

In Garden City, few parents questioned school board actions, and most meetings of the parent-teacher organizations were poorly attended. One community resident described parents as too overburdened by drug and crime issues and too naive about AIDS to demand HIV/AIDS education for the children. In defense of the parents, teachers and nurses cited parents' daily struggles and overwhelming poverty. The community was described as deferring to the school administration. "Parents trust us," said one educator. "It is traditional in our black community to leave the child in the hands of the school and to go away believing that the school will do what is best for the child."

Schoolchildren in Garden City frequently witnessed drug abuse and crime. Some teachers said the students "should be congratulated just for making it to class in the morning." With so many concerns, AIDS was accepted as part of the daily routine of life—just another problem in a troubled existence, no bigger and no smaller than any other hardship to be endured. However, some students' acquaintances and family members were dying of AIDS. Apathy in the community was being replaced by real concern because of the growing numbers of people affected by the disease. "Reality hit these kids," an educator suggested, "because they are seeing death and death is bringing fear with it."

Faculty members suspected that students were more aware of the seriousness of the AIDS situation than some of the teachers. "Many teachers live outside the community," one educator remarked. "They don't have to step over a junkie to get here, and they don't have to watch a friend or relative suffering from the effects of AIDS."

However, the children did not know about HIV transmission because the community did not discuss AIDS openly and perpetuated myths about it. Concerned faculty and administrators saw AIDS education as the first step in surmounting that problem. With pediatric and adolescent HIV infections on the rise, it was clear as day that the children would need every ounce of prevention they could get.

STAFF CONCERNS

By 1990, educators, nurses, and students more openly expressed personal fears and concerns. Scoffing at reports from administrators that the school board demonstrated genuine, ongoing interest in AIDS in the schools, educators and nurses denied receiving any formal input regarding training for self-protection, materials for class presentations, or special teaching considerations for HIV-infected children.

While nurses gleaned AIDS information through professional affiliations, teachers complained that they had to investigate the subject independently to better educate their students and protect themselves. One teacher, referring to rubber gloves and chlorine used routinely by school nurses, called it "lopsided protection." The teacher joked that in her school, "There are only two of them and 150 of us [teachers], but we have to figure things out [protective measures] for ourselves."

Many teachers reportedly purchased their own chlorine and rubber gloves to use as safety precautions. One can only imagine the effects on relationships in a classroom when the teacher greets the students with rubber gloves on. Despite teachers' insistence that these supplies were not provided for them, administrators were equally insistent that the gloves were readily available. Fifty-thousand pairs of gloves had been ordered for the district 2 years before, but many boxes sat on shelves in the administration office building.

The debate over the rubber gloves missed the point, however. There is no good reason for rubber gloves to be distributed to teachers because casual contact cannot infect teachers. Teachers' resentment over the apparent "preference" shown to nurses, however, indicated that they did not understand this.

Like the teachers, nurses complained that administration and board members gave too little guidance on AIDS and HIV. Aside from receiving rubber gloves and directives to use universal precautions, they had to use their own discretion with HIV-infected students—despite the fact that they treated nosebleeds and handled other body fluids in many school situations. Nurses quickly emphasized that any chlorine used for sterilization was personally purchased for self-protection.

GUIDANCE FROM THE GARDEN CITY HEALTH DEPARTMENT

Because the school district was autonomous, Garden City's health department had limited influence and limited contact with the school board. One official said, "If the department were in more of a position of responsibility with the school board, it could be of more help to the schools." He cited positive responses and high attendance by adolescents and parents at AIDS education meetings sponsored by the department. Occasionally, the school board did approach the health department for help. At a board-initiated training program for nurses and social workers in the district, the Garden City health department conducted a seminar attended by 60 to 70 people. Although invited, board members did not attend the session.

IMPLEMENTING THE CONFIDENTIALITY POLICY

Teachers and nurses felt oppressed by the lack of direction from the administration and the gnawing issue of confidentiality. Principals, too, felt stress and frustration. In isolated instances, the principal had to "man the front" alone when HIV-infected students were known to be enrolled in a school. Such situations were expected to be handled within confines of the school building. For this reason, school administrators were accused of stifling any information about AIDS- and HIV-infected students or about infected district personnel. In addition to keeping the information from the media and community residents, principals were required to reassure teachers who feared dealing with a child, as well as the nurse who provides health care for the child.

Despite the court-imposed confidentiality ruling, little happens in a school setting that escapes common knowledge, including suspicions of HIV infections. One principal described a teacher as "hysterical" after learning that an HIV-infected student was in her class. Despite reassurances from health officials and other knowledgeable sources, the teacher remained adamant about having the child removed from the class. The principal refused, but the child was treated with such discrimination that his behavior became a problem. The following year, the child advanced to another class and, with newfound acceptance, discontinued his bad behavior. At another school, an HIV-infected child was identified through rumors, according to several staff people. They further alleged that the principal was transferred to another school and reprimanded, and the parents reportedly filed a lawsuit for breach of confidentiality. The lesson learned from these incidents was to strictly adhere to the confidentiality ruling even in the most trying of circumstances. However, no lesson appeared to be learned by those who were supposed to provide leadership.

SUMMARY

Section I has described the emergence of the AIDS problem in Garden City and its schools. Efforts by the local government and the school board to protect their autonomy, as well as a denial of the severity of the AIDS crisis, allegedly impeded the development of comprehensive care and instilled mistrust and hostility in the community and the schools. Although the state made efforts to motivate Garden City officials, the state, too, was criticized as slow to respond and equally disorganized in its approach to the problem. Teachers and staff in the schools must adhere to policies for which they received little training and support. They must do this in addition to handling the many other problems that have made this a community under siege.

SECTION II

DEVELOPMENT OF LEADERSHIP AROUND AIDS AND HIV INFECTIONS IN SCHOOLS

COMMUNITY LEADERSHIP

A city committee on AIDS was established in 1987, and it appointed an educational chairperson, who spearheaded serious efforts to teach residents the facts surrounding AIDS and HIV infections. The city identified every group that would be affected by AIDS—churches, businesses, and schools, among others—to determine a locally based theme for the project and to provide a consistent approach. "Before the U.S. Surgeon General got into the act by sending direct mail on AIDS, the city decided to mail AIDS information to all residents to educate them and to diffuse panic," according to a spokesperson from the city's health department. Initially, the notices were to be included with utility bills. However, some groups, notably the churches, objected to the materials. The city then decided to use the water authority to distribute materials, because it was under the city's jurisdiction and the city did not need anyone's approval to include the material in mailings. Another method of distribution required the cooperation of the school board. The board agreed to give each student the materials to take home to their parents.

The city's AIDS committee was described as "not very active at that time." Although never formally disbanded, this committee quietly and almost imperceptibly stopped meeting in 1988. Its responsibilities shifted to a more formal AIDS task force under the auspices of Garden City's health department.

The state began to focus attention on adolescents in early 1989 by announcing plans for outreach programs, residential care facilities, and intensified AIDS instruction in the schools. A few months earlier, the city's AIDS task force initiated plans for a video aimed at teen dropouts, as well as adolescents inside the school system. Following the video, peer counselors engaged the spectators in one-on-one exchanges in an effort to encourage protective behavior. "The video is designed so that kids will be willing to sit back and listen (to the message)," emphasized the organizer. "The idea is that for 30 to 35 minutes, all components of the program will be addressed to serve as a training vehicle."

MEDICAL LEADERSHIP

AIDS efforts, spearheaded by the state health department, were coordinated with the hospitals, medical community, and other organizations in Garden City, as well as the city's health department. A Garden City Hospital AIDS Consortium, a nonprofit organization representing six hospitals, as well as state, county, and local health departments, was established to provide an outreach van for teen dropouts and for HIV testing. The consortium marked the first attempt by the participating groups to work together to address *any* health concern, according to state officials. This hard-won unity was further strengthened by countywide support from 50 provider agencies, and the Garden City AIDS Task Force was promoted by the Garden City council and health department.

City officials were slow to establish an AIDS case management unit. They did not name a coordinator until a year before foundation funding was to end. Nevertheless, the unit quickly expanded to include a secretary and two full-time assistants. To coordinate services for people with AIDS, the unit organized a seven-member committee to address concerns on behalf of adolescents, care providers, children, community-based and religious organizations, drug programs, gay and lesbian people of color, and women's organizations.

State and local officials acknowledged that much of the belated action was spurred by "the growing enormity of the problem. People are being forced to do something about it." Churches in particular had to alter their stance from condemnation to concern. "AIDS was considered a sign of God's wrath by the religious community," remarked one observer. "When the ministers had to bury aunts, uncles, parents, and so many other family members, they started to take a different look at AIDS and to invite speakers to educate the congregation."

CLARIFICATION OF SCHOOL POLICY

Following guidelines of the Centers for Disease Control (CDC), the state departments of health and education have adopted rulings assuring access to public schools for all children who have AIDS, ARC, or HIV infections. These regulations are seen in Figure 5.1. They stipulate that the child can be excluded from school on the basis of a lack of toilet training, uncontrolled drooling, or aggressive behavior that includes biting or harming others. Hospital representatives quickly point out that more has been learned about AIDS since the exclusionary stipulations were put in place. "We've learned saliva doesn't pose a risk," emphasized a medical spokesperson. "When you are dealing with kids, you'll find they are drooling because they are kids, not because they are showing symptoms of AIDS." Because recent findings on the transmission of AIDS conflict with these stipulations, the state health department is reviewing them and will pass its recommendations on to the department of education.

If the school physician and the child's personal physician do not agree that the child's behavior warrants exclusion from the public schools, an appeal may be made to a Medical Advisory Panel established by the state health department. "What's important to remember," noted an advocate of children's rights, "is that the Garden City schools will do

❖ A child shall not be excluded from school solely because he/she is infected with the AIDS virus.

❖ No child shall be excluded from school because a sibling, or any other member of the immediate family, is infected with the AIDS virus.

❖ Any child who is not 5 years old by December 31 will not be admitted to a school program, whether infected or not. (This is the general policy on age of admission.) This stipulation is in keeping with federal guidelines but is being reevaluated because it is viewed as a form of discrimination against "handicapped children," and AIDS and HIV infections are now viewed as legal handicaps. The state will comply with federal and CDC recommendations on this stipulation.

❖ Eligible preschool-age handicapped children will be provided an appropriate, non-school-based program, as designated in the child's Individual Education Program (IEP).

❖ Any school-age child who lacks control of bodily excretions, is significantly neurologically impaired, displays extreme aggressive behavior with biting, kicking, and/or scratching, or has uncoverable, oozing lesions may not be placed in a school program. An appropriate alternate program will be provided. (This is a general measure for infection control, not just for AIDS.)

❖ Upon the determination that a kindergarten-age child, a general admission, or a readmission student with the AIDS virus is seeking to enroll in the school district, all information on the child, including a medical evaluation and an approved-to-attend-school statement from the child's physician, shall be sent immediately to the appropriate Assistant Executive Superintendent (AES) for elementary or secondary programs, the Director of Health Education and Services, and the School Medical Inspector.

❖ The Assistant Executive Superintendent will forward the student information to the Office of the Assistant Executive Superintendent for Pupil Personnel Services. All personal data and health status information on the child shall be KEPT STRICTLY CONFIDENTIAL.

❖ A central review panel for the Board of Education that includes the directors of the divisions of Child Guidance and Special Education (or designees), the Director of Health Education and Service, the School Medical Inspector, the child's physician, and parents will determine if the student should be enrolled in school or provided an alternate educational program.

Figure 5.1. School Admission Guidelines for Children With AIDS, ARC, or HIV-Positive Designations
Source: Garden City School District.

> ❖ In making the determination of school placement, the panel will consider the behavior, neurological development, general student health status, and the expected type of student-to-student and student-to-staff interactions in the school settings.
>
> ❖ If school placement for the student is deemed appropriate by the Board of Education central review panel, a neighborhood school placement will be recommended. If the child requires a special education program, school placement will be determined by the Division of Special Education in consultation with the child study team.
>
> ❖ When agreement on the child's admissibility cannot be reached by the Board of Education central review panel, the Medical Advisory Panel of the state health department at the request of the County Superintendent will review the case and make a final determination on school admissibility. Pending a decision from the State Medical Advisory Panel, the child will receive home instruction or other appropriate alternate educational program.

Figure 5.1. *Continued*

all in their power to admit these kids, but they will keep in line with state and federal guidelines."

HIV-infected children often receive support from the state's Division of Youth and Family Service (DYFS), Department of Human Services. DYFS provides assistance to children based on their need for protection or welfare, not because they are diagnosed as having HIV infections. A large increase in the number of HIV-infected children under its supervision prompted many DYFS actions, including funding for nurses and social workers at hospitals across the state. DYFS was particularly cautious about protecting the confidentiality of infected children and released information to social service providers only on a "need to know" basis.

In addressing the concern in Garden City schools over confidentiality, children's AIDS advocates noted that, traditionally, parents and other caretakers were counseled to keep quiet about the infection to avoid discrimination and other problems. However, the AIDS program at Children's Hospital now encourages caretakers to voluntarily divulge this information to some school personnel, provided they feel the child will be well treated. At a minimum, the medical and education communities would like caretakers to inform the school nurse. Ideally, the child's teacher and the building principal, who have a "vested interest in the child," should also be told. The teacher can give the child emotional support and can deal with special learning needs. The principal needs to be informed about events in his building, in order to quell rumors, discourage discrimination, and provide leadership.

FINALLY—EDUCATIONAL LEADERSHIP

The school obtained a 5-year CDC grant to provide AIDS education and training, but no funds were available from CDC for the entire first year. Toward the end of the second year, the school district finally named an AIDS coordinator, a gifted school psychologist. The AIDS coordinator was a veteran of the Garden City schools. His tenacity and persistence on behalf of children were remarkable. He had simply refused long ago to fold up and go to the suburbs, even though he had alienated the school's administration. At first, he seemed like Don Quixote, fighting the windmills without a prayer of winning. Some speculated that the administrators probably gave him the AIDS assignment in hopes that it would get rid of him for good. Little did they know what he would achieve in this job.

Thanks in large part to the school's AIDS coordinator, the training project's strategies were aggressive and comprehensive. Initially, the main thrust of the program was teacher training. Student education became the focus once the staff were trained. Some direct education of children was ongoing, however. Community organizations and agencies such as Planned Parenthood provided some education while the teachers were trained.

A committee of 25 volunteers designed the initial training. The committee represented a cross section of personnel—principals, psychologists, social workers, guidance counselors, elementary and secondary school nurses, physical education staff, and general teachers. The committee was provided with strategies and activities to teach students about human sexuality, decision-making and problem-solving skills, refusal skills, assertiveness training, negotiation skills, and self-esteem enhancement. From the very beginning, activities and strategies were designed with the children's cultures in mind: African American, Latino, inner city. Cultural sensitivity training went hand in hand with AIDS instruction. The coordinator pointed out that, if he took this training program to the suburbs, he would have to change the student activities, and he would have to focus on marijuana and cocaine rather than crack and heroin—the drugs that pose the biggest threat to inner-city kids.

After the planning period, 20 teacher volunteers then received training in winter and spring of 1990. These volunteers, called "turn-key trainers," were selected based on their interest and enthusiasm, as well as their influence or potential influence with other teachers in their building. These trainers provided leadership on AIDS and assisted in training other teachers. In 1991, they trained over 1,000 teachers. This approach was chosen to use limited resources efficiently and to affect the situation quickly. Training materials for the turn-key trainers included all the information learned by the committee, specific lesson plans for teachers, and educational tapes from the American Red Cross and other agencies. Select people from the training committee became team leaders for the turn-key trainers. Pilot training for teachers was conducted over a 3-day period: two for secondary level teachers and one for elementary level teachers. In keeping with studies that show that people who are paid to attend training sessions tend to use that training more fully than those who are not compensated, the grant paid for 400 teacher volunteers to attend a summer session.

One important principle was to train as many different kinds of school personnel as possible, so children had a chance to hear the message from several sources. Coaches received customized training because of their unique relationship with student athletes. Nurses' training prepared them on the medical aspects of HIV-infected youngsters and positioned them as information resources for other school personnel. Other training sessions were tailored to school bus drivers, custodians, cafeteria workers, and other specialized employees. In each building, it is normal for children to particularly like certain custodians and other workers. Children will listen to them when the subject is HIV prevention.

The Garden City training program received national recognition because it had taken a fairly new approach for that time. Unlike training in other school districts, it was based on training children in assertiveness and skills for dealing with their peers, so that they could make healthful decisions. "Normally, these training programs are knowledge-based, but that only increases knowledge," remarked a committee spokesperson. "It doesn't affect attitude or behavior."

One of the basic concerns regarding AIDS education was the teacher's attitude. "If teachers are uncomfortable talking about alternatives to abstinence and other sensitive topics, they should not be forced into teaching these classes," emphasized a committee spokesperson. "This is not a reading curriculum, and if talking about gays makes a teacher wrinkle her face, it becomes self-defeating." Teachers who were uncomfortable were urged to swap subjects with other faculty members who were less inhibited about presenting the AIDS material. The AIDS curriculum focused on encouragement and support for the students, regardless of their lifestyles.

Opting for a more fully integrated AIDS curriculum well before the state's anticipated ruling for AIDS education at all grade levels, Garden City focused initially on its secondary level students. School officials established a student group to interact with students from Grades 6 through 12. The student trainers were selected from "high-risk kids who don't normally do well in school so that as these kids are trained, they will internalize to become more self-focused and more confident." Junior and senior students made AIDS presentations in informal study hall settings, whereas sophomores underwent training to replace graduating student trainers.

In an effort to "bring the community into the schools," another projected program focused on family workshops to promote student-parent communication.

SUMMARY

Local government remained uncoordinated and slow to respond to AIDS in Garden City. The picture remains grim and overwhelming. Nevertheless, a lot was accomplished by some genuinely concerned and dedicated people in education and health care. With support from state and federal sources, they developed culturally sensitive interventions that made good use of scarce resources. In the health care area, parents became resources for their children's care. Professionals asked them to judge who should know their children were HIV-infected. The parents were often in a good position to know who truly cared about their children and would treat them well. In the schools, teachers, nurses, and other staff were redefined as resources for AIDS education. As a group, they moved from rumor and unrealistic fear to active involvement in AIDS education for their colleagues and for the children. Even the building janitor became an asset for AIDS education, if he was a favorite with children. Finally, through peer education, these same children became positive actors to provide an effective prevention message. Key to these developments was a redefinition of teachers, parents, and children. Where previous policy treated them as bundles of needs and fears, these new strategies called upon their talents and capabilities.

 KEY ISSUE

IDENTIFYING AND BUILDING COMMUNITY CAPACITY

Communities have both assets and liabilities when they confront risks. Community liabilities in Garden City are visible everywhere: drugs, crime, poverty, substandard housing, substandard schools, no jobs, no future. Community assets include the variety of resources, skills, and commitments that community people can bring to the solution of a problem. These assets are often termed *community capacities* (Clark & McElroy, 1995). But what community capacity could we possibly identify in the Garden City case? Does the evidence force us to agree with the health official who said it was laughable to think of an inner-city school district taking effective action about AIDS? On the contrary, the case illustrates a critical point: Even the poorest and most needy communities have important capacities to confront risks. In this discussion, three general questions are addressed and related to the situation of Garden City:

▲ How do professional worldviews affect the definition of communities: as bundles of deficits or areas of strength?

▲ How can community strengths be identified to confront health risks?

▲   How can community strengths be built upon to confront health risks?

Worldviews: community deficits versus community capacities. Surprising community capacity in Garden City can be seen in three areas. First,
the school staff, when properly trained, educated their colleagues and
students about AIDS. In fact, they moved from uninformed fear, which
was impairing whatever relationships they were still able to build with
the children, to a condition in which they could better handle at least
some of the children's needs. Not all teachers were asked to provide
children with HIV education; all of us have individual strengths and
weaknesses, and some teachers were more comfortable than others with
the idea of discussing HIV and its relationship to sexual matters.

The second kind of community capacity was the judgment that
parents could bring to bear for disclosure of their child's HIV status.
Parents of HIV-infected children might be viewed as an unlikely community asset to some. With support from health professionals, however,
the parents decided whether to disclose their child's infection to school
staff. The assets they brought to the situation were their knowledge of
their children, the children's teachers, and the relationship between
teacher and pupil. They then used their judgment to decide who would
treat their child well, because the children needed support in school.

Third, local teens with training and support from prevention experts became important to Garden City's effort to prevent AIDS. The
model devised in Garden City was also employed elsewhere in the
country and found to be effective in reducing teens' self-reported HIV
risk behaviors (DiClemente, 1992). This model was originally used to
prevent the onset of teen smoking, as long ago as the 1970s (Flay, 1985).
Essentially, the model uses the peer pressure that is so influential with
teens, but for positive goals instead of risk taking or negative behavior.
Slightly older teens who are respected by their peers are trained in group
discussion methods and demonstration of refusal skills.

These three examples are fairly modest. No one would argue that
Garden City has eliminated or even greatly reduced its problems. But
the case demonstrates how professional worldviews affect the ability to
tap community capacity to solve problems. Professionals, and in fact
most of the public, tend to view poor communities as having nothing

but needs. However, they have important capacity as well. How professionals define community members dictates whether they can work with those capacities and build them (McKnight & Kretzmann, 1990). Everyone in decision-making roles viewed the citizens of Garden City as "problems" and as bundles of needs. Not until the AIDS coordinator redefined them as collaborators in confronting risk were their capacities recognized.

John McKnight (1995) notes that the helping professions tend to redefine the needs of communities, and especially poor inner-city communities, as bundles of deficits: "A need could be understood as a condition, a want, a right, an obligation of another, an illusion, or an unresolvable problem. Professional practice consistently defines a need as an unfortunate absence or emptiness in another" (p. 43). In McKnight's view, professionals aim to service these needs, and in the process, they often supplant community members who could provide the necessary support.

A focus on deficits instead of capacity can invade professionals' consciousness in subtle ways. Professionals perform needs assessments in public health and social welfare. More rarely do they perform "capacity" assessments. As McKnight and Kretzmann (1990) so cogently put it,

> [Needs surveys] are initiated by groups with power and resources who ask neighborhood people to think of themselves in terms of deficiencies. . . . They also teach people outside these neighborhoods that the most important thing about low-income people and their neighborhoods is their deficiencies, problems, and needs. . . . It is true that this map of needs is accurate. But, it is also true that it is only half the truth . . . every neighborhood has a map of riches, assets, and capacities. . . . the most significant difference about this capacity map is that it is the map a neighborhood must rely on if it is to find the power to regenerate itself. (pp. 16-17)

Identifying community capacity. Some areas of public health practice have started to focus on community capacity to address public health problems (Clark & McElroy, 1995). However, community capacity has rarely been studied directly in the context of confronting risks. It is true that community advisory groups and environmental activists can embody certain community skills and resources (Edelstein & Wandersman,

1987). But the case studies illustrate other types of community capacity that can constructively be brought to bear in confronting risks.

Sometimes, as in the Lakeview case study of Chapter 6, communities have many strengths to confront risks. In fact, a risk manager may feel pushed to the wall by cohesive and affluent communities that can draw on these strengths. Lakeview's community capacity included: an educated population, a tradition of volunteerism, access to a powerful congressman, a high stake in the property values of the area, and a sense that community members were able to critically evaluate even the most technical proposals to deal with pollution.

An important resource to identify community capacity is *Mapping Community Capacity,* a report by John McKnight and John Kretzmann (1990). Community capacity can be identified in line with McKnight's approach to finding community associations, outlined in the key concepts of Chapter 3.

Characteristically, McKnight suggests a focus on community assets that are most accessible to community people, wherever possible. However, other less accessible resources are also valuable to solving problems. The most easily accessible assets are located in the neighborhood and are for the most part under neighborhood residents' control. These include people, even people who are otherwise labeled as problems. For example, former gang members are active in several cities to promote positive activities and alternatives to gangs, as a means to prevent violence. Local newsletters, flyers, and other forms of communication fall into the category of locally controlled and easily accessible assets. The locally controlled citizens' associations are also accessible to build community capacity: citizen associations, business associations, and cultural, financial, or religious organizations. In particular, the African American church has taken the lead in more than a few major public health initiatives: for hypertension control (Kong et al., 1982), cholesterol reduction (Stoy et al., 1995), cancer control (Davis et al., 1994), and teens at risk (Rubin, Billingsley, & Caldwell, 1994), to name but a few (Thomas, Quinn, Billingsley, & Caldwell, 1994).

Somewhat less accessible assets are located in the neighborhood but controlled largely by outsiders. Public resources such as the schools, police, fire departments, parks, and libraries, as well as private and nonprofit organizations such as colleges or universities, hospitals, and social service agencies, can all be accessed to help solve a community problem. Even vacant land and energy and waste resources can cease to be a blight for neighborhoods and begin to be an asset with the proper approach. Gardening and recycling are offered as examples.

Potentially accessible assets are those located outside the neighborhood and over which the neighborhood does not have control. These could be brought to bear to solve problems: welfare monies that are currently expended for the maintenance rather than the solution of problems; public capital improvement expenditures that might be directed to specific uses in the neighborhood; and public information such as media-based efforts for health promotion.

Building community capacity to solve health problems. A resource on how the health professional can develop community capacity is a book edited by Neil Bracht (1990), *Health Promotion at the Community Level*. This resource outlines not only how to identify neighborhood and citywide resources, but also how they might be employed in health promotion and disease prevention.

Very valuable in the Bracht (1990) text is a review of theories of social change (Thompson & Kinne, 1990). Several of these theories are employed in later chapters to address specific public health aims in community. For example, the "A Su Salud" health promotion program for Mexican Americans on the border employs two theories: diffusion of innovations and use of role model stories, a strategy derived from social cognitive theory (Amezcua, McAlister, Ramirez, & Espinoza, 1990). In this program, as in several others developed by Alfred McAlister in partnership with communities, written and verbal stories are developed about people in the community who have taken positive actions on health. Volunteers share these role model stories with their neighbors. This method directly builds on community capacity that is closest to home (McAlister et al., 1982; see also Fishbein, Guinan, Holtgrave, & Leviton, 1996).

The chapter by Bracht and Kingsbury (1990) outlines how community organization principles might be employed in order to stimulate community change for health promotion. These can be adapted to the process of confronting risks. The principles developed for this purpose are reproduced in Figure 5.2.

1. Planning must be based on a historical understanding of the community. Conditions that inhibit or facilitate interventions must be assessed.

2. Because the issue or problem is usually one of multiple (rather than single) causality, a comprehensive effort using multiple interventions is required.

3. It is important to focus on community context and work primarily through existing structures and values.

4. Active community participation, not mere token representation, is desired.

5. For the project to be effective, intersectoral components of the community must work together to address the problem in a comprehensive effort.

6. The focus must be on both long-term and short-term problem solving if the longevity of the change is to endure beyond the project's demonstration period.

7. Finally, and most important, the community must share responsibility for the problem and its solution.

Figure 5.2. Community Organization Applied to Health Promotion
SOURCE: Neil Bracht & Lee Kinsbury, Community organization principles in health promotion: A five-stage model. In N. Bracht (Ed.) *Health promotion at the community level.* Newbury Park, CA: Sage, 1990.

Communities may need assistance to organize effective decision-making bodies to confront risk. Lines of authority and responsibility between professionals and community may also need clarification. The chapter by Bracht and Kingsbury (1990) outlines several models for these decision-making bodies, with advantages and disadvantages of each. Also helpful for environmental risk issues in particular is a review article by Lynn and Busenberg (1995) on citizen advisory committees.

Several common strategies in health promotion can be easily adopted to build community capacity to confront risk: training community members to influence other citizens, stimulate interest, and provide information and education. The teachers and staff of Garden City schools, as well as the teen peer leaders, offer examples of this form of capacity building specifically for HIV awareness and prevention.

A related strategy is to employ and pay community residents to take appropriate roles to confront risk. Although volunteers are an important resource, sometimes community expertise should be acknowledged and given status through payment. For example, employing lay helpers from the community is a strategy used fairly often in community-based health promotion (Leviton & Schuh, 1991). In any community, there will be individuals who are natural helpers, to whom community members may turn for advice or assistance. Often, the people skills of lay helpers can transfer easily to paid work on behalf of health promotion. In fact, there is evidence that paraprofessionals in this role can do many health education jobs at least as well as professionals (Cabral et al., 1996; Leviton & Schuh, 1991). However, they will require substantial support and backup from professionals, because they may face a variety of situations outside their realm of experience (Leviton & Schuh, 1991).

As lay helpers visit and talk with community members, they have important information to offer their organization about how the public perceives risk and about how the solutions are working. This feedback is another important strategy in community capacity building, making advocacy effective. Individual lay helpers cannot correct system-level problems that they see in their contacts with the community. Yet, information about the patterns they see, if properly documented, can be a powerful tool. Professionals and community leaders can use this information to become more effective advocates for specific improvements. Advocacy skills take time to master. The readings listed at the end of Chapter 6 will assist this process.

There are good reasons to try to identify new community capacity over time. Nascent leaders, new lay helpers, and new volunteers all revitalize community resources. People in these roles can become exhausted over time because of the demands placed on them. Lay helpers, for example, may benefit from rotating into other project responsibilities. Also, it is our observation that sometimes community leaders can become isolated from a variety of emerging community concerns or develop interests that are not identical with the interests of community. For all these reasons, community capacity building may need to include the identification and development of new community resources over time.

NOTE

1. In this case study, stakeholders were guaranteed anonymity. As a result, we changed names of places and withheld our documentation for quotations and sources.

CHAPTER **6**

SUPERFUND SHOWDOWN

The Management of Conflict Between the EPA and Community Activist Groups

STEPHEN E. KAUFFMAN

INTRODUCTION[1]

This case examines the development and resolution of conflict between a vocal community group and the U.S. Environmental Protection Agency (EPA). The conflict involved one of the most serious pollution problems ever recognized by the EPA's Superfund program. The community group was concerned about EPA's plan to deal with the public health threat posed by a large, unsecured hazardous waste landfill. In the early 1980s, the landfill was designated one of the top priorities of the EPA's Superfund program, whose mandate was to clean up and dispose of such hazardous sites.

The case nicely illustrates several points: (a) how history and physical setting affect reactions to health risks, (b) how community capacity for dealing with risk information affects its responses, (c) the importance of planning to facilitate public participation in decision making, (d) the crucial role played by informal relationships among stakeholders, and (e) the evolution of these relationships over time.

 ## KEY ISSUE AND GENERAL QUESTIONS

This case illustrates how relationships between health professionals and communities can improve when community participation is facilitated. However, obstacles to such relationships are all too predictable, given the nature of public health responsibilities, bureaucracies, and limited resources. The discussion of this case poses three general questions:

▲ What are the resources needed to improve and clarify risk communication?

▲ How can organizations improve their capacity to respond to communities?

▲ In an era of limited resources and fragmented public health responsibilities, what can be done to foster responsiveness?

 ## STAKEHOLDERS

Lakeview residents
State and local health departments
State and local environmental protection departments
Citizens and Neighbors Concerned About the Landfill (CANCAL)
Environmental Protection Agency (EPA)

TIMELINE

1958	Landfill operations begin
1963-1969	State department of health periodically inspects the site
1969	Two landfill fires caused by mishandling the waste
1970	Leachate observed migrating off-site
1971	Waste disposal ends
1972	State Department of Environmental Protection (DEP) files suit against Monson to clean up site
1974	Court actions force additional site cleanup
1979	EPA assumes coordination
	Athena Lake closed to fishing and swimming
1980	Federal Superfund enacted into law
1981	First EPA public meetings held
1982	EPA issues Record of Decision I
	Fence constructed around site and nearby creek
1983	EPA prepares community relations plan for site and establishes informational repositories in Lakeview
	Slurry wall and cap installed
1984	Public meeting held by EPA to address citizen concerns
1985	CANCAL founded
	Draft Remedial Investigation and Feasibility Study (RIFS) issued: Public comment period begins
	Series of public meetings
	CANCAL contacts senators, representatives, national environmental groups to examine technology and extend RIFS comment period
	EPA issues Record of Decision II
	Federal health assessment released

	Monson Health Committee formed at the suggestion of the EPA
1986	EPA establishes additional information repository with CANCAL
	EPA signs a letter agreeing "to clarify" the Record of Decision
	Public meeting held by EPA to discuss opposition to plans
	EPA agrees to $50,000 grant for technical assistance to Lakeview. Community advisory group, formed at request of EPA, to be grant recipient
	New EPA site manager assumes coordination
1987	Off-site RIFS released
1989	Health study released

SECTION I

BACKGROUND: A LAKE CLOSES

DESCRIPTION OF THE COMMUNITY

In the late 1980s, Lakeview Borough had a population of 10,000 spread across 2.5 square miles. Located only 30 miles from a major northeastern city, Lakeview was fairly affluent, with only 5% of the borough's population below the poverty level. The borough's residents were primarily white (98%) and middle or working class. Through development in recent decades, what was once an agricultural area became suburban in character.

Lakeview managed to maintain a small-town atmosphere, and residents attributed this to a historical sense of community. Civic commitment to Lakeview was seen in the many eager volunteers for all-community affairs. As one resident stated, "It's an all-volunteer community. People aren't paid, but when people get involved, it's all the way." Civic organizations of all sorts benefited, and their events were well attended. Concerts, barbecues, and parades were held frequently, especially during the summer months.

Active commitment to community also affected local politics. The mayor and borough council members served in unpaid positions, which was unusual for towns of similar size in the state. The lack of payment, however, was not a barrier to political participation. Local government positions were actively pursued in political contests.

Residents also pointed to nearby recreational areas as a reason for stability and for the high value placed on community. Foremost among these was Athena Lake. A large man-made body developed in the 1890s, the lake had a boardwalk, a bathhouse, a merry-go-round, and other attractions that drew people from the city throughout the summer months. Most of the lake's attractions fell into disuse earlier in the 1900s. Swimming, fishing, and picnics, however, continued to be enjoyed until recently. Swimming in the lake was banned after fecal contamination was discovered in the 1950s. Later, fishing was prohibited because of toxic contamination from the Monson landfill.

THE MONSON LANDFILL

Steve Monson, owner of the landfill, first used it as a sand and gravel pit. To backfill at the site, Monson accepted a variety of municipal, household, and liquid hazardous chemical wastes between 1961 and 1971. Liquid wastes usually arrived in barrels, which were often emptied or crushed on delivery. Monson accepted a tremendous volume of wastes during the years of operation: 12,000 cubic yards of solid waste, several thousand drums, and perhaps 3 million gallons of liquid wastes. This waste is composed of at least 74 different chemicals and metals that are known to be toxic. Several are known or suspected carcinogens.

The actual landfill site did not lie in Lakeview. Rather, it lay directly over the borough boundary in Extin Township. Before stringent environmental regulations, township or borough home rule allowed land use decisions to be made without consultation with surrounding communities. Consequently, the site, tucked in the southeast corner of the township and quite far from the residential areas of Extin, was located only one-half mile from some of Lakeview's nicest residential areas. The site itself topped a small hill and was surrounded by orchards. Between the site and Lakeview's residential areas lay a marsh and a creek. This creek connected nearby Athena Lake with a local reservoir. Beneath the site, below a clay layer, lay two aquifers from which some 20,000 area residents drew well water. Contamination from the site was believed to be kept out of the aquifers by the clay layer. However, it readily flowed off-site into the marsh, the creek, and Athena Lake.

LOCAL LEADERSHIP

In most areas of civic life, the Lakeview mayor and the borough council provided what townspeople considered to be adequate leadership. Residents attributed this leadership to the sense of community and the fact that, as a small, stable borough, residents and leaders knew each other well through years of contact.

Lakeview and Lake County were typical of the state, in which a patchwork of state and local health authorities held overlapping and confusing mandates. Lakeview had two primary organizations to deal with health issues. The first of these was the Lakeview Health Department, which confined its activities at the Monson site to some leachate, air, and water testing. Most borough activities concerning the landfill were the responsibility of the Lakeview Environmental Commission. Formed in 1984, the commission oversaw local environmental problems, including Monson, gypsy moths, open space, wildlife, recycling, shade trees, site planning, education, water resources, and air quality. In the late 1980s, the commission conveyed citizen concerns about the landfill. Prior to 1986-1987, however, the focus of the commission was much more narrow. Problems associated with the landfill, although discussed, were primarily left to state or federal agencies. Many in the community saw this limited activity as a leadership void that was later filled by a local activist group.

Lake County had two agencies that historically dealt with environmental health. The Lake County Planning Department focused primarily on environmental impacts of development. Much of the early testing of the Monson site was done by this agency during the construction of new homes near Athena Lake. The Lake County Health Department, however, had a more active role in the full range of health issues affecting the county. The department assisted the state and federal government in environmental testing and monitoring of potential health threats.

These activities were no small task: Lake County had three Superfund cleanup sites, including the Monson landfill. The county health department tested, monitored exposure, and provided information to concerned citizens. Once the state and federal authorities took responsibility for the sites in the 1980s, the county health department continued to provide information. The department often received calls and questions about the sites, their safety, and area property values.

STATE LEADERSHIP

The state had long been a leader on environmental issues. With an extensive history of chemical production and manufacturing, the state was one of the first to recognize the toxic threats associated with the disposal of chemicals and chemical by-products. Two state agencies addressed toxic health concerns: the state health department and the Department of Environmental Protection (DEP).

The state health department had a fully developed program for monitoring and assessing health effects associated with all types of environmental health problems. With a staff of qualified epidemiologists and scientists, the department often conducted sophisticated health studies for communities that were concerned about toxic exposures. The state health department regularly inspected the Monson landfill during its operation in the 1960s. Little, however, was known about the potential health effects of such a site at that time. Nor were any licensing or monitoring requirements in effect. Consequently, the health department did not impede the site's operation.

The DEP operated a large-scale program for remediation of toxic waste sites that did not qualify for federal cleanup assistance. The DEP also regularly worked with the federal government on sites that fell under EPA jurisdiction. Prior to the creation of the federal Superfund, most initial remedial activities at the Monson landfill were directed by the DEP.

By the late 1960s, toxics disposed at the landfill were observed to be migrating off-site. At the same time, people living near the landfill noticed unpleasant odors and symptoms such as headaches and nausea, which they attributed to the landfill. Several fires were also reported at the site. These problems led Mr. Monson and some of the nearby residents to contact the DEP in 1969 to determine whether the landfill posed a hazard. As a precaution, Mr. Monson voluntarily stopped accepting liquid wastes in December 1969. However, liquid containing the toxic wastes continued to migrate off-site at rates later estimated at around 100,000 gallons per day. Large pools of multicolored leachate were found throughout the marsh.

In 1971, the DEP closed the landfill to all waste disposal and, in 1972, filed suit against Mr. Monson to clean up the site. In part voluntarily, but also as a result of the court actions, Monson dug ditches to catch the contaminants and spread lime over the surface to reduce odors. These actions had little effect, and wastes continued to flow from the site.

Throughout the late 1970s, DEP activities were generally confined to site monitoring and testing. With EPA involvement, which began in 1979, the DEP moved to a less active role. Today, the DEP works with the EPA in a supportive capacity.

NATIONAL LEADERSHIP

Before the late 1970s, the federal government was not well prepared to deal with toxic environmental problems of large scope. The federal government had only limited authority to address these issues at all. Three laws, described in Figure 6.1, changed the federal role. In the mid-1970s, Congress passed the Resource Conservation and Recovery Act and the Toxic Substances Control Act. These laws were designed to help control present and future chemical production and disposal. It was not until the Comprehensive Environmental Response, Compensation, and Liability Act (Superfund) was passed in 1980 that a national mechanism was established to address the problem of past hazardous waste disposal. The legislation directed the EPA to identify, characterize, and clean up existing hazardous waste sites. Funding was to come from taxes on hazardous wastes produced by manufacturing and from lawsuits or negotiation with polluters when they could be identified.

The Superfund legislation was strongly supported by communities such as Lakeview that had environmental problems. Not surprisingly, the congressman for the Lakeview area was a vocal advocate for passage of Superfund. Until recently, he sat on committees that had oversight responsibility for EPA and the Superfund.

Although the legislation promised much, a variety of problems hurt successful implementation. An important early problem, during the Reagan administration, was an ideological opposition to environmental protection, manifested in the appointments of Anne Burford as EPA Director and Rita Lavelle as Superfund Administrator. In the words of

Three federal laws affect domestic hazardous waste production and disposal. These are:

1. The Toxic Substances Control Act of 1976 (TOSCA): The intent of this act was to prevent harmful substances from entering the marketplace. The act required manufacturers to test materials before production and distribution to ensure that these materials could be safely produced. A mechanism was also established by which materials already on the market could be evaluated, and, if necessary, removed from production.

2. The Resource Conservation and Recovery Act of 1976 (RCRA): This act allowed the government to set standards and regulate the disposal of hazardous wastes. It established a "cradle to grave" philosophy of oversight for such wastes as they moved through the production cycle. This act did not address past disposal practices or abandoned toxic waste sites already in existence.

3. The Comprehensive Environmental Response Compensation, and Liability Act of 1980 (CERCLA): This act, known as "Superfund," directed the EPA to identify, characterize, and clean up existing hazardous waste sites. Funds for the process were to be derived from taxes on hazardous wastes produced in the country or through legal action or negotiation with polluters when they could be identified. The act initially was to be funded until 1986. It was, however, very poorly implemented in its early years, and by the mid-1980s, a push was on to reauthorize and expand the scope of the legislation. The reauthorization and expansion came with the passage of the Superfund Amendments and Re-Authorization Act of 1986. This act, known as SARA, produced several beneficial changes, including the expanded opportunity for individuals to obtain Technical Assistance Grants (TAGs).

Figure 6.1. Federal Hazardous Waste Legislation

one EPA official, they "systematically set out to dismantle" all EPA programs, including Superfund. Operating budgets were slashed, administrative structure was in constant flux, legal actions nearly ceased, and negotiations with polluters resulted in what have been characterized as "sweetheart deals." For their efforts, Burford and Lavelle were forced from their positions in 1983, and Lavelle was prosecuted for criminal activity. As a consequence, EPA morale plummeted and many Superfund operations never really got off the ground.

Later experience revealed that other forces hampered Superfund remedial efforts as well, including legal and technical difficulties and an extremely complex implementation process. Of the hundreds of sites identified for cleanup by Superfund, only a handful were fully remediated by 1990. Most of the remainder were mired at some earlier point.

THE SUPERFUND IMPLEMENTATION PROCESS

The complexity of the Superfund implementation process deserves special attention for its effect on the Monson site. Figure 6.2 outlines the overall process. In general, sites undergo a long process of characterization and evaluation before remediation can start. Two complex documents must be written and disseminated: a Remedial Investigation (RI) and a Feasibility Study (FS). If the documents are combined, as they were for the Monson site, they are called a RIFS. The RIFS is an important document. It defines the problem and presents cleanup alternatives. Also included are evaluations of the alternatives based upon effectiveness, comparative cost, public health considerations, and technical feasibility. The final remedial action must (theoretically) be selected from the options presented in the RIFS.

Proper evaluation of the alternatives requires a great deal of information. Therefore, site characterizations, monitoring studies, and technical aspects about the problem and the proposed solutions are included in the RIFS. With all this information, the RIFS is usually several hundred pages long. Much of its information is very sophisticated technically.

Communities and interested individuals are encouraged throughout the development of the RIFS to provide input into the decision-making process. In addition, after the RIFS is prepared and released, concerned individuals may comment upon or question any aspect of the information it contains. Comments are accepted verbally at a public meeting or through written correspondence with the EPA within a specific time. Officially, Superfund regulations require only a 21-day public comment period. Often, this time is extended, but in the early days of Superfund, the extension rarely exceeded 5 or 6 weeks.

At the end of the comment period, the EPA releases a Record of Decision (ROD). The ROD presents the selected remedial alternative and the EPA's reasons for choosing this alternative. In addition, comments or questions received from the public during the comment period must be addressed in the ROD. These are contained in what is called a

1. Sites receive a Preliminary Assessment (PA).
2. If needed, they then receive a Site Inspection.
3. They are then scored by the Hazard Ranking System.
4. If the score is high enough, they are placed on the National Priorities List (NPL), and they become eligible for remedial action by the government, if necessary, or by responsible parties identified as having created the uncontrolled toxic waste site.
5. The site then receives a Remedial Investigation and Feasibility Study (RIFS).
6. The public may then comment on the RIFS and the EPA's preferred alternative of technology for the cleanup.
7. The EPA then issues a Record of Decision (ROD) that says what remedial action has been chosen and why.
8. A site may be split into several aspects, with different RIFS and RODs.
9. Then, the actual remedial action begins.
10. RODs may also be modified when new information is found or difficulties are encountered.
11. Finally, the site will be removed from the NPL.

Figure 6.2. The Superfund Process

"citizen's responsiveness summary." Several RODs may be appropriate for a given site if the scope of the problem is large, and it may take years to complete the entire process, just to decide what is to be done.

In theory, the Superfund implementation process is supposed to encourage public input into the decision-making process. Comment periods, public meetings, community relations plans, advisory groups, and information dissemination guidelines are all specified for EPA officials through Superfund legislation or EPA regulations. Most of this process was used in the Monson cleanup. The EPA held public meetings to explain its activities as early as 1980. In addition, EPA set up a community relations plan for the site in 1983. As part of this plan, informational depositories were set up in Lakeview to receive relevant EPA documents for public review.

The actual Superfund process at any site may involve a dozen or more agencies, businesses, or contractors in addition to the EPA. Site characterizations, health studies, legal aspects, construction work, and community relations may be handled by different organizations. The coordination and administration of this process, however, usually falls to one individual known as the site manager. The site manager is not the sole contact with other agencies and the community; however, he or she often serves as the "point man" for both coordination and criticism. In the early days of Superfund, site managers were hired primarily for their technical or administrative skills. EPA gave little priority to community relations experience.

SUPERFUND AT THE MONSON SITE

The Monson site was identified early in the Superfund program as requiring remediation. The degree of contamination, potential for health damage, and political power of the area's congressman contributed to its designation in 1980 as a top priority for site cleanup.

When the EPA and Superfund took responsibility for the site, the Lakeview community was greatly relieved. It was widely believed that the Superfund program would clean up the site in fairly short order. Early relations between Lakeview and EPA were generally good. At one of the first public meetings about the Monson site, in November 1981, the attending crowd cheered as the EPA site manager and others described their long-term plans for the site.

In 1982, EPA issued its first ROD for the site, including two emergency actions. A chain-link fence would limit access to the site, and shortly thereafter a slurry wall and cap would be installed around and over the site. The slurry wall, built deep into the ground, reduced the movement of liquid contaminants off-site by 98%. Air contamination was essentially eliminated by the site cap. Everyone (the EPA and Lakeview) recognized that the slurry wall and cap were short-term solutions. During the next 6 years, the focus turned to plans for long-term remediation. Two sets of RIFS and RODs were planned for the site: one set to address the on-site contamination, and one set to address contamination of the marsh, the creek, and Athena Lake.

DEVELOPMENT OF A
COMMUNITY ORGANIZATION: CANCAL

Before 1985, local leadership and oversight of state and federal activities fell almost exclusively to the Lakeview borough council and the environmental commission. In a July 1984 public information meeting for the borough, public records indicate that town leaders were very pleased with EPA progress. A number of residents who lived near the landfill expressed their concerns at this meeting, however. These included: doubts about the integrity of remediation and containment technologies employed to that point; the length of time necessary for the process and for cleanup; the possible health effects due to years of exposure to the toxic wastes; whether the lake would be restored; and the perception that despite the EPA's community relations efforts, citizens had difficulty obtaining records of EPA activities. Concern escalated in the months following the meeting. During this time, the EPA was preparing its on-site RIFS. Some community members felt that EPA gave vague and elusive answers to several questions they raised. This perception became stronger as EPA officials put forth little effort to discuss, address, or otherwise follow up the concerns presented by the community.

At a follow-up meeting in January 1985, community members repeated these questions and concerns. The EPA had had 7 months to prepare answers or plan a way to address these concerns, but EPA offered no further insight. This angered some Lakeview residents. They believed local government was not applying the type of pressure to EPA that would ensure attention to community concerns. Some believed that the borough council and the Lakeview Environmental Commission should have provided more leadership and a voice for the community in EPA activities.

Many Lakeview residents who lived closest to the site decided in June 1985 to form the Citizens and Neighbors Concerned About the Landfill (CANCAL). CANCAL intended to make sure that EPA fully addressed community concerns. Their primary goal was to make certain that EPA adequately remediated the threat presented by the landfill. For many CANCAL members, removal of the health threat meant removal of the wastes altogether. If removal was not possible, they wanted an alternative technology that would satisfy them that the community was fully protected.

MEN IN MOON SUITS

The Monson landfill posed a potentially severe health threat to Lakeview. Several agencies tested the site extensively in the 1970s and 1980s. They found contamination from a variety of chemical compounds and metals, not only on the site itself, but in the marsh areas and in the surface water and soil of Athena Lake as well. The toxicological effects of these substances and their sheer quantity greatly worried the community. Known or suspected carcinogens found both on- and off-site include arsenic, benzene, bis (2-chloroethyl) ether (BCEE), chloroform, and 1,2-dichloroethane. In addition, chromium, ethylbenzene, lead, mercury, nickel, toluene, xylenes, and zinc have known toxicities. These compounds and metals, when evaluated for their impact on health in risk assessments of the Monson site, had the potential to cause cancers and other illnesses.

Most of the Lakeview concern focused on BCEE. This chemical is believed to be a carcinogen at low exposure levels. BCEE was found in the creek and in Athena Lake during site characterization studies in 1979-1980. As a result, warning signs were posted around the lake and stream, and fishing in the lake was prohibited. Closing their lake to recreational use drove home for Lakeview the potential for health problems. So did Lakeview's observation of EPA activity, as men in fully encapsulating "moon suits" worked around the landfill. Residents tell stories of families having backyard barbecues when moon-suited workers would pass by the neighborhoods directly adjacent to the marsh areas. People living along the creek continued to feel persistent symptoms, such as headaches, nausea, and dizziness. Citizens attributed a variety of health problems to the landfill, ranging from school absenteeism to cancers.

SUMMARY

By 1983-1984, the potential for harmful toxic exposure had been known or suspected by at least some in the community for almost 14 years. Many others in the community grew increasingly concerned about the health threat. CANCAL was created out of fears of an ongoing toxic exposure and a growing perception that the local government was not providing sufficient oversight of EPA activities. CANCAL's members sought to ensure that the EPA's plan for cleanup was adequate and to strongly voice community concerns in light of what it perceived as inadequate reactions by the local government.

SECTION II

A STRUGGLE TAKES SHAPE

WAS EPA UNRESPONSIVE?

Seven months later, the EPA released its draft on-site RIFS. This draft shattered hopes for a solution the community could accept. In the RIFS, four general strategies were evaluated. Of these alternatives, the EPA preferred batch flushing. This technology would force water into the site, pump it out with contaminants, treat it, and then release the water back onto the site or elsewhere. Sludge from the operation would be returned to the landfill. The treatment was anticipated to take 15 years to complete.

This recommendation immediately enraged many in the community, and especially several members of CANCAL. The EPA had rejected the option of removing the wastes from the site, which many had wanted, expected, and viewed as the most effective way to eliminate the health threat. In the RIFS, EPA rejected removal because it was deemed too expensive and would create additional risks to the workers and the community. Moreover, at the time, the EPA did not believe federal regulations would allow them to remove such a large amount of waste from the Monson site.

An EPA staffer has noted that, unfortunately, the EPA officials did little to build a case for the efficacy of batch flushing when they presented the RIFS to Lakeview in August 1985. Instead, it appeared to several members of CANCAL that the EPA officials leading the meeting were unprepared. They could not answer questions about many details of batch flushing. More important, the officials could not say whether the site would stay clean after flushing was completed. Residents also noted that the EPA staff still could not answer questions posed a year earlier about health concerns, the probability of continued contamination, information availability, or the plans for off-site remediation.

Many of those attending felt that the EPA officials ignored or redirected the questions presented to them. In the eyes of one CANCAL member, their unresponsiveness bordered on outright belligerence: "We went to this meeting and there was this guy who wasn't receptive to our questions—explaining things, he was very antagonistic. He basically told my wife she was an idiot."

As the meeting progressed and at all subsequent public meetings about the on-site process over the next 2 years, CANCAL members became increasingly angry and frustrated over EPA's apparent lack of responsiveness. The exchanges at these meetings were marked by much yelling and shouting. EPA staff, too, became frustrated. Said an EPA official, "These (early) meetings were unreal—they would last for hours and involve hundreds of concerned people asking questions about health, technology, whatever, with really irrational tones. People would attribute any health concerns to the toxic exposure." Said a community member, "You could see that these guys (the EPA) had been through so many of these meetings and they had been yelled at so many times, it became, OK, we've got to get through this meeting."

CANCAL members' contacts with the EPA outside of the public meetings increased their anger and frustration. CANCAL's correspondence with EPA on specific questions or concerns often obtained no response, a vague response, or a deferred response until "the problem could be studied further." As a result, CANCAL members perceived EPA officials as wholly insensitive to the community's concerns. If they had cared about the community, said CANCAL, they would have listened and made a greater effort to respond. EPA staff, including the site manager at this time, did not help to improve this perception. Although the site manager was a well-qualified administrator and technician, Lakeview residents pointed to his appearance as a "bureaucrat," his use of technical jargon, and his "lack of communication skills," which did little to create trust.

BARRIERS TO PARTICIPATION

The difficulty of making informed comments about the RIFS also increased community anger. The RIFS contained several hundred pages of technical material in which EPA defended the choice of batch flushing. Analyzing this information and critiquing it required a great deal of technical understanding. For CANCAL members, the comment period the EPA allowed between the distribution of the RIFS and the distribution of the ROD made adequate analysis impossible. Said a member of CANCAL,

> To be a part of the process, you have to understand the process. There are stacks and stacks of technical documents, and how can you be part of the process if you're given these documents 2 or even 30 days before a meeting?

To make matters worse, access to information posed a continuing problem. Even with hundreds of pages of material, the RIFS did not contain all of the information that CANCAL members thought important. Complete site characterizations, raw data, information about methodologies, and results of site testing appeared to be absent or glossed over. Thus, CANCAL members did not believe it possible to evaluate the document fully.

The access problem extended well beyond the RIFS. Documents about the cleanup, if made available at all, routinely arrived for CANCAL's scrutiny much later than its members requested. Often, documents arrived several months after they became available to the EPA or its contractors. Furthermore, these documents sometimes did not address any of the issues or the chemicals with which CANCAL members were most concerned.

CANCAL'S ACTIONS

After the release of the RIFS, CANCAL members began an active campaign to make the EPA responsive to their concerns. First, they sought informed analysis of the flushing technology by developing networks with other, more experienced environmental groups. Second, CANCAL contacted their elected representatives in Washington to request an official analysis of the technology. Third, CANCAL asked area legislators to exert pressure on the EPA to delay the ROD until CANCAL had sufficient time to make informed comments. Finally, CANCAL used the media and set up education networks to organize the larger community. This allowed them to ask for help from larger numbers of people. In the words of one CANCAL member, the community is "more likely to get involved if you spell things out for them."

In spite of these efforts, the EPA issued its ROD in September 1985, choosing the flushing technology as expected. However, CANCAL's strategies had produced an unending stream of phone calls and letters from Congress, the public, and others. In response, EPA extended the time for which comments on their plans would be accepted. EPA also announced that it intended to "clarify" the ROD and reevaluate its choice of flushing technology. This move was prompted by new information about the flushing technology and methodological flaws in the RIFS. CANCAL had gathered this information with help from local politicians and technical sources, including the Citizen's Clearinghouse for Hazardous Waste, Clean Water Action, and the federal Office of Technology Assessment (OTA). OTA had conducted an analysis at the request of the community's senators and representatives.

Of greatest concern to CANCAL and the other groups was the fact that batch flushing was an experimental technology that in theory should be effective, but for which actual site experience was limited. Nevertheless, EPA did not abandon the flushing technology even after reevaluation. EPA did, however, incorporate a few minor changes into its clarified ROD. It shortened the projected length of the process from 15 to 8 years. EPA also agreed to use some other technology if flushing did not work as expected.

HEALTH EFFECTS STUDIES

The community had important health concerns—after all, its residents lived next to a landfill with perhaps 3 million gallons of waste, composed of at least 74 different chemicals. The community shared these concerns with EPA and congressional representatives during the development of the on-site RIFS. EPA prepared and released two exposure assessments, in October 1985 and October 1986, respectively. These exposure assessments actually increased community anger. The 1985 report used excessively technical jargon and presented "nothing useful," in the words of one community member. The community was even more severely critical of the 1986 report. It ignored almost all of the chemicals of major concern at the site, instead focusing on pesticides and in particular on chlorodane contamination. Chlorodane, although a potential health problem in the state as a whole, was not one of the chemicals in the landfill. None of the most feared chemicals in the landfill was even mentioned except in appended data.

UNINTENDED CONSEQUENCES

CANCAL's activities had two unintended consequences. First, every time questions were directed to EPA and whenever the EPA was required to amend or change its plans, cleanup was delayed. Everyone—CANCAL members, the EPA staff, local government officials, and non-CANCAL community members—found these delays quite frustrating. EPA staff members saw the flushing technology as the best solution and were impatient to implement it. Many non-CANCAL community members were less concerned about the technology and just wanted some movement on cleanup. All parties were especially worried because the original authorization period for Superfund was just about over. By late 1985, future funding of the cleanup seemed uncertain, especially for off-site remediation.

A second unintended consequence of CANCAL's activities was a growing hostility between CANCAL and local government. CANCAL accused the local officials of failing to represent the community's interests to the EPA. For their part, the local government officials thought CANCAL had arrogated to itself activities that were the borough's responsibility. Exchanges between CANCAL and the town council were sometimes openly angry. Said one CANCAL member, "The borough council saw us as a group trying to do something politically . . . there was a concern that it would make the council or the environmental commission look bad."

SUMMARY

CANCAL believed that the EPA's toxic waste site remedial action was inadequate. Problems of access to, and interpretation of, EPA information made comment on EPA activities difficult. EPA staff workers apparently possessed few skills to deal constructively with the public and ineptly carried out their mandate for public participation. CANCAL's members believed that the EPA was unresponsive and insensitive and that it was preparing to use an ineffective technology to address a clear health threat. As a result, CANCAL applied consistent pressure on EPA to become responsive, pressure that had begun to work.

SECTION III
MOVING TOWARD SOLUTIONS

With the signing of the On-Site Remedial Action ROD in late 1985 and its clarification in early 1986, the EPA began to address some of the community's concerns. However, the mistrust and frustration that characterized relations between CANCAL and the EPA certainly did not disappear overnight. Changes in EPA procedures evolved over a 3-year period. Not until at least mid- to late 1988, after numerous, continuous contacts among the various groups, could relations between the EPA, Lakeview, and CANCAL be called "good."

MONSON HEALTH STUDY

In early 1986, at EPA's suggestion, the Monson Health Committee was created with representation from CANCAL, two federal health agencies, the Lake County Health Department, the EPA, the state health department, Lakeview, and the surrounding townships. The aims of this group were to summarize the health questions that the community wanted answered and to plan a systematic assessment of the health effects of present and past exposures at the site. A subcommittee to evaluate specific health issues included representatives of CANCAL, state and county health departments, the Lakeview Environmental Commission, and the Lakeview and Extin Boards of Health. The EPA was not represented on the subcommittee but provided technical expertise to the group.

The subcommittee decided to study residents' health in cooperation with the state health department. A registry was created of those who had been exposed to the waste. Two types of health effects were evaluated: cancers and low birth weight. These were selected because data were available from state registries, and because both health effects had been previously found to be associated with certain chemicals at the site. Low birth weight, in particular, was considered one of the most sensitive indicators of toxic exposure.

As the lead agency on the project, the state health department shaped the Monson Health Committee by inviting members and providing technical information. However, committee members said that their actual decision making was very much by consensus. Representatives from the community and CANCAL were encouraged to participate just as much as the health experts.

When the committee confronted technical or methodological problems, health experts spent many hours explaining why certain choices had to be made. Information about exposure was limited. Also, it was not possible to attribute some health problems to toxic exposure conclusively. If these limitations had not been explained carefully to the committee, they could have undermined the credibility of the study to the larger community.

Educating nontechnical group members allowed genuine community participation in decision making. It allowed the members to feel they "owned" the study. In the words of a health department participant: "It was satisfying after a while when you could see that individuals were understanding more and more of the technical issues; then [they would] explain these issues to others, newcomers to the group, the community, or the press."

The study was completed in early 1989. The study found no significant excess of cancer cases due to exposure to chemicals at the site. However, more leukemia cases appeared than would be expected by chance. Birth weights were also significantly lower in 1971-1975 than other years. This period preceded construction of the slurry wall and is considered to be the time of greatest exposure.

With CANCAL and EPA's local history in mind, the state health department and the subcommittee took steps to ensure the credibility of the study. First, the study's findings, data, and methodology were submitted to an external peer review panel. The panel suggested several changes in the conclusions and recommended further study of some gaps in the data. The health subcommittee decided that research would continue beyond the release of the findings in hand.

Another important step was to make sure that committee members fully understood the findings and implications of the study. In the words of a state health department committee member,

They were essentially the community's elected representatives; they would be seen as the peer group. They were the people I would talk to if I lived there. These people would interact with the community on an ongoing basis. Because they were not scientists, they could better relate to the community.

The subcommittee prepared to release the study's findings at a public meeting in Lakeview. Anticipating the usual uproar at public meetings about the Monson site, the state health department looked for a spokesperson who had good listening skills, did not appear lofty, and was good at explaining complex issues to an audience that was not sophisticated about chemical exposure and its relationship to health. The health department prepared the spokesperson for likely questions with a "dry run" using experts as the audience to judge community reaction.

Findings were presented to Lakeview at a well-attended meeting in February 1989. Everyone on the subcommittee, even CANCAL and community representatives, made an effort to answer all questions fully and completely. According to a state health department committee member: "They (community representatives) actually chimed in and provided information to educate that person. They really owned that decision and weren't so much defending it as providing all the missing pieces from what they had learned."

In addition, full copies of the report were available to anyone who wanted one. According to the state health department administrator,

Giving people the option to have a full copy of the report to take home and read was also good. This gave the impression that there was nothing hidden; if they wanted something, it was there. Giving them the report communicated that we didn't want them to make just a snap impression.

Participants say that the meeting was completely unlike other public meetings with the EPA. Questions expressed concern and occasional frustration, but little anger or conflict. Although the study could not answer all questions about specific health problems, Lakeview largely accepted the fact that an honest effort had been made to investigate health risks about which they were concerned.

As successful as the meeting was, not everyone was completely satisfied. Problems with the study methodology left many health questions unanswered. The actual exposure levels were unknown. Also, the community continued to worry about specific cancer cases among individuals who lived near the landfill. The unanswered questions left some people frustrated and others feeling they had learned nothing new.

At the end of the meeting, some community members had questions that required additional attention. One subcommittee member, a county health officer, announced he would be available for such questions the following day. Because he happened to have lived in Lakeview for many years, he was familiar with the community and well known to residents. In private, he offered to answer questions that individuals might have and that they did not want to ask in the impersonal surroundings of a public meeting. The health officer explained that he knew the strengths and weaknesses of the study. Because residents knew him, they would trust his answers more than the answers of an outside expert. Several in Lakeview took advantage of his offer. After the meeting, he became an information resource for the community, often receiving phone calls about residents' health concerns.

TECHNICAL ASSISTANCE GRANT

After EPA distributed the on-site RIFS, CANCAL asked EPA and Congress for help to interpret the volumes of technical material. With pressure from Congress, the EPA agreed in May 1986 to give Lakeview and CANCAL a Technical Assistance Grant of $50,000. The money allowed Lakeview to hire an expert of its own choosing to review and interpret the piles of documents produced by the remedial process. EPA stipulated that the community had to assure broad citizen participation in using the funds. Local government created an advisory group to act as the formal grant recipient, including members of the Lakeview Environmental Commission, CANCAL, the public, and the borough council. The advisory group conferred another benefit: It forced all community factions to discuss their positions and work toward common goals. It also relieved the tension between CANCAL and the local government; CANCAL could provide the leadership it saw as necessary, while the local government regained its political authority.

Yet another advantage of the Technical Assistance Grant was that it forced EPA to work with the community. Because the regulations were unclear, neither EPA nor Lakeview knew how to apply for the funding. Over the following year, EPA officials helped Lakeview to put the grant application into the correct format. The process used in Lakeview later was incorporated into Superfund regulations.

A NEW SITE MANAGER

In mid-1986, when conflict was at its height, a new manager assumed responsibility at the site. The site manager was new to EPA and brought with him a very different perspective about community relations. To Lakeview, he simply appeared to be less of a bureaucrat and more of an environmentalist. In the words of a CANCAL member,

> He was more in tune with listening and communicating. He was an environmentalist in the true sense—he didn't wear the traditional blue suit. And he was a nice guy. Very intelligent—he didn't agree with everything we said, but he defended himself well.

Equally important, he created a new management style based on communication and mutual interest. In his words, he brought "a spirit that I would treat people as I would want to be treated if it was me that lived next to the landfill."

This attitude produced some tangible changes. Most important was the development of an ongoing dialogue between EPA and the community. The new site manager encouraged informal communication, made EPA more accessible, and instituted procedures to resolve unanswered questions. For example, before he made any formal contact with Lakeview, the new site manager asked for stakeholders' questions and concerns so they could be answered appropriately at the time of formal contact. The manager also held a series of informal "public availability days" during which EPA staff, their contractors, and community relations specialists could answer questions. He organized a series of small group meetings with the local politicians and CANCAL that could be more focused (with less screaming and yelling) than the big meetings. Finally, the manager improved access to information, assuring a timely and complete sharing of documents that CANCAL saw as critical. Monitoring reports, for example, were revised to make sure that chemicals of greatest concern to the community were included. Moreover, important findings or documents were distributed to key stakeholders prior to public distribution or presentation in the context of a public meeting. This allowed CANCAL to organize questions for the public meetings and to present them from a more informed position. These improvements in both formal and informal communication may have been the most important change in the relationship between CANCAL and the community. In the words of a CANCAL leader, "Maybe all the things [the health study and the Technical Assistance Grant] wouldn't have worked if you didn't have a guy with good communication skills. He brought us into the process and won us over."

SUMMARY AND EPILOGUE

EPA and the community developed an ongoing dialogue about the cleanup, addressing Lakeview's concerns as they arose. Not everyone was happy about every decision, but the conflict was resolved, and management problems became the new focus. The best evidence of this shift was the disappearance of CANCAL from the scene. At the end of the case, CANCAL existed in name only; the principal leader of CANCAL was elected to the borough council. His election and attention to Monson activities by the local environmental commission have helped disparate groups to speak as one voice in the management of this public health problem.

 KEY ISSUE

IMPROVING ORGANIZATIONAL CAPACITY TO CONFRONT RISKS

LAURA C. LEVITON

STEPHEN E. KAUFFMAN

The National Research Council (1989) emphasizes that risk communication is a two-way exchange of information. In fact, it implies that failure to engage in true dialogue and problem solving with the public puts our society at risk: "To remain democratic, a society must find ways to put specialized knowledge into the service of public choice and keep it from becoming the basis of power for an elite" (p. 15). This discussion therefore addresses three questions about how organizations that confront risks might increase their own capacity to work constructively with communities:

▲ What are the resources needed to improve and clarify risk communication?

▲ How can organizations improve their capacity to respond to communities?

▲ In an era of limited resources and fragmented public health responsibilities, what can be done to foster responsiveness?

Although this discussion focuses on organizational improvements, some readers may have taken on the other role in this relationship, that of a frustrated community activist struggling with an unresponsive bureaucracy. For community activists, some additional suggested readings appear at the end of the discussion.

Resources to improve effectiveness and clarity of risk communication. The need for such improvements, and the organizational obstacles, are all too common. Many have commented on the lack of responsiveness produced by legal and regulatory requirements, the difficulty of communicating scientific information, and the frequent lack of public relation skills in those who must communicate about risk to the public (National Research Council, 1989).

The early years of the Lakeview case provide a textbook example of how not to do risk communication. The Lakeview community blocked action for years on the Superfund cleanup of the nearby Monson landfill, one of the highest priorities for environmental cleanup in the nation. The community did so because EPA experts had failed to respond to their concerns and did not provide adequate opportunity to review the cleanup plan. Therefore, the community was dissatisfied with its opportunities to participate in decision making, opportunities that were mandated by federal law. A great deal of time and money were spent before the EPA altered its approach to the community, spent time in both formal and informal dialogue, and arrived at a negotiated solution.

Citizens often encounter certain barriers when they attempt true participation in risk communication about environmental problems. Several of these characterized the Lakeview situation:

1. There was no legal requirement that the citizens' choice must be the one selected.

2. The bureaucracy made decisions in routinized ways that did not readily allow true citizen participation.

3. The agenda of some government participants may have been to co-opt the public into a decision that the government had already made.

4. Mechanisms for participation (for example, public hearings) were not structured in such a way that they truly promoted participation.

5. Mechanisms for participation did not facilitate a dialogue, only a one-way communication process.

6. Information that was provided did not make the government's assumptions explicit.

7. Information was not easily available.

8. Decisions required understanding complex technical information. This body of information was overwhelmingly large for citizens to digest and required technical expertise that communities did not have.

9. The officials were trained as scientists or technicians, not in people-oriented skills.

Much has been written about making risk communication clear and accessible and ensuring meaningful participation of the public in decisions about health risks. This information is readily available to the reader. Material developed by researchers at Rutgers University is a helpful start for this purpose. They have produced guidelines that should alleviate some of the obstacles to which Kauffman alludes (Chess et al., 1988; Covello et al., 1988). It is helpful to have the explicit rules for communication these authors set forth (e.g., Be open and honest).

Other resources are available to promote clarity and effectiveness of risk communication. A treasured resource (and free) is the National

Cancer Institute (1989) publication, *Making Health Communication Programs Work.* This is a lucid presentation of the tools required to produce relevant, effective, and clear communications to a target audience. Techniques, including the use of focus groups and pretesting, are presented. To this day, such techniques are sadly neglected in many areas of risk communication. In addition, the National Cancer Institute publication focuses on the issue of readability, of critical importance whenever long, technical terms invade communications with the public. It is always feasible to reduce reading complexity. One author (Leviton) has reduced the reading level of risk communications from that required for postgraduate training to 8th grade level or less. It was not easy, but it was possible. Computer programs are also available to calculate reading level and will make suggestions to simplify language as well.

In general—no matter who the intended audience may be—it is useful to reduce the complexity of reading material. Think about physicians for example: They have to read complex information all day long. They are educated enough to read very complex information—but reading and understanding are more likely the simpler the language can be. One knowledgeable source quipped that when doctors leave the office, they won't even read the prospectus for an investment. As a class exercise, we have asked students to gauge the readability of a manual for "right to know" regulations, aimed at businesspeople. The reading level was the equivalent of first-year graduate school. Is it any wonder that small business owners "go ballistic" over government regulations? They need a full-time translator just to keep informed.

Simplifying language does not have to insult the reader's intelligence, provided that it is done appropriately. Recall Churchill's pithy sentence, "We will fight them on the beaches." The only word with more than one syllable was *beaches.* Good, plain, Anglo-Saxon terms will mostly get the point across.

Sometimes risk communications are unnecessarily complex and unclear to the readership because the authors have not paid sufficient attention to their own goals, much less to the interests or needs of the audience. In particular, the difficulty may arise from a felt need to portray adequately the complexity of science or findings in all communications that stakeholders receive. However, as long as stakeholders have access to more complex and thorough presentations, not every communication they receive has to be complex. Stakeholders can be provided with access to more technical documents placed in libraries or other local repositories, if they seek this level of detail (some will). The tendency toward unnecessarily complex writing may also come from a need to sound scientific or technical, in the belief that this ensures credibility. However, remember who you are writing for. The appearance of science is not the same as the actuality; in fact, unnecessary jargon that obscures the meaning of a risk communication falls into the category of "scientism"—the trappings and outward form of science without its substance. It takes real writing skill to achieve clarity as well as technical quality.

Improving organizational capacity to respond to communities. Bureaucracies' style of interaction is in some ways the antithesis of community. Bureaucracies typically have strong pressures to routinize and regularize their contacts with the public (Blau, 1963; Downs, 1967). This feature of bureaucratic life is driven by law and regulation in an effort to assure due process, accountability, and regularity in government. However, the routines of government do not necessarily encompass the dynamics of confronting risk. Where bureaucracies need routine and hierarchy, communities are spontaneous and informal in much of their communication (McKnight, 1995).

When risk communication or health problem-solving formats are mandated by regulation or law, even greater restrictions are placed on how bureaucracies can interact with communities (National Research Council, 1989). EPA was constrained by procedure in Lakeview. Administrators were constrained first to contact elected community officials when entering Lakeview. Publicizing the opportunities for public comment brought out a diverse group of people, but it was only afterward that a subset of those people could be seriously engaged over time on the issue.

In general, we can contrast the formal opportunities for dialogue with informal ones in Lakeview. For example, the limits of town meeting formats are clearly demonstrated; town meetings became formats for the expression of community frustration and name calling.

An informal communication process grew up side by side with the formal process in Lakeview, and was largely responsible for the eventual acceptance of the cleanup plan. In particular, communication and preparation between public meetings were a key to success in Lakeview. The study of health problems that might be linked to the Superfund site provides a good example of the value of informal communication. The coordinator of the state-sponsored study approached community members informally from the beginning and remained in contact with them and with their concerns. In providing the results to community members, the coordinator went beyond the public meeting format in which he shared the overall results of the study. Knowing that some people would not be willing to ask questions about their own health in a public forum, he invited them to respond to the results in private. Rather than specifying the form in which the public had to obtain information, he provided it to them in the form they required. This is what is called a *public servant*.

Informal communications do not replace the formal procedures set forth in law and regulation. In fact, there would be great danger in doing so—accountability requires hearings, meetings, and formal contacts. However, these do not appear to be sufficient for effective risk communication or problem solving.

One resource that can sometimes improve organizational capacity is a citizen advisory committee. However, as we saw in Chapter 3, such advisory bodies will not be effective if they are a pro forma exercise to comply with regulation or provide the appearance of bureaucratic responsiveness. A recent article summarizes what we know about citizen advisory committees for environmental issues (Lynn & Busenberg, 1995). The characteristics of effective committees and the pitfalls of work in this area are outlined. Recommendations include: outlining specific goals for the committees, assuring neutrality through broad representation, using facilitators, and taking a utilization-focused approach to research and its findings. Parenthetically, these authors note that only in 1995 was the EPA considering the incorporation of citizen advisory committees into its Superfund community relations program.

A citizen advisory committee, if properly formulated from the beginning, would have alleviated much of the time and cost devoted to dealing with the Lakeview problem. Such a committee eventually emerged in any case, but it was "home grown." It educated itself about the technical issues and was able to communicate them to the rest of the citizenry. In addition, this committee served several vital functions that helped to overcome some of the obstacles engendered by the EPA's situation. It was a stable force and an institutional memory, whereas EPA personnel shifted regularly. It was a source of informal communication and help, whereas the EPA was required to communicate primarily through formal channels. These obstacles were caused in part by the nature of federal bureaucracies. Overcoming these obstacles is the focus of our second key concept.

Another important feature of federal bureaucracies in agencies such as EPA is fairly regular turnover of staff. Unless a deliberate effort is made to share institutional learning and preserve trust, turnover will impair agencies' ability to maintain improved relationships with communities. In the Lakeview case, for example, there was very little continuity of staff to interact with community. The Lakeview community saw a procession of "suits" who seemed interchangeable but in fact were not. Important experience and information about Lakeview were lost when these staff left the project. Also, and critically, turnover in staff disrupted the informal lines of communication built up with community. In a real sense, this is public health infrastructure that may go ignored unless we understand its worth.

Community advisory committees can also help to overcome this problem. Although staff may turn over, advisory committees do not have to do so. Or they can turn over at a different rate, allowing individuals to share and preserve both institutional learning and agency-community relationships.

Coping with public health disarray. As shown by EPA's turnover problem, public health and environmental organizations are often limited— sometimes severely—by their own capacity to confront risk. During the period in question, the EPA did not have much experience in Superfund issues, had serious political constraints from the administration in power, and, it is fair to say, had limited talent on hand for communicating with the public. These forces derive from a larger national trend. The Institute of Medicine (1988) has concluded that, in general, infrastructure for public health is in serious disarray. Capacity is sometimes inadequate to carry out essential public health functions. Services and benefits of public health are not distributed equally among our population. Organizations designed to protect public health are fragmented or submerged in agencies with other missions, such as welfare or environmental protection. Certainly, the Lakeview case describes a proliferation of state and local agencies with responsibility for confronting risks.

Citizens have come to expect disappointment in their bureaucratic encounters concerning public health problems. Perrow and Guillen (1990) have described how organizations in the New York City area generally failed to cope with the AIDS epidemic. According to these authors, it is almost as though the disease had been designed to highlight weaknesses in our social and governmental structures. Edelstein and Wandersman (1987) have made the same point in discussing how bureaucracy and local government cannot seem to adequately assist people in dealing with toxic exposures.

Do public health organizations recognize the limits on their capacity? Not always, and not systematically. It is especially noteworthy that EPA personnel either did not recognize their lack of capacity to communicate with Lakeview or did not feel that consultation with communications experts was important.

For a better understanding of what public health organizations can and cannot accomplish, public health professionals have developed an important guide. A collaborative project of national, state, and local health organizations produced the APEXPH model (Assessment Protocol for Excellence in Public Health) (National Association of County Health Officials, 1991). The model guides readers through a two-part assessment process requiring participation of all portions of the organization. First, public health organizations assess their internal capacity for carrying out public health functions. Second, the organizations assess their capacity for working with the communities affected by public health problems.

Institutional learning about risk communication is possible. Capacity building about these issues is feasible. However, growth in the relevant organizations is more likely to occur if the organizations make use of community resources, such as citizens advisory committees and the public health infrastructure of trust.

NOTE

1. In this case study, stakeholders were guaranteed anonymity. As a result, we changed names of places and withheld our documentation for quotations and sources.

SUGGESTED READINGS FOR COMMUNITY
ACTIVISTS INVOLVED IN ENVIRONMENTAL HEALTH*

Amy, D. (1987). *The politics of environmental mediation*. New York: Columbia University Press.

Bobo, K., Kendall, J., & Max, S. (1991). *Organizing for social change: A manual for activists in the 1990s*. Cabin John, MD: Seven Locks Press.

Boyle, H. C. (1989). *Commonwealth: A return to citizen action*. New York: Free Press.

Hadden, S. G. (1989). *A citizen's right to know: Risk communications and public policy*. Boulder, CO: Westview.

Legator, M. S., & Strawn, S. F. (Eds.). (1993). *Chemical alert! A community action handbook*. Austin: University of Texas Press.

Ross, D. K., & Nader, R. (1973). *A public citizen's action manual*. New York: Grossman.

Staples, L. (1984). *Roots to power: A manual for grassroots organizing*. New York: Praeger.

Wasserman, G. (1982). *The basics of American politics* (3rd ed.). Boston: Little, Brown.

* Adapted from Needleman, C. (1995). Nursing advocacy at the policy level. In Institute of Medicine (Eds.), *Nursing, health, and the environment* (pp. 253-262). Washington, DC: National Academy Press.

CHAPTER 7

COMMUNITY TEAMWORK ON AIDS CARE

LAURA C. LEVITON

INTRODUCTION[1]

This case describes a city in which community leaders came together to solve problems of AIDS care. The relatively low number of AIDS cases forced different types of arrangements and resources than we saw in the coastal cities. The solutions were innovative and demonstrated a collaborative style that is typical of the city's leadership. Although not everyone was perfectly satisfied with the result, the city boasted an excellent record on AIDS care.

The case illustrates several points concerning community problem solving.

1. It describes a process whereby previously marginal groups became players in community leadership, while

establishment leaders became stakeholders in a so-called gay disease.

2. It illustrates the advantages and perhaps the limitations of a nonconfrontational problem-solving style.

3. It shows what can be done about health problems, even in communities that have few apparent resources and perceive many higher-priority problems.

4. It demonstrates that constructive action can turn a political "no-win" issue to stakeholders' advantage.

KEY ISSUE AND GENERAL QUESTIONS

This case illustrates the advantages of conflict resolution, negotiation, and collaboration in restructuring services for people living with HIV and AIDS. How these processes are conducted, and their key roles in constructive problem solving, are still underappreciated by professionals who confront public health risks. The discussion addresses three general questions:

▲ What are the advantages of conflict resolution, negotiation, and collaboration?

▲ What power do various stakeholders possess? Why is this important?

▲ What is the collaborative process?

STAKEHOLDERS

People living with AIDS
River City AIDS Task Force
Other River City AIDS service organizations
River City Health Department
State health department
State Department of Public Welfare (DPW)
River City hospitals
River City nonprofit nursing homes
River City Council (and city-run nursing homes)

Unionized nursing home workers
River City foundations
Media
Blue Cross

 TIMELINE

1981	First AIDS case diagnosed locally
	Reagan era budgets reduce funds for health planning
1982	Decentralization and budget cuts for federal public health begin
1983	AIDS-related problems begin in River City
1984	River City AIDS task force is organized
1985	Task force begins advocacy efforts
	County nursing home sees first AIDS patient
	Task force develops bylaws and elects board
1986	Acute care settings see decline in fear and discrimination
	River City Community Consortium on AIDS (RCCCA) is formed
	Intense local media attention begins
	Demise of federal funding for health system planning
	State health department scrapes up funds for planning
1987	Many organizations join RCCCA
	Demise of local health systems agency
1988	Task force hires executive director and paid staff
	DPW begins interagency task force meetings
	Foundation-funded meeting on AIDS patients in long-term care
	DPW hosts regional meetings on caring for people with AIDS
	Governor gives his first speech on AIDS

SECTION I

BACKGROUND: "TROUBLE IN RIVER CITY"

DESCRIPTION OF THE COMMUNITY

River City was typical of many midsize metropolitan areas that saw the "second wave" of AIDS cases. Located in the middle Atlantic states, the metropolitan population of about 3 million and city population of about 400,000 were primarily white and derived from a mix of European nationalities. The population of the surrounding counties was primarily rural. For decades, River City lost a large proportion of its population, as younger people sought jobs elsewhere. The older citizens were left behind. River City also underwent a dramatic economic transition from a heavy industrial base to primarily white-collar employment. In spite of this shift, much of the blue-collar population remained, especially the older people. Neighborhoods were extremely stable and traditional. The white-collar worker generally adhered to conservative norms of behavior.

This situation offered both advantages and disadvantages to River City. Social support networks for longtime residents were strong, neighbors were friendly and supportive, the crime rate was fairly low, and the environment was generally safe. At the same time, people kept stubbornly to tradition, often showing active prejudice against outsiders and those who deviated from the norm.

According to River City AIDS activists, these prejudices applied especially to homosexual and bisexual men, although comparisons with other cities would be very difficult to make. Nationally, definitions of civil rights did not include sexual preference. Legally, gays could be denied housing, child custody, and marriage and could be fired from their jobs or from the military. The River City Council had recently failed to pass a local ordinance enforcing the civil rights of homosexuals. However, many activists were surprised that it was even raised and debated.

Most gay and bisexual men in the metropolitan area were hidden. Conservative community values made it difficult for gays to admit their sexual preferences to their families. The AIDS epidemic forced many of them out of the closet. After an initial shock, most River City families helped relatives with AIDS. Many people with AIDS came back to River City after becoming ill. In spite of prejudice, River City families were often willing to look after their own.

COMMUNITY AND STATE LEADERSHIP

The River City style of dealing with community problems was "don't make waves." Cooperation was the approved strategy. Community members tended to form committees to work out problems, rather than engaging in public name calling or seeking publicity for their cause at the expense of others. Public confrontations did occur, especially in politics. However, low-key, behind-the-scenes negotiation was the norm for most community concerns. "Team players" were valued by those active in community life. A fairly small number of players—almost a clique—were likely to deliberate on any public issue. They knew each other and had worked together on other issues in the past.

Foundations and corporations exerted a major influence on many aspects of life in River City. In fact, many would claim that River City was the home of corporate social responsibility, given the dramatic improvements since the 1950s in the environment, the physical appearance of the city, and the quality of education, health care, and cultural life. Although foundations and corporations were less powerful than they once had been, they continued to be extremely influential in the community and, in particular, exerted influence on nonprofit and voluntary agencies.

County government, headed by three commissioners, was especially important to AIDS care in River City because it controlled many services important for people with AIDS. For example, it funded a fairly large independent health department, regarded as one of the stronger county health departments in the country. However, it had recently been necessary for the health department to cut back on services, and specifically those services relating to patient care. The health department maintained a large, active program on sexually transmitted disease (STD) that early on became key to AIDS services planning. Like most health departments in the nation, however, it had few resources to deal with AIDS health care.

Although the county government did not fund any hospitals or acute care settings, it did administer four large public nursing home facilities. The large aging population of the region was greatly increasing the demand and need for these nursing homes, at the same time that the area was losing its tax base of younger employed citizens. Other county social service administrators complained that the nursing homes consumed many resources in an era of public fiscal constraints.

Fiscal woes for the local government were also reflected at the state level. The state health department had experienced deep budget cuts and attrition of staff during the late seventies and early eighties. Federal Reagan-era budget cuts and the loss of health planning authority made the situation even worse. The state health department gave some support to specific programs such as AIDS education but clearly could not take a leadership role.

The state Department of Public Welfare (DPW) was much more powerful than the state health department. DPW staff said that the DPW budget was larger than that of many Third World countries. Through Medicaid, DPW paid for much of the public medical care in the state. DPW also provided direct services at state hospitals, mental hospitals, centers for delinquent youth, and mental health and mental retardation units. DPW contracted with still other agencies for many services, including public assistance payments, day care for children, mental retardation and mental health services, personal care homes, children and youth agencies, and adoption agencies. All these organizations were likely to encounter people with AIDS.

THE HEALTH CARE SYSTEM
IN RIVER CITY

The health insurance market was dominated by a fiscally sound Blue Cross and Blue Shield. However, "the Blues'" market share had started to erode as large companies tried to contain health care costs. Blue Cross made important contributions to civic life, and few insiders would doubt its reputation for corporate responsibility. To meet concerns over cost containment, Blue Cross developed a for-profit subsidiary aimed at managing use of hospital-based services.

Medicaid paid health care for the poor. Controlled by both federal and state regulations, Medicaid placed limits on service, especially services for nursing homes and personal care. Patients requiring such care were often forced to spend most of their personal resources before becoming eligible for Medicaid. Nursing homes in the state generally claimed that Medicaid did not pay them enough. In the mid-1980s, state per capita payments for long-term care were far below the national average.

Nonprofit community hospitals and tertiary care centers dominated the River City health care system. These hospitals strongly identified with communities that were intensely loyal to them. A single for-profit hospital in the area was "beyond the pale," in the view of many. No public or charity hospital was needed because by long-standing agreement, all institutions shared the burden of indigent and Medicaid patients.

Hospitals had become less cooperative and more vulnerable to problems in recent years. The decline in population over three decades led to downsizing, mergers, and joint ventures. Institutions launched aggressive marketing campaigns to attract patients. In addition, hospitals had to cope with national cost-containment measures under Medicare. With the stated aim of controlling these trends and assuring continued access and quality of health care, local foundations and corporations worked with hospital management leadership and boards of directors to develop a community plan for hospital restructuring.

Nursing homes were of three types. Patient care at the large county nursing homes was paid by Medicaid. Although the for-profit and nonprofit homes took some Medicaid patients, the county nursing home was the major source of care for individuals who had exhausted their own savings. For-profit homes were in fairly good supply, but they were expensive. Several religion-affiliated nonprofit homes had excellent reputations and were seen as taking the lead for innovation and addressing community concerns. Long waiting lists were common for a bed in nonprofit homes, although the recent opening of several new for-profit homes had led to several months in which even Medicaid patients were actually able to "shop around" for what they perceived as the best facility.

Nursing homes distinguish between skilled care, in which people need round-the-clock nursing care, and intermediate care, in which patients need supervision and protection. In River City, a chronic problem was the supply of intermediate care beds, especially in light of the aging population. For many years, families often had to seek care for sick relatives in other states. Although this situation had been alleviated somewhat, a new problem took its place: A sicker patient was being seen in the skilled care facilities, due to cost-containment in the hospitals. Long-term care problems were also compounded by the relative lack of suitable alternatives to nursing homes. These alternatives include home health services and other supportive home services; personal care boarding homes, and adult day care. Reimbursement levels and limits on home health care in particular continued to be a problem. Furthermore, in the absence of a supportive family member or friend, many people simply did not have the help they needed to continue to live at home. These problems were compounded if suitable housing was not available to an individual—the case for many people with AIDS.

AIDS IN RIVER CITY

The medical director of the county health department's STD program managed one of the first AIDS cases identified in the nation. In the view of many, this episode reflected the high degree of scientific and technical expertise on AIDS that served the community extremely well. The STD medical director also served on the faculty of the River City Medical School, and he later become a coinvestigator on all medical school projects dealing with AIDS. He worked with area hospitals on the AIDS issue and became a prime mover to educate the general public about AIDS.

In River City, work began on the virology and epidemiology of AIDS in 1982. Several major projects for treatment served as an important base for organizational and community action. Cases occurred primarily in the homosexual and bisexual population. The number of reported cases in the River City area was one of the lowest in the nation for cities of comparable size. Even though the available information was flawed, this makes sense. River City was not a major destination for tourism, transportation, or migration. Young people had moved away. Now, people with AIDS were coming home to die.

River City became nationally known for its good fortune to have medical and public health professionals and researchers who took an early interest in AIDS and achieved eminence in the field. This interest was not typical of medical schools or researchers in the nation as a whole (Panem, 1988; Shilts, 1987). Much larger cities had few medical researchers willing to provide technical resources, and a notable lack of interest continues in several hard-hit cities to this day.

SUMMARY

A traditional, blue-collar community in transition, River City faced many pressing problems besides the AIDS epidemic. The number of AIDS cases was very low until well into the 1980s. The public health agencies were in financial trouble and had been stripped of their mandates for health planning and for medical services. The medical care system faced lean and mean times in which the welfare of marginal patient groups posed some major concerns. Yet, the community also offered important resources for coping with the epidemic and the continuing need for health planning.

SECTION II

SECURING HEALTH CARE FOR PEOPLE WITH AIDS

HOSPITALS' TREATMENT OF PATIENTS WITH AIDS

In 1983 and early 1984, advocates saw overwhelming gaps in service to people with AIDS, problems that typified AIDS care nationwide. Information about the disease and its prevention were minimal early in the epidemic. People had nowhere to turn for specialized care or for advice on issues such as finding funeral homes and applying for Supplemental Security Income from the federal government. In hospitals, AIDS patients were ignored and did not receive proper therapy; nurses refused to serve them, and meals were not brought to them. By 1985, advocates began to see a decline in health professionals' fear and ignorance regarding HIV transmission. However, fear and consequent problems for patient care still occurred regularly, and many institutions were not consistent in their treatment of people with AIDS.

Among health professionals, those working in acute care hospitals had made the most progress in dealing with adverse reactions to people with AIDS. Most hospitals had advocacy committees that provided a way to get action on cases of fear or discrimination. The committees also forced the hospitals to look at existing policies and see how they applied to people with AIDS.

River City hospitals agreed that all members of their trade association would share in the treatment of AIDS patients. This agreement was consistent with the general pattern in the region, that all "problem" cases were in principle shared among institutions. In the case of AIDS, however, it gave hospitals "safety in numbers"—some assurance that other patients, staff, and physicians would not shun any single institution that treated a lot of AIDS patients.

Although the hospitals shared AIDS cases in principle, the distribution was still fairly uneven, in the view of at least one advocate. One hospital saw many AIDS patients due to its link to well-funded research efforts. Another hospital saw many AIDS patients due to its association with a physician who was familiar and comfortable with sexual minority health issues. Through word of mouth, the hospital gained a reputation for competent and compassionate care for people with AIDS.

CONTINUING GAPS IN SERVICE

Once hospitals began to cooperate, the most important gaps in service became housing and long-term care services. Many disabled people with AIDS had no home to which they could return after leaving the hospital. They lost their homes because they lost their jobs, or because of repeated medical expenses. They lost apartments because the landlords found out they had AIDS. Many did not have the kind of family or friends with whom they could live. Yet, having a home opened the door to a wider range of services. For example, home health services were generally available to people with AIDS who had health care coverage. Some people believed that it was easier for people with AIDS to get home therapy than to get nursing home care because it was cheaper. Others speculated that home care agencies were more willing to serve people with AIDS because patients treated at home did not know each other, as they would in nursing homes.

The exact level of need for nursing homes was unclear in the mid-1980s. Policy analysts believed that 50% of people with AIDS would need short-term skilled care at some point each year, whereas 20% would need longer-term care in either skilled nursing facilities or intermediate care facilities. Even so, very few AIDS patients were discharged to nursing homes. According to one analyst, the nursing home shortage meant that AIDS patients competed directly with the elderly for available beds. By the time that many people with AIDS acknowledged the need for a nursing home, they were already quite deteriorated. In River City, Blue Cross's experience was that relatively few patients needed a nursing home, whereas many more needed home care. The general pattern for people with AIDS was a slow deterioration in the hospital. Long-term care facilities saw people with AIDS when they were quite frail and disabled.

People with AIDS were most likely to need nursing home care when they experienced HIV encephalopathy and AIDS dementia. Patients who were no longer ambulatory were also candidates for nursing homes. People with AIDS dementia had special needs and tended to fall between the cracks. Neither the long-term care system nor the mental health/ mental retardation system was prepared to serve the demented person with AIDS. Nursing homes stated that they were not able to care for an AIDS dementia patient, fearing biting, spitting, and wandering problems. AIDS advocates responded that the homes already served patients that were demented for other reasons. Why should AIDS patients be different?

Nursing home staff did require some special training about AIDS. According to a state planning document, people with AIDS needed frequent medical reevaluation for development of opportunistic infections. Staff workers needed to become familiar with the drugs used to prevent and treat such infections. They needed to recognize drug side effects, and they needed to follow universal precautions to minimize their own exposure to blood and body fluids.

The typical AIDS patient in a nursing home was a man in his mid-thirties. That made it rather easy for other residents to figure out the diagnosis, because the average nursing home patient was an 84-year-old woman. Nursing home administrators had no idea how they would handle this problem.

A SLOW RESPONSE AND
A LEADERSHIP VACUUM

Gaps in service caused several AIDS advocacy organizations to form. Typical of the nation as a whole, these organizations filled a leadership vacuum (Altman, 1988). The consensus was that River City was slow to recognize an epidemic and especially slow in providing services to people with AIDS. Although the scientific and medical community were actively involved from the very start, neither the public agencies nor the traditional nonprofit agencies took much initiative in providing services. Most advocates believe this was not primarily because AIDS was a new disease. Rather, there was no interest because AIDS patients were gay. Politicians, for example, believed AIDS was a losing issue because the gay stigma was attached. The county commissioners delegated leadership to the health department, not recognizing any special need for service.

The state health department's responsibility was for reporting, preventing, and planning, not providing service. However, the drastic loss of staff for state health planning meant that there could be no proactive planning for AIDS care. Also, the state had no time or resources to adjust, and AIDS services did not fit well into any of its existing structures.

A community leader who moved to River City in 1985 was struck by the minimal reaction to AIDS. Where she came from, some of her friends were dying of AIDS. She noted that many more pressing health care problems were perceived to exist in River City. Some critics have pointed out that, given the magnitude of the other health problems, the reaction to AIDS may have been appropriate. The numbers of the elderly, the indigent, and people without insurance certainly outweighed the number of AIDS cases. The director of the STD clinic agreed that people felt no urgency about dealing with AIDS problems. On the other hand, River City was able to study the experiences of the cities that had been hard hit by AIDS already. This provided the city with the opportunity to plan and prepare for prevention and for services to people with AIDS.

THE RIVER CITY AIDS TASK FORCE

An AIDS researcher at the university stimulated much of the initial coordination and integration of services for people with AIDS. He knew that to study the epidemic successfully, he needed the cooperation of the gay community. He collaborated with several gay physicians and formed a community advisory board with substantial gay representation. Recruiters and some staff for the study were also gay.

The staff and community board quickly found themselves becoming the focal point for information and referrals about AIDS in the city. People would call, desperate for assistance in getting services, and with a wide variety of questions concerning AIDS. The staff and community board discussed this problem, and in late 1984, five of them formed the River City AIDS Task Force, an advocacy and service organization for people with AIDS. The university research project provided many resources for startup in the form of space, post office boxes, mailing, and other services. Association with the study and with a university lent prestige and credibility to the task force, in the view of one of its founders and board members.

The task force began as a completely voluntary agency. Individuals were identified as leaders because of their compassion and visibility, because they fit in with the group, and because they had skills to champion the cause of people with AIDS. During the first year, the task force developed from a strictly informal grassroots organization, in which decisions were arrived at by consensus, into an organization with bylaws and a board elected by the membership.

The task force took on three major advocacy issues: education to overcome health professionals' fears, quality of care, and discrimination.

Initially, local advocates concentrated on acute care settings, especially on talking with individual nurses, physicians, and other providers. Later, the tactics changed in that they concentrated on building the skills of health care workers. Self-help groups and assertiveness training for people with AIDS served an advocacy role as well.

The chair of the task force was deeply involved in medical staff education about AIDS and felt that the best antidote to fear of AIDS was firsthand experience. She believed that people eventually become desensitized to unrealistic fears of infection. Also, because staff can be stigmatized by their roles in treating people with AIDS, trainers need to address the concerns of family members and spouses. Other advocates said that if individuals persist in being unrealistically fearful of people with AIDS, there may be some underlying homophobia.

Quality of care and discrimination issues encompassed more systematic difficulties in a health care organization. The executive director of the task force described the sequence of events in advocating for people with AIDS: a problem arose, it came to the attention of advocates, advocates made sufficient noise to get an agency to respond, education and training were provided to staff, problems were negotiated between advocates and the agency, the agency gained experience in dealing with the issue, and change resulted.

The task force deliberately chose a style of advocacy that was different from AIDS advocacy groups in other cities. The task force preferred to operate in a nonconfrontational, low-key manner. When service providers discriminated or mistreated people, the task force documented the problem and tried to locate a reasonable person in the service organization with whom to work. If this did not work, the task force advocacy committee "raised a ruckus" with the organization involved, along with a not-so-subtle threat to expose discrimination and poor service. This was rarely necessary. The task force advocacy committee used social worker volunteers who were familiar with the health care system and were used to serving as advocates in that system.

Some individuals took a more confrontational approach, including family members who felt service was denied to loved ones and younger, more militant gays, who tended not to be leaders of the gay community. One respondent mentioned that the more militant individuals served a valuable function, especially if they coordinated their goals with those who worked "in the system." They brought attention to community problems, and they also made other advocates look more reasonable.

The task force also used a buddy system for advocacy, to assure quality of care and to provide emotional support. Buddies were assigned to people with AIDS and helped them in dealing with the system. If difficulties arose, the buddy's job was to act as an advocate or to call in additional help from task force advocacy specialists, supervisors, or case managers. Attorneys volunteered in difficult cases of discrimination.

The local media gave almost constant attention to AIDS, beginning in 1986. Relations with the media were complex, given their focus on drama and victimization. However, the task force worked with the media to bring the epidemic to the public's attention and to indicate problems of service delivery to people with AIDS.

Although raising controversy might have led to more attention to their problems, the task force worried about a backlash against people with AIDS. Their media relations were therefore deliberately non-alarmist and "responsible," in the words of one task force member. The approach was to provide facts about the extent of the epidemic and about prevention. In fact, one respondent from the task force believed that the media wanted the task force to be more alarmist than it was.

This approach to advocacy and to the media fit the overall style of community action in River City. Several advocates doubted a more confrontational approach would work very well in this community. A backlash might have come from confrontation due to the community's attitudes about homosexuality. River City's approach contrasted with that of a larger nearby city, where AIDS advocates not only launched public protests at the offices of service providers but publicly denounced each other as well.

TASK FORCE GROWING PAINS

The growth in AIDS cases required a change in the task force. A paid director, receptionist/secretary, and director of client services were brought on. The organization was in conflict about this change, because its volunteers were a vital resource. At the same time, volunteers could no longer do everything, and some members of the task force were resisting this idea. The organization faced several dilemmas. One was how to create a new and more effective organizational structure that still maintained the connection to human issues. The second was how to maintain lines of authority when individuals simultaneously had to be leaders and grassroots people, or board members and hands-on volunteers. Third, the growth in cases meant that some issues had to take priority over others. The task force could no longer do everything. Finally, the task force had to handle volunteers' perception that their importance was decreasing. Staff expansion was necessary given the increased demand for services. An increase in volunteers from 18 in 1985 to 400 in 1989 meant that someone had to manage the volunteers.

The increase in cases also brought great frustration over paying for services. State health department funding for community services came extremely slowly. Although the state ranked 7th in the number of AIDS cases at the end of the 1980s, it ranked 38th in state-contributed payment for AIDS services. In addition, the state health department had delays in the release of monies when they were available. In some instances, contracts were not signed until well after projects were to have started. The state also established an "equal share" strategy for distribution of available funds among 13 community-based AIDS organizations. The River City AIDS Task Force, working with the second-highest number of cases in the state, received essentially the same number of dollars as AIDS task forces in smaller communities and rural areas where the epidemic was just beginning.

Fund raising for the task force illustrated the degree to which the organization was able to gain public acceptance. It also illustrated the limits on public acceptance. Although the gay community continued to provide the lion's share of funding, other establishment organizations slowly began to do so. The task force held annual public auctions, first held at a gay bar and later at a prestigious suburban country club. The City Council provided a grant for task force operations in 1987, made possible only because of the support of one councilman. The River City Foundation gave a grant, as well as low-key support to coordinate and plan AIDS services. A few other local foundations expressed a mild interest in supporting AIDS-related activities. Federal dollars came slowly and, prior to the Ryan White Act, went mostly to research, not community services.

DEVELOPMENT OF OTHER
AIDS SERVICE ORGANIZATIONS

The year 1986 brought the development of other organizations designed to address the problem. In the view of some, this meant a diffusion of responsibility for AIDS services, planning, and coordination. Others saw the development in a more positive light, pointing out that one did not see the same range of AIDS advocacy groups that would exist, for example, in San Francisco or Boston.

Besides the task force, three other organizations developed services for people with AIDS. One was a long-established mental health center that counseled sexual minorities. Its mission expanded to counsel people with AIDS, their families, and significant others. A second organization was a drop-in center created by and for people with AIDS/HIV and supported by a local religious organization. The drop-in center served family members, friends, and caregivers and focused on opportunities to socialize. The third organization was the Hemophilia Center, which provided medical, social, and counseling services for its HIV-infected clients and their families. The center also played a discreet public advocacy role on behalf of AIDS care.

A small interagency task force was charged with planning and coordinating county agency AIDS services, but it was not very active and did not include private community-based AIDS organizations. The county government delegated responsibility for AIDS to the health department, even though the health department had neither the mandate nor the resources to affect health and social services.

In 1986, the task force and other AIDS service providers created the River City Coordinating Council on AIDS, or RCCCA. RCCCA was to be a communication and planning network: to prevent duplication, identify gaps in service, and coordinate services to people with AIDS. RCCCA identified the need for a local AIDS hotline and the need for recreation activities for people with AIDS. Many community organizations joined RCCCA, but most did not encounter people with AIDS very often. RCCCA provided a forum for discussing AIDS and served as a seal of approval for members, but it had no authority to coordinate service and never gained official recognition from political leadership.

SUMMARY

AIDS advocates were fairly successful in overcoming individual fear and prejudice and increasing hospitals' responsiveness. The AIDS task force experienced growing pains as the number of AIDS cases grew. They chose a nonconfrontational style, in line with the general style of the River City community. AIDS organizations proliferated as support for AIDS became fashionable, but their effectiveness was questionable and planning became diffuse. Most important, their power to create and pay for services was very limited. Who did have the power, and would they use it on behalf of people with AIDS?

SECTION III

ADDRESSING GAPS IN SERVICE

LEADERSHIP FROM BLUE CROSS

A former vice president of Blue Cross was one of the first community leaders to bring up the AIDS issue. He saw how the epidemic affected health care in other cities, and quite early in River City's experience, he insisted that Blue Cross develop a reimbursement and case management strategy. AIDS was changing, and Blue Cross was faced with a group that was living longer and could be served outside a hospital. Blue Cross often paid for alternatives to hospital care for subscribers, even if such alternatives were not normally part of the medical insurance plan, provided that such care was both appropriate and less expensive than hospitalization.

Case management made sense for people with AIDS, because they could use the level of care that was appropriate for their needs. In the absence of other services, people with AIDS might stay in hospitals for months. Both quality of life and health care suffered when other services were not available and people with AIDS had to remain in the hospital. Under the case management system, Blue Cross could add services to the subscriber benefit package, provided that the services would be more beneficial and save money. Blue Cross paid only for medical services, although case managers could and did help people with AIDS to secure other services. For example, they helped one man to find housing.

Blue Cross case managers also identified the most cost-effective settings for care. For example, drug therapy was cheaper at home than in an institution. The case managers used their knowledge of benefits and health care systems to work effectively with the patient. No patient was compelled to abide by the case manager's recommendation. Case management was less costly to subscribers through their premium payments, and most important, people with AIDS did not exhaust their benefits as quickly. In other cities, people with AIDS were quickly spending their life savings on unnecessary hospital care.

Normally, employers would pay for case management services from Blue Cross, but for people with AIDS, case management is "a community service," indirectly paid by all Blue Cross subscribers. This protected the confidentiality of people with AIDS. To inform employers that their organization even had a person with AIDS would put undue pressure on Blue Cross to reveal the person's identity.

Early in the development of case management for people with AIDS, Blue Cross staff sought out the community organizations in town, to let them know what the case management system would involve. They did so in order to explain exactly what could be provided in the way of services, the manner in which confidentiality would be preserved, and the fact that acceptance of case management was strictly voluntary. By approaching the community organizations, Blue Cross staff aimed at helping them feel comfortable talking with their clients who had Blue Cross coverage, in case any person with AIDS was distrustful of Blue Cross or reluctant to participate.

On the other hand, Blue Cross was a business. There was a limit to what they could provide to subscribers. This created some concern on the part of AIDS advocates and a lingering skepticism of Blue Cross. Health insurance was for health care needs, not daily living needs. Most people did not understand insurance benefits, and when they suffered

a catastrophic health problem, understanding became even more difficult. This was true for all people, not only people with AIDS.

LEADERSHIP FROM THE
COUNTY NURSING HOME

The four county nursing homes were some of the first nursing homes in
the country to admit people with AIDS. The county homes were taking
a risk, because even in a publicly paid institution, fear of AIDS on the
part of staff or patients could have produced serious consequences.
Thanks to good planning and preparation, this did not happen.

Referrals of people with AIDS came so quickly to the county nursing
homes that there was very little time to implement an education and
training program. Only staff, not patients, were trained, because of the
urgency. It was difficult to notify and educate patients in advance. A
full-time infection control officer was on staff, made possible because of
the sheer size of the county homes. A leader in the field of infection
control for long-term care, this individual was consulted by many other
nursing homes regarding AIDS and won a national award for her work.
Her credibility as a nun made her effective as a trainer; staff felt she
would not hide dangers from them. Her style of teaching also conveyed
her sincerity. She used case studies and couched the information in such
a way that the lowest-paid staff could understand.

Education and training about AIDS seemed "almost routine" in
terms of the staff's acceptance. Although the union might have raised
concerns in other circumstances, the AFL-CIO had recently published
guidelines on AIDS in the workplace. Therefore, management was able
to refer employees back to the union-produced guidelines.

An example indicates the general approach to handling employee
skepticism about HIV training. A toilet clogged up in the room of a
person with AIDS. Although the plumbers had received substantial
training from the county home, they refused to fix the toilet, because it
would force them into bodily contact with the fluids of a person with
AIDS. The director of the county health department intervened. When
he could not persuade the plumbers, he offered to fix the toilet himself,
if the plumbers would show him what to do. When the plumbers saw

the director was ready to put himself in their place, they agreed to fix the toilet.

Managers of the county home facilities were anxious when at last they admitted a person with AIDS. However, staff became fairly attached to this person, who was warm and very personable. The man was only in the facility for a week before he died, but several staff attended his funeral. One manager said he expected to be deluged with phone calls when his facility took a person with AIDS. He had expected family members of patients to come to him saying, "What's going on here?" but this did not really happen very much.

COMMUNITY LEADERS AND THE NONPROFIT HOMES

By 1988, the River City AIDS Task Force was serving notice to local nursing homes that people with AIDS needed their services. Thanks to the efforts of the task force, public bodies with some clout also began to intervene, including the Office of Civil Rights of the U.S. Public Health Service, DPW, and the State Human Relations Commission. Nursing homes in general had avoided AIDS admissions, often citing the contagious disease regulations concerning tuberculosis. The task force dealt with this obstacle by obtaining an interpretation of those regulations, as they did or did not apply to AIDS, from the state health department. This not only provided advocates with ammunition in writing, but alerted the health department to the problem and made the health department and nursing homes aware that an advocacy group with some level of sophistication was watching.

Although it seems adversarial, this activity remained in line with the advocates' low-key approach. Especially for the nonprofit homes, this helped; one administrator mentioned that his colleagues respond better to need than to pressure.

In early 1988, the River City Foundation organized a meeting of AIDS advocates, health experts, and the executives and board members of local nursing homes. The foundation also made money available to these homes for training of their staff in the area of AIDS. The meeting served notice that long-term care for people with AIDS was now important to the wider community, as well as to AIDS advocates. The hospitals and the county home shared their experiences. Blue Cross administrators encouraged nursing home admissions for people with AIDS, by offering to consider a higher rate of payment.

One foundation officer noted that it was very important to have a private sector physician take the lead in giving the facts about AIDS to this group. Although the county's STD officer made an excellent public speaker on AIDS, he would not have been persuasive to leaders in the nursing home field. The county and state health departments regulated nursing homes, so that there was an adversarial relationship. A private and well-respected physician, on the other hand, found a receptive audience among nursing home administrators and board members.

At this meeting, participants also challenged several beliefs that had impeded serving AIDS patients. First, some in the audience expressed concern about infection control. A state official pointed out that nursing homes had to certify that they could handle all types of infection control. If they could not do so in the case of AIDS, then their certification was in doubt. Second, allegations were made that people with AIDS were more costly for nursing homes than other types of patients. A local nursing home administrator challenged this assumption, because managed care had pretty much eliminated any group of patients that was not quite sick. Although some studies claimed to show that AIDS was more costly than other conditions in a nursing home, a state report concluded that the costs were not excessive for AIDS patients.

The hospital trade association had been attempting to encourage mergers and closer ties between hospitals and nursing homes for some time. The nursing homes were concerned about infection control, as well as transfers of AIDS patients back to acute care hospitals. The hospital association pointed to the AIDS situation to persuade nursing homes that they needed hospital affiliation, which would help them to manage infection control and patient transfers and to access superior technical expertise in treatment. In summer 1988, a conference was organized to encourage joint ventures between hospitals and nursing homes, for caring for people with AIDS.

Four nonprofit homes agreed to consider taking people with AIDS and trained their staff for that purpose. All nursing homes that made the commitment to take AIDS patients acted in a very low-key manner. They felt it was a little easier for the county homes to announce their policy than it was for the nonprofit homes. Medicaid patients and their families could not walk away from the county homes—they needed care. But private pay patients at a nonprofit facility could well afford to do so. The administrators expected some trouble, but there was none. There was no mass exodus of patients through fear of infection.

The nursing homes all realized that they would eventually be forced to take people with AIDS. Some were threatened with action by the Office of Civil Rights. Also, they are aware of a case pending in another state in which a nursing home was sued for a failure to admit a person with AIDS. The goal of the River City nursing homes was to produce a joint statement that they would all take some people with AIDS. In the "safety in numbers" approach, no one institution was singled out as the "AIDS facility." All shared the responsibility and would not suffer financially by the departure of their other patients.

Most of the participating homes took AIDS patients within the year. Although relatively few patients were admitted, River City was well ahead of all other communities in dealing with this issue. In cities with a high number of AIDS cases, segregated facilities served long-term care needs. The low number of cases precluded this choice in River City and communities of similar size.

LEADERSHIP FROM DPW

Like Blue Cross, DPW had incentives to make sure that the appropriate and less costly care was available. DPW applied for a waiver from the federal system to permit Medicaid payment of case management for eligible AIDS patients. Also funded under the waiver were services: homemaker visits, extended home health visits, services of home health aides, supplies, and nutritional services. These were not normally paid by Medicaid. AIDS advocates from River City and around the state cooperated with DPW in the development of the plan for this waiver. It was unusual for DPW to develop plans in conjunction with advocacy groups. DPW benefited from the advice of AIDS advocates because it obtained a more realistic idea of the nature of AIDS services.

However, AIDS advocates disagreed with DPW on several issues. DPW would not permit case management organizations to deliver services as well. Advocates pointed out that the organizations closest to the problem were currently providing services and would be most sensitive to the case management needs of people with AIDS. Advocates saw such regulations as somewhat arbitrary on the part of the state and the federal government. DPW representatives pointed out, however, that their hands were tied whenever the federal Medicaid program insisted on rigid requirements and procedures. Medicaid was concerned about use of services and saw an independent case management agency as its best guarantee of control over services.

Most of the service agencies funded by DPW were likely to encounter people with AIDS or HIV-infected individuals. The fearful reactions seen in health settings repeated themselves in welfare offices, child welfare settings, and many other social service agencies, disrupting access by eligible state citizens. DPW set about correcting this situation in several ways. A special unit within DPW developed a network on AIDS matters and contacted various program administrators and contractor agencies when they were felt to be acting inappropriately regarding AIDS. This unit also trained the 32,000 DPW employees about AIDS, as well as contractors and agencies that were paid by Medicaid for services to eligible patients. Through this training, the DPW hoped to deal with service providers' fears, as well as the special fears of the managers and board members of such organizations.

The DPW special unit formed a statewide task force of agencies serving people with AIDS. Although these agencies generally competed sharply for resources, the DPW unit had convinced them that developing good policy on AIDS was in their own best interest.

The special unit handled discrimination against people with AIDS in the DPW system. The unit intervened and provided education and supervisory support. Staff were warned that continued discrimination would lead to disciplinary action. In one case, an HIV-positive person was admitted to an institution, and the staff walked out at 3 p.m. on a Friday afternoon. They would not serve the individual. The special unit had to provide service for the people who were at this facility.

The unit required each contractor agency to designate an AIDS coordinator, who was supposed to provide training and see to it that no discrimination occurred. The unit also developed policies for contractors to prevent future discrimination. The unit disapproved any plan that agencies developed unless staff were trained to their satisfaction and services were provided to people with AIDS.

DPW officials were intrigued to learn how River City leaders had persuaded nursing homes to take people with AIDS. Many areas of the state have very few nursing homes, and the public is not sophisticated about AIDS. Provider fears of being shunned as the AIDS facility are even greater in such areas than they would be in River City. The River City Foundation offered to fund regional meetings for DPW contracting agencies and their boards of directors. These meetings had the same format as the nursing home meeting in River City. Local community leaders went on record to advocate facilities' sharing services to people with AIDS. Although these meetings met with good acceptance, it remains to be seen whether the safety in numbers strategy can work in more rural areas of the state.

At long last, in June 1988, the governor gave a speech on AIDS. This was the first significant public address that included the promise of funds and programs. Yet, DPW had acted to ameliorate the problems of people with AIDS long before the governor's speech.

SUMMARY

The proliferation of cases, as well as their impact on service systems and health care reimbursement systems, eventually meant that the wider community got involved in planning for AIDS care. In typical River City fashion, much of the decision making was done by committee. The town committed itself to case management for AIDS care, to expanded services for AIDS patients after they left the hospital, and to their admission to nursing homes. These developments were followed closely by state level decision makers, who collaborated with AIDS advocacy groups.

 KEY ISSUE
CONFLICT RESOLUTION, NEGOTIATION, AND COLLABORATION

We end with the River City case because it is in many ways the most complex: Many stakeholders were active on AIDS issues, and their actions made it possible to improve the way the community treated people with AIDS. Discrimination was kept to a minimum, AIDS services organizations generally worked well together, and nursing home care for people with AIDS was the envy of communities everywhere.

On the surface, everything looked pleasant and positive in this case study. Yet, no stakeholders gave in to any solution that was contrary to their interests. Moreover, it was clear where the stakeholders' interests lay. Stakeholders may collaborate, but they never do so against their own interests. The River City stakeholders skillfully used conflict resolution, negotiation, and collaboration. This discussion addresses three general questions:

▲ What are the advantages of conflict resolution, negotiation, and collaboration?

▲ What power do various stakeholders possess? Why is this important?

▲ What is the collaborative process?

At the end of the discussion, some additional readings on conflict resolution, negotiation, and collaboration are offered to the interested reader.

Conflict resolution and negotiation: Needed skills in confronting risk. Often, competing interests rise to the surface and create conflict over risks. The cases in this book are rife with conflicts about the risk, its causes, potential solutions, social construction, and side effects. The conflict can prevent discovery of options that may satisfy stakeholders. Conflict leads to hardening of positions, in which stakeholders may end up reiterating demands and failing to listen. Often a zero-sum game is assumed: a winner and a loser. The possibility of benefits to all stakeholders is not considered. Solutions that use an adversarial approach are often expensive and rarely satisfactory to all stakeholders (Gray, 1989).

These messy and complex situations require skilled conflict resolution and negotiation. In the seminal book *Getting to Yes,* Fisher, Ury, and Patton (1991) set forth a variety of principles to assist in overcoming conflict. The key to conflict resolution is to avoid what the authors term *positional bargaining,* that is, the tendency to get committed or locked into solutions and preferences. This process wastes time, can ruin productive relationships, and can end in a stalemate or a solution that is not satisfactory to anybody.

To avoid positional bargaining and reach solutions that all parties can accept, the authors recommend separating personal and professional relationships from the problem at hand. In the case study of Chapter 4, for example, workers exposed to a carcinogen became estranged from their attorney when they disagreed with his proposals about settling lawsuits. Destroyed through their disagreement was a satisfactory long-term relationship in which he had represented workers' families for years. *Getting to Yes* recommends, "be soft on the person and hard on the issue." In other words, it is not necessary to give in to the other side to keep a productive relationship, or at least keep lines of communication open. In River City, AIDS activists were often powerful but rarely strident. They were able to talk to agency heads, offer suggestions for training, and speak to the consequences of continued discrimination without name calling. Activism in several other case studies had proven highly stressful, often because the activists focused on personalities, not issues.

A second important point in *Getting to Yes* involves getting a good understanding of stakeholders' interests. This cannot be done very well if positions have hardened so that a negotiator cannot understand or identify those interests. We all make assumptions about other people that may or may not be grounded in reality. Those can drive our own positions or harden them, and they need to be checked. In River City, plumbers at the county nursing home initially believed they were being put at risk of HIV infection by professionals who would never venture to do the job themselves. They were only persuaded when the county health director volunteered to unplug a toilet himself. *Getting to Yes* recommends, "Don't deduce their intentions from your fears."

A key to successful negotiation is that "interests define the problem" (Fisher et al., 1991). Once one understands stakeholders' real interests, it becomes easier to develop solutions that satisfy everyone's interests. Positional bargaining does not reveal those interests, because demands are stated without the necessary background. In River City, the low number of AIDS cases meant that stakeholders did not initially see an interest in collaboration on AIDS care. Later, these interests emerged in sharp focus. For example, Blue Cross had an interest in making sure that subscribers preserved their benefits as long as possible. This interest coincided with task force efforts to extend services for people with AIDS; although they had few illusions about the insurer, the task force abided by its ground rules for case management. The nonprofit nursing homes had an interest in providing services in line with their mission. Yet at the same time, public fear of AIDS meant that they might lose paying patients—even be ruined—if they took people with AIDS.

River City also offers a good example of what Fisher et al. (1991) call principled negotiation, that is, negotiation that appeals to objective criteria or principles. The task force negotiated for AIDS services on the basis of principle: that people with AIDS were entitled to services under the law. While acknowledging agency and staff fears, the task force argued from the facts: The fears were groundless.

Collaboration. The stakeholders in River City went beyond negotiation to collaboration. In an extremely helpful text, *Collaborating: Finding Common Ground for Multiparty Problems,* Barbara Gray (1989) describes key features of collaboration:

> Collaborative processes protect each party's interests by guaranteeing that they are heard and understood. In addition, the processes are structured to ensure that ownership of the solution remains with the participants since ratification hinges on their reaching agreement among themselves. (p. 22)

McKnight and Kretzmann (1990) would say that community leaders in River City were successful in accessing important institutional capacities on behalf of AIDS care. Strength built on strength. The health department had expertise in the epidemic and shared it early on to anticipate likely experience. The university shared its research-based resources to help develop the task force. Blue Cross wanted to clarify service and save subscribers benefits and therefore assisted the task force. The county nursing home had a positive experience with its first AIDS patient and made this known to others. The hospitals provided a model for how to share AIDS cases in a collaborative way.

Individuals also contributed by the way they conducted themselves. AIDS advocates were not generally strident. Turf issues developed but were minimized in public. What if the first AIDS patient in the county nursing home had been someone less likable? A good first impression may have increased staff willingness to house AIDS patients. The health department director was willing to do the same job for an AIDS patient that he asked plumbers to do. The integrity of the infection control officer increased people's trust in the safety of admitting AIDS patients.

Gray (1989) describes several incentives that stakeholders have to collaborate. Three of these often apply to confronting risks: blurred boundaries for authority and responsibility (as in the case of AIDS care) where policy dialogues can clarify these issues; declining or unavailable governmental revenues (for example, to address AIDS care or worker screening), which encourages the development of public-private partnerships; and dissatisfaction with legal and regulatory ways to deal with disputes.

Gray (1989) describes several other ways of settling differences, but they often lead to unsatisfactory results. Adversarial strategies can be time consuming and costly. Also, court-settled disputes often exclude important stakeholders who might have something to contribute to a collaborative solution. Resolution by experts may not address stakeholder concerns and may not obtain buy-in from all concerned.

Understanding stakeholder power. Key to collaboration is shared power. Stakeholders rarely collaborate when they have the power to achieve their objectives independently. However, emerging issues (such as AIDS in the 1980s) make it less likely that single organizations can reach a solution independently. In the River City case study, no single group had the power to achieve its aims alone—collaboration helped them share power to achieve negotiated goals. Under collaborative arrangements, "a group of stakeholders have mutually authorized each other to reach a decision" (Gray, 1989, p. 119). Power may be shared to define the problem, to propose a solution, or to implement the solution.

Think about who had power in the River City case study. Certainly, Blue Cross, the DPW, and local foundations had power over the other stakeholders. They could reward and punish others with money. In addition, DPW could impose legal requirements. However, some types of stakeholder power were surprising. For example, the AIDS task force, through its informal, low-key discussions, exercised several kinds of power. Certainly, they had the power to embarrass. No institution wanted to appear less than beneficent, given the city's "go along, get along" team-player orientation. The task force needed only to imply a threat of potential media exposure or legal action to gain a forum for its concerns. A second source of power was the threat of legal action. Finally, the task force had a resource these institutions knew they needed: the capacity to train staff on many aspects of AIDS care.

Another unlikely stakeholder group with power were the hospital and nursing home workers. They had the ability to wreck AIDS care and confidentiality, if they were not consulted. The administration paid them and could fire them—but as DPW learned, workers can also walk out en masse, leaving AIDS care to the bosses. The incident between plumbers and the director of the health department shows vividly that workers were more persuaded by leadership and the power of example than they were by either risk communication or the threat of sanctions.

The role of these workers illustrates the point that some stakeholders have more power at the implementation stage, once agreement is reached, than at the negotiation or problem-solving stage. One can imagine, for example, what would have happened if the AIDS task force and other advocates had used court action to force institutions to accept people with AIDS. They would have complied—but in all likelihood, the effort would have been sabotaged at the level of implementation. The spirit of an agreement would have been violated, if not the letter. We saw this kind of violation in Garden City, where teachers complied with directives to include HIV-infected kids in class but used rubber gloves and disinfectant in the class as well.

The collaborative process. Figure 7.1 outlines Gray's (1989) description of the collaborative process. She identifies three distinct stages, each with its major objectives and activities: problem setting, direction setting, and implementation.

In problem setting, a key activity is to get the various stakeholders to the table. Examples of "tables" are seen throughout the River City case, ranging from informal discussions between institutions and the AIDS task force, to quasi-public meetings of nursing home providers

Phase 1:	Problem setting
	common definition of problem
	commitment to collaborate
	identification of stakeholders
	legitimacy of stakeholders
	convener characteristics
	identification of resources
Phase 2:	Direction setting
	establishing ground rules
	agenda setting
	organizing subgroups
	joint information search
	exploring options
	reaching agreement and closing the deal
Phase 3:	Implementation
	dealing with constituencies
	building external support
	structuring
	monitoring the agreement and ensuring compliance

Figure 7.1. The Collaborative Process
Source: Barbara Gray, *Collaborating,* San Francisco, CA: Jossey-Bass, 1989, p. 57. Reprinted with permission.

and AIDS advocates, to public sessions between the state DPW and its providers and contractors.

Stakeholders must develop a common definition of the problem. In the River City case study, the problem was initially ill defined—what is to be done with people with AIDS?—and became crystallized as: How can people with AIDS gain access to nursing homes and other services? Identifying stakeholders and recognizing their legitimacy in collaboration are also important activities at this stage.

Gaining the commitment to collaborate involves stakeholder judgments of five issues, according to Gray (1989). We explore those judgments for one stakeholder group in the case study, the nonprofit nursing homes:

1. *Does the present situation fail to serve my interests?* For nursing homes it did, because they might eventually be forced to accept AIDS

patients with or without collaboration among the homes and with or without the resources that other stakeholders could provide to ease the transition.

2. *Will collaboration produce positive outcomes?* This would not have been clear to nursing homes initially. However, when the public nursing home took an AIDS patient and nothing bad happened, the nonprofit homes became more willing. Also, they got expert advice on infection control and training—the best available.

3. *Is it possible to reach a fair agreement?* Once several nonprofit homes agreed to take people with AIDS, the safety in numbers approach assured fairness—no one would become known as the AIDS facility and lose paying patients. This expectation of fairness was reinforced by the sponsorship of powerful community interests who would react strongly to any indication of bad faith. It was also strengthened by the long-standing hospital tradition of sharing indigent care.

4. *Is there parity among the stakeholders?* Parity refers to whether the stakeholders have relatively equal power in the situation. Certainly some of the other players had more power, but this was the best deal the nursing homes were going to get.

5. *Will the other side agree to collaborate?* The answer was yes. Several nursing homes agreed to take part.

The role of the convener is very important to this process. Gray (1989) notes,

> Delicate shuttle diplomacy by a third party or by the convening stakeholders is frequently necessary to decipher the obstacles to collaboration and to tease out a problem definition that is sufficiently broad or ambiguous to incorporate the agendas of multiple stakeholders. (p. 58)

In this case study, the convener for nursing homes could not be a state or local health official; however, the foundation community was able to fill that role. However, in other circumstances, health department officials often make excellent conveners. Particularly when a new or emerging community problem is affecting health, public health officials can gain much by collaboration that extends the amount and type of resources to address the problems. Public health departments can sometimes gain in stature by convening problem-solving efforts.

Stakeholders must be perceived as legitimate; this occurred over time for AIDS services organizations as the epidemic progressed. Also, resources are needed to keep the collaboration on track: for the collection of data, for example. In River City, foundations agreed to provide these resources; later during implementation, DPW and Blue Cross became important to assist in the development of training materials and public relations strategies for other nursing home residents.

The second phase, direction setting, involves important activities that are a prerequisite to action, as well as specific problem-solving activities. Establishing ground rules is especially important when relations have become adversarial in any way. Setting the agenda means reaching agreement about what issues can be discussed. This is also helpful when conflict has been prevalent in the past; although it was not necessary, agenda setting in River City might have included the stipulation that no one discuss the origins of the AIDS epidemic or speculate about whether it was God's punishment of homosexuality. Agenda setting is useful to separate the issues that can be resolved from those that cannot.

Subgroups may be organized to reflect stakeholder interest and expertise. For example, a subgroup in River City might examine infection control issues; a second subgroup, reimbursement of nursing home care; and a third group might examine how to explain the presence of HIV-infected patients to other nursing home residents. Joint information search assures that everyone is operating from the same information and assumptions. It is a prerequisite for developing options that can then be explored. Finally, this phase includes reaching agreement (formal or informal) and closing the deal.

At the implementation phase, stakeholders must first explain the agreement to their constituencies. For example, the AIDS task force needed to explain the agreement to its membership, which then assessed whether the plan was acceptable to them. Nursing homes had to begin the process of training staff and educating residents as to what would happen. External support must be built. In this case, the River City collaboration gained the interest and support of DPW, which then attempted to replicate it elsewhere in the state. The newspapers and hospital association also endorsed the agreement. Structure is needed in order to execute the agreement, especially if it is not automatic. In the River City case, participants agreed to a timetable for introducing AIDS patients into the nursing home settings, as well as a format for staff training. Finally, it is helpful to plan for mechanisms of monitoring the agreement and ensuring compliance. In the River City case, monitoring would be carried out by the AIDS task force and other AIDS service organizations, as well as DPW and, if necessary, the courts.

NOTE

1. In this case study, stakeholders were guaranteed anonymity. As a result, we changed names of places and withheld our documentation for quotes and sources.

SUGGESTED READINGS ON CONFLICT RESOLUTION, NEGOTIATION, AND COLLABORATION*

Avery, M. (1985). *Building united judgment: A handbook for consensus decision making.* Madison, WI: The Center for Conflict Resolution. Address orders to: New Society Publishers, P.O. Box 582, Santa Cruz, CA 95061-0582.

Bagwell, M., & Clements, S. (1985). *A political handbook for health professionals.* Boston: Little, Brown.

Biagi, B. (undated). *Working together: A manual for helping groups work more effectively.* Amherst, MA: Center for Organizational and Community Development. Address orders to: 225 Furcolo Hall, University of Massachusetts, Amherst, MA 01003.

Brown, C. R. (1990). *The art of coalition building: A guide for community leaders.* New York: The American Jewish Committee.

Sparks, D. B. (1982). *The dynamics of effective negotiation.* Houston, TX: Gulf Publishing Company.

---

*Adapted from Needleman C. (1995). Nursing advocacy at the policy level. In Institute of Medicine (Eds.), *Nursing, health, and the environment* (pp. 253-262). Washington, DC: National Academy Press.

CHAPTER 8

RISK CONFRONTATION

Tasks, Criteria, and Evaluation

LAURA C. LEVITON

MAURICE A. SHAPIRO

This last chapter is by no means the final word on issues of importance when confronting risks. It is instead an essay in the original sense of the word: an attempt. We will essay a synthesis of the points made in the book, identify needs for changes in practice, and propose methods to evaluate risk confrontation.

Confronting risk is defined as a problem-solving process in which stakeholders attempt to cope with several consequences of a risk. These consequences include physical or medical consequences posed by the health problem. They also include a variety of other consequences caused by society's reactions to the problem—the way the problem is defined socially. In Chapter 1, we made a case that confronting risk is a complex undertaking. The current formal definitions of risk assessment, risk management, and risk communication place boundaries around some very messy problems. However, these definitions do not encompass the array of issues and tasks that are necessary to plan and implement successful methods to confront risk.

Successful risk confrontation occurs when negative consequences are avoided and positive ones are optimized. Positive and negative consequences are defined by consensus of the stakeholders where this is possible. Where no consensus is possible, these can still be identified as potential consequences for debate and discussion. Finally, they can be defined as positive or negative using as criteria the balance of ethical principles outlined at the end of Chapter 4: beneficence, autonomy, justice, and efficiency.

WHAT CONSTITUTES
RISK CONFRONTATION?

Risk confrontation is defined as a problem-solving process. The process includes several major elements that are outlined in this book. In this section, we describe the elements, indicate the advantages of taking them into formal consideration, and speculate about why they seem to be neglected in public health practice. The central point is that by considering them, it is sometimes possible to craft a better problem-solving process.

History of the risk problem. The problem's history is both scientific (technical or physical) and social (or socially constructed). For example, lead exposures in Port Royal (Chapter 3) came about because of the history of emissions from nearby industry. However, the Port Royal community also shared a social history that highlighted past failures of government to address the problem. The history of a problem can be almost completely local in focus, as in the history of HIV in the schools of Garden City (Chapter 5). Alternatively, it can involve national players, as when the Classic Chemical workers (Chapter 4) became a national symbol of workers' right to know about exposures that might harm their health. The history can be a shared interpretation so that there is a common understanding, as in River City concerning AIDS care (Chapter 7). Often, however, the problem's history will be filtered through individual and community worldviews, so that one wonders whether the same set of events is really being described by different people (for example, Chapter 4). Finally, history continues: The risk problem and efforts at solution continue to evolve over time (for example, Chapters 2 and 6).

The social history of risk problems often seems neglected, to the detriment of constructive risk confrontation. Or if understood, it is interpreted within a technical, physical, or medical framework. Social issues are addressed primarily as they affect that framework. These are not particularly new assertions, as outlined in Chapter 2. Why, then, do these tendencies persist?

The way that projects are currently organized, staffed, and funded contributes to this tendency. Experts tend to be called in for a specific period of time and to treat the problem in an episodic fashion. Categorical funding and time-limited projects in public health programs contribute to a short-term view. Furthermore, turnover in government organizations contributes to this tendency, because institutional memory is flawed and haphazard. New employees will only rarely be briefed in detail concerning the social history of the risk problem. It is noteworthy that, in both case studies that concerned the AIDS epidemic, certain professionals were involved with community concerns over a long period. Their ongoing involvement may have assisted them to develop innovative solutions (Chapters 5 and 7). In the same way, the successful worker notification program of Chapter 2 benefited form NIOSH wisdom developed in Chapter 4.

Stakeholders. The process of confronting risk also has stakeholders, defined as those who have a stake in the problem or its solution. Stakeholders themselves have several key attributes: interests, power, legitimacy, and participation. It is not entirely obvious who the stakeholders are; nor is their legitimacy always self-evident. Sometimes legitimate stakeholders can be excluded inadvertently, as in Port Royal, where researchers simply did not know who the real power brokers in the community were (Chapter 3). If recognized, their interests and power still may or may not be well understood. Even if interests and power are understood, stakeholders may still be excluded from decision making concerning the risk, as seen in Lakeview (Chapter 6). If included formally, they may or may not prevail in negotiations.

It is rare that experts systematically seek out all relevant stakeholders when they confront risks. Granted, this task can be somewhat difficult, and community insiders themselves may not have identified all the legitimate stakeholders. It is rarely sufficient to put an announcement in the paper requesting comments on regulation or announcing a public hearing. It may be necessary to seek out stakeholders more actively, something that government agencies may not have resources to do. Indeed, regulation or law may preclude them from doing so. For this purpose, third parties can be especially effective, as in Hilltown (Chapter 2) or River City (Chapter 7). Yet, their participation must be planned.

Decision-making venues. The process has decision-making venues, which may be formal, as in the case of the Hilltown Chemical workers' advisory committee in Chapter 2. They may also be informal, as when the River City AIDS Task Force (Chapter 7) sat down with agencies to solve problems of access or discrimination. Sometimes, formal and informal venues may function side by side, as when the EPA and Lakeview residents finally developed a committee for mutual education that functioned in parallel with EPA's official Superfund process (Chapter 6).

Decision-making venues often require a convener who is able to bring various stakeholders to the table. As seen in the case studies, the choice of a convener can be critical. In Chapter 2, a neutral university group had to convene the Hilltown Chemical worker advisory group. In Chapter 7, the health department could not convene nursing homes to negotiate on AIDS care, because it already had an adversarial relationship due to the need to inspect and enforce standards. In other circumstances, the health department is an ideal convener when perceived as an agency without interests that compete with those of other stakeholders.

Risk assessment, risk management, and risk communication have most often relied on the formal and more public decision-making venues. However, for various reasons, these venues are unlikely to be conducive to the processes of conflict resolution, negotiation, and collaboration. Within the more public venues, stakeholders may not be willing to forgo positional bargaining. They may not be willing to admit to their real interests. Brainstorming and development of options are often hindered by public venues and may be precluded by the rules of procedure in many formal venues. To the extent that these processes are valuable to the development of constructive solutions, it may be desirable to foster informal venues, side by side with the formal ones. It is understood that informal decision venues have their own abuses: Open public hearings were created largely to avoid secrecy, exclusion of citizens, and backroom deal-cutting. However, the public forum for confronting risks does not always operate as it should to include citizens, foster their understanding of issues, or reach constructive conclusions. To ensure true participation, both formal and informal venues are necessary.

Organizational and community capacities. Both communities and organizations have capacities that can be accessed for the problem-solving process. Capacities can include resources, power, talent, and leadership. As illustrated in Chapter 5, even the poorest community has capacity that can be developed to solve risk problems. As seen in Chapter 6, more advantaged communities have at their command a wide variety of resources that can be brought to bear on the problem. When recognized and developed, these capacities can contribute to constructive and innovative solutions.

Declining organizational capacity to address public health problems is a cause for serious concern. Not every health department can confront risk successfully, given reduced budgets, limited time, and a dearth of experienced staff. We do not wish to tantalize professionals with goals they cannot reach, given the resources available. At the same time, this situation argues even more powerfully for the need to identify, engage, and develop relevant capacity in both community and professional partners. We have seen public health professionals convene meetings to address a problem, then achieve excellent implementation together with other agencies and volunteers, extending their influence far beyond the available staff.

If community and organizational capacities are truly limited, then planning and implementation need to take that into account. However, it is worthwhile to check one's assumptions. Professionals sometimes dismiss community capacities and focus on deficits. This is unfortunate, because by themselves, professionals may have limited ability to achieve their goals. Assumptions about organizations can also be harmful. Although health departments are not rich in resources, they may still have untapped capacity that they can bring to bear. For example, in Chapter 6, the study of a toxic dump's potential health effects was directed by a health officer who was a veteran of partner notification for sexually transmitted diseases. His prior experiences led him to develop interpersonal skills that were highly beneficial to communicate the study's results sensitively. In Chapter 7, various River City professionals employed by county government had demonstrated their ability to achieve cooperation and consensus because of their track record of trust and their leadership by example.

Cognitive and interpersonal tasks. Risk confrontation also involves several cognitive and interpersonal tasks, including: reaching a shared definition of the risk problem, generating proposals for action, debating those proposals, and implementing the proposals. Because risk problems evolve, there may be several iterations of this sequence of tasks. The definition of the risk problem changes over time, as new information and experience emerge. This was seen clearly in Chapter 7, as River City gained more experience in caring for people with AIDS. The problem can be defined strictly in terms of the physical risk, as in Chapter 3, where lead contamination seemed logically to require study and screening. Despite this assumption by the experts, the need for these activities was by no means clear to residents of the affected area. In general, we believe that definition of the problem will be more complete, informative, and useful when the idea that risks are socially constructed is at least considered, and when it is recognized that there are multiple valid perspectives on the problem and its consequences.

The tasks of generating, debating, and implementing proposals for action often do take social consequences into account. Nevertheless, the primary focus is usually on the abatement of physical risk or prevention of disease. Those who manage risks often seem uncomfortable with, and may even feel helpless to influence, the social consequences of a risk. They understandably prefer to recommend actions on the more scientific problems of exposure, disease or likely disease, and quantified probabilities. Social consequences seem less certain, less predictable, "mushy," and difficult to weigh in the balance.

The social definition and consequences of risk have become legitimate scientific problems. Also, they clearly influence the options available for risk management. Nevertheless, these social consequences are often not anticipated when they might be. When they are anticipated, they are often viewed as improper or impossible to control, whereas the physical and medical consequences of risk are thought to be more controllable.

These habits of thought are not helpful. Social consequences of public health risks do lend themselves to prediction and also to some control (or at least, amelioration). As outlined in Chapter 2, the scientific study of risk perception is now well-developed. A good deal is known about how humans perceive probabilities; about the way they process risk information; and about specific knowledge, lack of knowledge, and misunderstandings concerning the operation of health and environmental risks. Furthermore, as described in Chapter 7, the dynamics underlying conflict resolution, negotiation, and collaboration are well understood. As seen in Chapter 3, the analysis of communities and of stakeholder groups has advanced at least far enough to allow anticipation of interests, likely power, and perceived legitimacy.

Therefore, it is argued that the social consequences of confronting risk can be anticipated and ameliorated to a greater degree than is the common practice for planning, debating, and implementing solutions to risk problems. The consequences of planning for worker notification in Hilltown (Chapter 2) and for AIDS care in River City (Chapter 7) demonstrate that this is possible. The way in which findings on health effects were shared in Lakeview (Chapter 6) demonstrates that negative social consequences can be minimized when due care is taken. Other examples are available (e.g., Tillet et al., 1986).

WHAT ARE THE CRITERIA FOR SUCCESSFUL RISK CONFRONTATION?

To begin a discussion of criteria, it is essential to review the definition of risk confrontation. It is a problem-solving process that addresses both health and social consequences of a health risk. To establish criteria for success is to assign value to this process and to its consequences. We can begin by contrasting risk confrontation and risk communication. The

National Research Council (1989) distinguished two general approaches to risk communication. These two approaches focus on the role of government and can be labeled *informational* and *interventionist*. In the first approach, the goal is an informed public that can make its own decisions about how to solve a risk problem. Successful disclosure of information to the public was the criterion. The other approach is more activist, involving attempts to influence people's compliance with public health recommendations. In this view, the appropriateness of influence attempts depends on the particular risk situation. The criteria for success would include both successful behavior change and public acceptability of efforts to induce such change. In addition, appropriateness of persuasive attempts by government depends on the balance of ethical principles outlined in Chapter 4. Autonomy must be balanced against beneficence, justice with efficiency.

Confronting risk inevitably requires intervention, if not by government, then by someone. It requires intervention by definition: It is a problem-solving process that develops options to take action (although one option is always to do nothing). By definition, it also addresses a wider range of consequences that go beyond those identified as a result of information or persuasion. Although it is possible that government could limit itself to providing information for decisions, or even to persuasion, it is not possible to limit the consequences of risk confrontation to the ones identified for risk communication. Because it requires action, we reject the idea that risk confrontation amounts to the same thing as public relations. Certainly, public relations ought to be part of the tool bag of public health practitioners, just as risk communication should be.

While maintaining that risk confrontation ought to be evaluated against a wider range of consequences, we can adopt the two criteria used for the interventionist approach to risk communication: public acceptability and application of the ethical principles of public health. However, using these criteria is not easy. It requires judgments about what was possible to achieve as well as what was achieved. Such judgments are feasible only when the judges have enough experience to recognize opportunities that were seized or ignored.

The result can be fairly subtle. For one thing, a good problem-solving process ought to expand or optimize the available decisions, as often occurs in negotiation and collaboration. One could inform the public exceedingly clearly about a risk, leaving decisions up to them. But what if their decisions are all limited to brutally unpleasant options? Can that be good public health practice? What about opening some options that were otherwise not available? Throughout this volume, actions of stakeholders operated to increase available options or, tragically, to preclude them.

Because the consequences involve more than information for health decisions, it becomes critical to define what constitutes acceptable activity and successful consequences. These case studies have described a variety of consequences that were alleviated, left unchanged, or worsened by confronting risk. Some of these consequences apply to individuals, others to communities, and still others to societies. Consequences for the individual and community can be classified as:

- ❖ Medical: ignoring an opportunity to protect personal health, Chapter 3; increased access to care, Chapter 7
- ❖ Economic: job loss, Chapter 2; property values, Chapter 6; preservation of insurance benefits and savings, Chapter 7
- ❖ Environmental: Superfund decisions, Chapters 2 and 6
- ❖ Educational: teacher-student relations, Chapter 5
- ❖ Personal: stress and its influence on interpersonal relations, Chapters 2 and 4

Some consequences affect society's long-term ability to cope with problems. These include

- ❖ Changes in the public's trust of government (reduced in Chapters 2 and 4; increased in Chapters 6 and 7)
- ❖ Changes in the cooperative relationships between institutions and communities (Chapters 2, 4, 5, and 7)
- ❖ Changes in community capacity to cope with problems (diminished in Chapters 4 and 6; enhanced in Chapters 5 and 6)
- ❖ Changes in public health services infrastructure (improvement, Chapter 5; impairment, Chapter 2, section 1)

These are only a few of the ways to characterize the societal consequences of risk confrontation. To do a comprehensive classification, additional study is required that uses the collective wisdom of seasoned public health practitioners.

EVALUATING RISK CONFRONTATION

This section addresses three challenges for evaluation that arise because of the need to address a wider range of consequences. These three challenges include: identifying all the consequences that stakeholders judge to be relevant and then assigning value to those consequences; evaluating the problem-solving process; and relating the quality of the process to the identified consequences—in particular, to public health outcomes.

Challenge 1: Identifying and valuing the consequences. It is not possible to anticipate all consequences, identify them in a timely fashion, or control their effects on communities. Some can be anticipated, as when residents fear for their property values or parents fear for children's health. These seem to take priority on a fairly regular basis when communities confront health risks. As experience is gained with a wider variety of risk situations, the frequency and severity of these consequences, and others, ought to be established empirically. Empirical study will assist the professional to anticipate and ameliorate the consequences. It is important to discover additional consequences and to document their association with particular kinds of physical risk and problem-solving activity. The use of the case survey method, as described by Yin (1984), might be appropriate. In this method, features of many case studies are content-analyzed; to examine risk confrontation, we might content-analyze the variety of consequences and the attributes of the problem-solving process. Certainly, numerous case studies of environmental risk problems are available. Unfortunately, they do not all document the elements of problem solving as one might wish.

Current methods of study cannot definitively attribute success to the way stakeholders confront risk. These activities occur in open systems, not in controlled studies. Until this issue can be better addressed, we would endorse Michael Scriven's (1967, 1991) emphasis on evaluation as the assignment of value to a program or product. In

Scriven's terms, all the attributes of a risk situation can be assigned a value. They are good or bad in themselves, just as *Consumer Reports* can assign good and bad attributes of a toaster: price, safety, durability, quality of toast, and so forth. In this use of the term *evaluation,* it is not necessary to limit ourselves to any stated objectives of risk problem solving. Indeed, we should not do so, given stakeholders' current tendency to define the objectives primarily in technical or medical terms. This perspective frees the evaluator to detect and assign value to the variety of consequences that may affect the public.

The consequences of confronting risks can be assigned values. To discover the consequences and their attributes, exploratory and qualitative methods are required. One way to develop a sense of these attributes is to interview a variety of stakeholders, building a list of potential consequences, until redundancy of information is achieved— that is, no additional consequences or attributes are discovered. Then, the list might be shared with all stakeholders, and individual perceptions of consequences could be verified by other stakeholders. A modified delphi technique can be employed, in which the revised list of attributes could be assigned values by the stakeholders and by independent judges familiar with similar situations.

This method would respect and recognize the fact that not all consequences can be anticipated. The method would work best when there was at least some consensus among stakeholders regarding the facts. It would work better in the case studies of Chapters 2 and 7, for example, than in the case studies of Chapters 3 and 4. Where stakeholders disagree about the facts concerning consequences, then independent verification might be sought through documentation or key informants. Where stakeholders agree on the facts but disagree on the value assigned to consequences, such disagreements should be documented and preserved, rather than aiming for a false consensus (Mitroff & Kilmann, 1978).

Challenge 2: Evaluating the problem-solving process. A variety of process features can be evaluated when we confront risk. These might serve as a checklist for evaluation. For each question, standards of evidence might be employed, similar to those used in verifying the list of consequences. The key aspects of process reviewed in this book include:

1. Have the professionals studied the social and technical history of the risk problem?

2. Do professionals understand that the risk has a socially constructed definition as well as a technical one?

3. Have the relevant stakeholders been identified?

4. Are the stakeholders' interests understood?

5. Is the stakeholders' power understood?

6. Have stakeholders been invited to a decision-making venue or forum?

7. Is stakeholder legitimacy to participate understood by other participants?

8. Has the decision-making forum been convened by a neutral, respected party? Is this necessary?

9. Have experts charged with technical or medical problem solving built relationships with other stakeholders through phone calls and personal contacts?

10. Is the responsibility of the experts clear? Are expectations realistic?

11. Is the mandate or responsibility of government clarified? Are limitations on government action clearly understood?

12. Do interests conflict? If so, have leaders attempted conflict resolution and negotiation?

13. Have stakeholders had an opportunity to offer potential solutions?

14. Are resources adequate to the proposed solution?

15. Have relevant community capacities been identified?

16. Have relevant organizational capacities been identified?

17. Is the rationale for the proposed solution justified by a balance in the four principles of public health activity: beneficence, autonomy, justice, and efficiency?

18. What is the balance that is struck among these principles?

19. Is this balance clearly understood by stakeholders?

20. Is it satisfactory to all stakeholders? If not, do the dissatisfied stakeholders understand reasons for the solution chosen, and do they feel their views were considered in reaching the decision?

It is likely that additional elements will be added to the checklist as experience is developed. One would encourage such a process. Just as health and social programs refine their process based on experience and study, one expects the process of confronting risk to be refined on this basis as well.

Challenge 3: Relating the problem-solving process to public health consequences. There are no guarantees of success in risk confrontation. The evaluator might get glowing responses from stakeholders on the process, and yet the list of negative consequences might be grave indeed. This may be particularly problematic for health consequences. It is possible that the problem-solving process could receive high marks with little or no effect on the health problem in question. Take, for example, a hypothetical program to improve prenatal care for inner-city women in a metropolitan area with high infant mortality. The program might have an advisory board of community residents with a great deal to say about how the program is implemented. The program might employ community residents as outreach workers, giving jobs and teaching marketable skills. Such a program might improve relations between the health department and inner-city communities. It might provide good publicity for a mayor who could be seen as doing something about infant mortality. All these are positive features of the way the community chose to confront risk. Yet, if no effect is seen on use of prenatal care (much less infant mortality), we would not regard this program as successful. We would evaluate the way the community confronted risk as reasonable. Yet, problem solving did not result in positive health consequences.

An essential public health question therefore is this: For which public health goals are these attributes and process elements helpful? When community capacity is developed, for what public health goals will it improve outcomes? Our hypothesis is that these elements will promote public health goals (a) provided that the goal is attainable at all, (b) to the degree that community forces are relevant, and (c) to the degree that organizational capacity is relevant.

The movement to introduce fluoride into water systems provides an illustration of a program for which these processes are clearly relevant. Fluoridation works to prevent dental caries—a strictly technical and medical issue, for an attainable goal. Yet, some communities still resist the idea of fluoridating *their* drinking water. Community leadership is needed to overcome this resistance; organizational capacity within health departments and related units of government is needed to work skillfully with community leadership on this issue. The technology is relatively simple; the physical effects of fluoride have been known for a long time. Yet, acceptance depends almost completely on the social construction of risks and benefits. Implementation depends on the problem-solving process of confronting risk.

Most professionals would acknowledge the point in the fluoride example. Indeed, we are hard-pressed to find an example of a public health goal that can be achieved independent of community consent. However, working with communities is often time consuming. Can the health department justify the expenditure of staff time, in light of potential returns on the investment? It is the cost-effectiveness of the process that is often in question, not its incremental effectiveness.

We would maintain that this is a critical empirical issue. Certainly, in the case studies presented, one could point to savings from a good process and waste of money from a bad one. Let us take the case study of Chapter 2, concerning a small Superfund site in a rural area. At no time did the EPA contractors consult individuals who had worked on-site. Had they done so, at least two costly accidents might have been avoided. In Chapter 6, the community of Lakeview was flexing its muscle. Once a contract was awarded for cleanup, EPA really could not afford many delays. An injunction imposed by the courts would have stopped cleanup in its tracks, with little prospect for early resolution. Finally, in Chapter 7, collaboration among various community leaders definitely operated to increase access to lower-cost health care options for people with AIDS. A failure to plan for such care in other cities has meant a quicker exhaustion of people's savings and greater reliance for their care on state and federal sources.

Across case studies and identified consequences, it is likely that a good problem-solving process will be associated with improved consequences. However, it remains important to study the conditions under which an investment in risk confrontation is worth the reward—the cost-effectiveness issue.

CONCLUSION

Confronting risk lends itself to empirical study of several kinds. First, the variety of social consequences can be documented and evaluated by stakeholders and independent judges. Second, the process of confronting risk can be evaluated, by the presence, absence, and quality of the features of problem-solving. Third, it is possible to evaluate whether a constructive problem-solving process contributes incrementally to achieving public health goals. Such evaluation is uncommon at present, and is needed if public health professionals are to make optimal use of their engagement with communities.

The benefits of empirical study are particularly promising for public health practice. The resources for public health in the United States are diminishing; to extend them farther, both community and organizational capacities need to be identified and developed. Improving the problem-solving process is likely to result in better social consequences, and in many cases, in the better achievement of public health goals.

Should public health practitioners wait for additional studies before they attempt skillful risk confrontation? Certainly not! Practitioners learn by doing, and public health demands that they be fully engaged in risk confrontation, building up their own personal portfolio of experiences and skills. Reflective practitioners, the ones who can benefit from additional studies, draw on their own set of experiences—even the mistakes—to extract meaning from studies.

REFERENCES

Altman, D. (1988). Legitimation through disaster: AIDS & the gay movement. In E. Fee & D. M. Fox (Eds.), *AIDS: The burdens of history* (pp. 301-315). Berkeley: University of California Press.

Amezcua, C., McAlister, A., Ramirez, A., & Espinoza, R. (1990). A su salud: Health promotion in a Mexican-American border community. In N. Bracht (Ed.), *Health promotion at the community level* (pp. 257-277). Newbury Park, CA: Sage.

Beauchamp, D. E. (1985). Community: The neglected tradition of public health. *Hastings Center Report, 15,* 28-36.

Becker, S. M. (1996). *Environmental accidents and their human service implications: Lessons from the Camelford drinking water contamination case.* Ph.D. dissertation, Bryn Mawr College, Bryn Mawr, PA.

Berger, P. L., & Luckmann, T. (1967). *The social construction of reality: A treatise in the sociology of knowledge.* Garden City, NY: Anchor Books.

Blau, P. M. (1963). *The dynamics of bureaucracy* (rev. ed.). Chicago: University of Chicago Press.

Bok, S. (1983). *Secrets: On the ethics of concealment and revelation.* New York: Vintage.

Bracht, N. (Ed.). (1990). *Health promotion at the community level.* Newbury Park, CA: Sage.

Bracht, N., & Kingsbury, L. (1990). Community organization principles in health promotion: A five-stage model. In N. Bracht (Ed.), *Health promotion at the community level* (pp. 66-88). Newbury Park, CA: Sage.

Cabral, R. J., Galavotti, C., Gargiullo, P. M., Armstrong, K., Cohen, A., Gielen, A. C., & Watkinson, L. (1996). Paraprofessional delivery of a theory-based HIV prevention counseling intervention for women. *Public Health Reports, 111* (Special supplement 1), 75-82.

235

Chess, C., Hance, B. J., & Sandman, P. M. (1988). *Improving dialogue with communities: A short guide for government risk communication.* New Brunswick, NJ: Environmental Communication Research Program, Rutgers University.

Clark, N. M., & McElroy, K. R. (1995). Creating capacity through health education: What we know and what we don't. *Health Education Quarterly, 22,* 273-289.

Cole, P. (1994). The moral bases for public health interventions. *Epidemiology, 6,* 78-83.

Covello, V. T., Sandman, P. M., & Slovic, P. (1988). *Risk communication, risk statistics, and risk comparisons: A manual for plant managers.* Washington, DC: Chemical Manufacturers Association.

Dake, K. (1992). Myths of nature: Culture and the social construction of risk. *Journal of Social Issues, 48,* 21-38.

Davis, D. T., Bustamante, A., Brown, C. P., Wolde-Tsadik, G., Savage, E. W., Cheng, X., & Howland, L. (1994). The urban church and cancer control: A source of social influence in minority communities. *Public Health Reports, 109,* 500-506.

DiClemente, R. (1992). *Adolescents and AIDS: A generation in jeopardy.* Newbury Park, CA: Sage.

Douglas, M., & Wildavsky, A. B. (1982). *Risk and culture: An essay on the selection of technical and environmental dangers.* Berkeley: University of California Press.

Downs, A. (1967). *Inside bureaucracy.* Boston: Little, Brown.

Edelstein, M. R., & Wandersman, A. (1987). Community dynamics in coping with toxic contaminants. In I. Altman & A. Wandersman (Eds.), *Neighborhood and community environments.* New York: Plenum.

Erikson, K. T. (1976). *Everything in its path: Destruction of community in the Buffalo Creek flood.* New York: Simon & Schuster.

Etzioni, A. (1993). *The spirit of community.* New York: Crown.

Faden, R. (1987). Ethical issues in government-sponsored public health campaigns. *Health Education Quarterly, 14,* 27-37.

Faden, R. (1990). Ethical issues in life-style change and adherence. In S. A. Shumaker, E. B. Schron, & J. K. Ockene (Eds.), *The handbook of health behavior change* (pp. 438-445). New York: Springer.

Fischhoff, B. (1989). Risk: A guide to controversy. In National Research Council, *Improving risk communication* (pp. 211-319). Washington, DC: National Academy Press.

Fischhoff, B., Bostrom, A., & Quadrel, M. J. (1993). Risk perception and communication. *Annual Review of Public Health, 14,* 183-203.

Fishbein, M., Guinan, M., Holtgrave, D. R., & Leviton, L. C. (Eds.) (1996). Behavioral science in HIV prevention [Special issue]. *Public Health Reports,* Special supplement 1.

Fisher, R., Ury, W., & Patton, B. (1991). *Getting to yes: Negotiating agreement without giving in* (2nd ed.). New York: Penguin.

Flay, B. (1985). Psychosocial approaches to smoking prevention: A review of findings. *Health Psychology, 4,* 449-488.

Fowlkes, M. R., & Miller, P. Y. (1987). Chemicals and community at Love Canal. In B. B. Johnson & V. T. Covello (Eds.), *The social and cultural construction of risk: Essays on risk selection and perception* (pp. 55-78). Dordrecht, Holland: D. Reidel.

Freudenburg, W. R., & Pastor, S. K. (1992). NIMBYs and LULUs: Stalking the syndromes. *Journal of Social Issues, 48,* 39-63.

Gans, H. J. (1982). *The urban villagers: Group and class in the life of Italian-Americans* (expanded edition). New York: Free Press.

Gardener, J. W. (1991, June 24). *Community.* Address delivered to the W. K. Kellogg Foundation, Battle Creek, MI.

Gray, R. (1979). *A history of London.* New York: Taplinger.

Gray, B. (1989). *Collaborating: Finding common ground for multiparty problems.* San Francisco, CA: Jossey-Bass.

Haddix, A. C., Teutsch, S., Shaffer, P. A., & Dunet, D. O. (1996). *Prevention effectiveness: A guide to decision analysis and economic evaluation.* Oxford, UK: Oxford University Press.

Harris, D. (1984). Health department: Enemy or champion of the people? *American Journal of Public Health, 74,* 428-430.

Haynes, R. B., Sackett, D. L., Taylor, D. W., Gibson, E. S., & Johnson, A. L. (1978). Increased absenteeism from work after detection and labeling of hypertensive patients. *New England Journal of Medicine, 290*(14), 741-744.

Hornsby, J. L., Sappington, J. T., Mongan, P., Gullen, W. H., Bono, S. F., & Altekruse, E. (1985). Risk for bladder cancer: Psychological impact of notification. *Journal of the American Medical Association, 253,* 1899-1902.

Houts, P., & McDougall, V. (1988). Effects of informing workers of their health risks from exposures to toxic materials. *American Journal of Industrial Medicine, 13,* 271-279.

Ibsen, H. (1965). *Three plays: An enemy of the people, the wild duck, Hedda Gabler.* New York: Heritage Press.

Institute of Medicine. (1988). *The future of public health.* Washington, DC: National Academy Press.

Johnson, B. B., & Covello, V. T. (Eds.). (1987). *The social and cultural construction of risk: Essays on risk selection and perception.* Dordrecht, Holland: D. Reidel.

Jones, J.H . (1981). *Bad blood: The Tuskegee syphilis experiment.* New York: Free Press.

Kasperson, R. E., Renn, O., Brown, H. S., Emel, J., Govle, R., Kasperson, J. X., Ratic, S., & Slovic, P. (1988). The social amplification of risk: A conceptual framework. *Risk Analysis, 8,* 177-204.

Kohler, H. G. (1990). Henrik Ibsen's *An Enemy of the People* and Eduard Meissner's expulsion from Teplitz. *British Medical Journal, 300,* 1123-1126.

Kong, B. W., Miler, J. M., & Smoot, R. T. (1982). Churches as high blood pressure control centers. *Journal of the National Medical Association, 74,* 920-923.

Leviton, L. C., Marsh, G. M., Talbott, E. O., et. al. (1991). Drake chemical workers' health registry: Coping with community tension in health protection. *American Journal of Public Health, 81,* 689-693.

Leviton, L. C., & Schuh, R. G. (1991). Evaluation of outreach as a program element. *Evaluation Review, 15,* 420-440.

Lynn, F. M., & Busenberg, G. J. (1995). Citizen advisory committees and environmental policy; What we know, what's left to discover. *Risk Analysis, 15,* 147-162.

McAlister, A., Puska, P., Salonen, J. T., Tuomilehto, J., & Koskela, K. (1982). Theory and action for health promotion: Illustrations from the North Karelia Project. *American Journal of Public Health, 72,* 43-50.

McKnight, J. L. (1987). Regenerating community. *Social Policy, 17,* 54-58.

McKnight, J. L. (1988). *Getting connected: How to find out about groups and organizations in your neighborhood.* Evanston, IL: Center for Urban Affairs and Policy Research, Northwestern University.

McKnight, J. L. (1991, September). Address to participants, Kellogg Community-Based Public Health Initiative workshop, Itasca, IL.

McKnight, J. L. (1995). *The careless society: Community and its counterfeits.* New York: Basic Books.

McKnight, J. L., & Kretzmann, J. P. (1990). *Mapping community capacity.* Evanston, IL: Center for Urban Affairs and Policy Research, Northwestern University.

Meyerowitz, B. E. (1993). Assessing quality of life when planning and evaluating worker notification programs: Two case examples. *American Journal of Industrial Medicine, 23,* 221-227.

Meyerowitz, B. E., Sullivan, C. D., & Premeau, C. L. (1989). Reactions of asbestos-exposed workers to notification and screening. *American Journal of Industrial Medicine, 15,* 463-475.

Miles, M. B., & Huberman, A. M. (1994). *Qualitative data analysis.* Thousand Oaks, CA: Sage.

Mitroff, I. I., & Kilmann, R. H. (1978). *Methodological approaches to social science.* San Francisco: Jossey-Bass.

Morgan, M. G., Fischhoff, B., Bostrom, A., Lave, L., & Atman, C. J. (1992). Communicating risk to the public. *Environment, Science, and Technology, 26,* 2048-2056.

National Association of County Health Officials. (1991). *APEXPH: Assessment protocol for excellence in public health.* Washington, DC: Author.

National Cancer Institute, Office of Cancer Communications. (1989). *Making health communication programs work: A planner's guide* (NIH Publication No. 89-1493). Bethesda, MD: U.S. Department of Health & Human Services.

National Research Council. (1989). *Improving risk communication.* Washington, DC: National Academy Press.

Needleman, C. (1993). Worker notification: Lessons from the past. *American Journal of Industrial Medicine, 23,* 11-23.

Needleman, C. & Needleman, M. L. (1996). Qualitative methods for intervention research. *American Journal of Industrial Medicine, 29,* 329-337.

Oppenheimer, G. M. (1988). In the eye of the storm: The epidemiological construction of AIDS. In E. Fee & D. M. Fox (Eds.), *AIDS: The burdens of history.* Berkeley: University of California Press.

Panem, S. (1988). *The AIDS bureaucracy.* Cambridge, MA: Harvard University Press.

Perrow, C., & Guillen, M. F. (1990). *The AIDS disaster: The failure of organizations in New York and the nation.* New Haven, CT: Yale University Press.

Public Health Service. (1990). *Promoting health/preventing disease: Year 2000 objectives for the nation.* Washington, DC: U.S. Department of Health & Human Services.

Rayner, S. (1987). Risk and relativism in science for policy. In B. B. Johnson & V. T. Covello (Eds.), *The social and cultural construction of risk: Essays on risk selection and perception* (pp. 5-23). Dordrecht, Holland: D. Reidel.

Renn, O., Burns, W. J., Kasperson, J. X., Kasperson, R. E., & Slovic, P. (1992). The social amplification of risk: Theoretical foundations and empirical applications. *Journal of Social Issues, 48,* 137-160.

Risse, G. B. (1988). Epidemics and history. In E. Fee & D. M. Fox (Eds.), *AIDS: The burdens of history.* Berkeley: University of California Press.

Rosen, G. (1958). *A history of public health.* New York: MD Publications, Inc.

Rubin, R. H., Billingsley, A., & Caldwell, C. H. (1994). The role of the black church in working with black adolescents. *Adolescence, 29,* 251-266.

Russell, L. B. (1986). *Is prevention better than cure?* Washington, DC: Brookings Institution.

Ryan, W. (1971). *Blaming the victim.* New York: Basic Books.

Sands, R. G., Newby, L. G., & Greenberg, R. A. (1981). Labeling of health risk in industrial settings. *Journal of Applied Behavioral Science, (17)*359-374.

Schulte, P. A., Boal, W. L., Friedland, J. M., Walker, L. B., Connally, L. B., Mazzuckelli, L. F., & Fine, L. J. (1993). Methodologic issues in risk communications to workers. *American Journal of Industrial Medicine, 23,* 3-9.

Scriven, M. (1967). The methodology of evaluation. In R. W. Tyler, R. M. Gagne, & M. Scriven (Eds.), *Perspectives of curriculum evaluation* (pp. 94-142). Chicago: Rand McNally.

Scriven, M. (1991). *Evaluation thesaurus* (4th ed.). Newbury Park, CA: Sage.

Shadish, W. R., Cook, T. D., & Leviton, L. C. (1991). *Foundations of program evaluation: Theorists and their theories.* Newbury Park, CA: Sage.

Shilts, R. (1987). *And the band played on: Politics, people, and the AIDS epidemic.* New York: St. Martin's.

Sigmond, R. M. (1989). A catalyst for change: A new book depicts the hospital as an instrument for forming social policy. *Health Progress, 70,* 40-42.

Silver, P. T. (1992). *Occupational disease and the low wage worker: A case study of lead poisoning among secondary lead smelter workers.* Ph.D. dissertation, Bryn Mawr College, Bryn Mawr, PA.

Simons-Morton, B. G., Greene, W. H., & Gottlieb, N. H. (1995). *Introduction to health education and health promotion* (2nd ed.). Prospect Heights, IL: Waveland Press.

Slovic, P., Fischhoff, B., & Lichtenstein, S. (1987). Behavioral decision theory perspectives on protective behavior. In N. D. Weinstein (Ed.), *Taking care: Understanding and encouraging self-protective behavior.* Cambridge, UK: Cambridge University Press.

Stoy, D. B., Curtis, R. C., Dameworth, K. S., Dowdy, A. A., Hegland, J., Levin, J. A., & Sousoulas, B. G. (1995). The successful recruitment of elderly black subjects in a clinical trial: The CRISP experience. *Journal of the National Medical Association, 87,* 280-287.

Sullum, J. (1996). What the doctor orders. *Priorities, 8,* 8-16.

Thomas, S. B., Quinn, S. C., Billingsley, A., & Caldwell, C. (1994). The characteristics of northern black churches with community health outreach programs. *American Journal of Public Health, 84,* 575-579.

Thomas, W. I. (1966). *W. I. Thomas on social organization and social personality: Selected papers.* Chicago, IL: University of Chicago Press.

Thompson, B., & Kinne, S. (1990). Social change theory: Applications to community health. In N. Bracht (Ed.), *Health promotion at the community level* (pp. 45-65). Newbury Park, CA: Sage.

Tillet, S., Ringen K., Schulte, P., McDougall, V., Miller, K., & Samuels, S. (1986). Interventions in high-risk occupational cohorts: A cross-sectional demonstration project. *Journal of Occupational Medicine, 28,* 719-727.

Walsh, E. J. (1987). Challenging official risk assessments via protest mobilization: The TMI Case. In B. B. Johnson & V. T. Covello (Eds.), *The social and cultural construction of risk: Essays on risk selection and perception* (pp. 85-101). Dordrecht, Holland: D. Reidel.

Wandersman, A. H., & Hallman, W. K. (1993). Are people acting irrationally? Under-
    standing public concerns about environmental threats. *American Psychologist, 48,*
    681-686.
Wandersman, A., & Hallman, W. (1994, April). *Environmental threats: Perception of
    risk, stress, and coping.* Paper presented at the Spanish Congress of Environmental
    Psychology, Tenerife, Spain.
Ward, C. (1972). A doomwatch for environmental pollution. (a). Pollution of land—an
    enemy of the people. *Royal Society of Health Journal, 92,* 173-177.
Warren, R. L. (1978). *The community in America* (3rd ed.). Chicago: Rand McNally.
Yin, R. K. (1984). *Case study research: Design and methods.* Beverly Hills, CA: Sage.

Name Index

241

Subject Index

ABOUT THE AUTHORS

Laura C. Leviton is Professor of Health Behavior in the School of Public Health, University of Alabama at Birmingham. She is well known in the evaluation of disease prevention programs and is the coauthor of *Foundations of Program Evaluation*. She has conducted evaluations of occupational health programs and worksite health promotion programs. She has also conducted evaluations of HIV prevention in women and infants, homosexual and bisexual men, and injection drug users. More recently, she has collaborated on evaluations of education campaigns on symptoms of heart attack, dissemination of physician practice guidelines on premature birth, urban health programs, and clinical care for sexually transmitted diseases. She has served as a consultant to the federal Centers for Disease Control and Prevention (CDC), the National Institute for Occupational Safety and Health (NIOSH), and the Agency for Toxic Substances and Disease Registry (ATSDR). She is currently a member of CDC's national advisory committee for HIV and STD prevention. She won the 1993 award from the American Psychological Association for Distinguished Contributions to Psychology in the Public Interest.

Carolyn E. Needleman holds a Ph.D. in socology from Washington University in St. Louis. She is currently a professor in the Graduate School of Social Work and Social Research at Bryn Mawr College, where she teaches courses in social policy and evaluation research. At Bryn Mawr, she directs a doctoral social work concentration in occupational and environmental health, focused on the family and community impact of occupational and environmental health hazards. She is a well-known researcher in the fields of occupational and environmental health and often serves as a consultant to state health departments, labor unions, corporations, the National Research Council, and federal agencies such as NIOSH, ATSDR, the Occupational Safety and Health Administration, the National Institute for Environmental Health Sciences, the National Cancer Institute, and the Department of Energy. She is active in the American Public Health Association, having served on its Governing Council and Action Board. Her publications include numerous articles and monographs in the areas of public health, risk communication, occupational safety and health, and environmental issues. She is co-author, with Martin Needleman, of *Guerrillas in the Bureaucracy: The Community Planning Experiment in the United States*.

Maurice A. Shapiro is Emeritus Professor of Environmental Health Engineering of the Graduate School of Public Health, University of Pittsburgh. Among many achievements, he implemented one of the first air pollution graduate education programs in the nation. He has advised numerous state and local health departments on the range of issues dealing with environmental health and public health leadership.

ABOUT THE CONTRIBUTORS

Stephen E. Kauffman, Ph.D., is Associate Professor at Widener University's Center for Social Work Education, where he teaches social policy and research. The two major areas of his scholarly research are citizen involvement in governmentally sponsored problem remediation efforts, and ideology and its role in policy development and research. Presently he is working with several community organizations in Chester, PA, to examine the effectiveness of their programs in education, housing, childhood lead screening, and substance abuse prevention.

Martin L. Needleman, currently on the faculty of Bloomsburg University in Pennsylvania, holds a Ph.D. degree in sociology from the State University of New York at Buffalo. He has many years of experience in community-based research related to environmental health and other social issues. His publications include a coauthored books on community planning and a number of articles and monographs.

Regina R. Reitmeyer has been a reporter and freelance writer in the areas of health and education for many years. She also has a small consulting firm dealing with educational policy and media relations.